WALLACE STEVENS
AND POETIC THEORY

WALLACE STEVENS

AND POETIC THEORY

Conceiving the Supreme Fiction

by B. J. Leggett

University of North Carolina Press

Chapel Hill and London

Library of Congress Cataloging-in-Publication Data

Leggett, B. J. (Bobby Joe), 1938–
  Wallace Stevens and poetic theory.

  Bibliography: p.
  Includes index.
  1. Stevens, Wallace, 1879–1955—Aesthetics.
I. Title.
PS3537.T4753Z6744   1987   811'.52   86-16125
ISBN 0-8078-1718-X

Designed by Naomi P. Slifkin

FOR CORINNE

CONTENTS

ACKNOWLEDGMENTS

I am grateful to the Huntington Library for the fellowship that served as the point of origin for the following chapters. I also wish to thank the Huntington for permission to quote from unpublished materials in the Wallace Stevens Archive and from marginal notations in Stevens's private library. John D. Kendall and Royann Hanson of the University Library, University of Massachusetts at Amherst, also provided much assistance in my review of the Stevens material held there. I am grateful as well for permission to quote from marginalia in that portion of the Stevens library now in the University of Massachusetts Special Collections. Grants from the John C. Hodges Fund of the English Department of the University of Tennessee and from the Graduate School of the University of Tennessee provided funds for travel to the Huntington and the University of Massachusetts, as well as time in which to complete these chapters, and I am indebted to the department, especially to Joseph Trahern, and to the Graduate School for their generosity.

My indebtedness to other readers of Stevens is great, although with the passage of time difficult to sort out and to identify. No doubt what I think of as my own reading of Stevens has been largely shaped by earlier commentary, both by direct borrowings and by reactions against views I have taken to be misreadings or misdirected approaches. I am perhaps the least qualified to disentangle these influences; however, I recognize the presence of two distinguished critics of Stevens in these pages, and it is frequently their readings of Stevens against which I set my own, even when this is not made explicit. The first of these, Helen Vendler, I regard as the reader who has been the most faithful to the spirit and the letter of Stevens's major poems and the most generous in providing a larger audience access to the difficult long poems. Her latest studies represent an attempt to rescue Stevens's poetry from the epistemologist and the theorist, and I hope that my own study will not be regarded as a setback to that effort. The second of these critics, Harold Bloom, is perhaps the most willful and the least generous of Stevens's readers in that he has to some extent appropriated Stevens for his own theory of poetry, and in the process given us a debilitated Stevens whose greatness arises from the scandal of repression and melancholy (to borrow Bloom's provocative terminology), a Stevens who has become our prime example of the anxiety of influence. Yet the provocative nature of Bloom's brilliant criticism continually forces a response, necessitates a new reading of Stevens if only for the purpose of combatting Bloom's powerful misreading; in that regard he is the most enlivening and inspiring of contemporary critics, and the critic who has most contributed to Stevens's present stature as *the* strong poet of modern American poetry. A portion of Chapter Three serves as an example of the sort of response Bloom provokes, and parts of my readings of *Notes toward a Supreme Fiction* and "The Auroras of Autumn" are set against Bloom's influential views of these greatest of Stevens's long poems.

I wish to thank *Studies in Romanticism* for permission to reprint, with slight alteration, the material that comprises Chapter Two, and *The Wallace Stevens Journal* for permission to reprint material included in Chapter Four. Quotations from *The Collected Poems of Wallace Stevens* are used by permission of Alfred A. Knopf, Inc. Stevens's works will be identified in the text by the following abbreviations: (CP) *The Collected Poems of Wallace Stevens* (New York: Knopf, 1954); (L) *Letters of Wallace Stevens*, ed. Holly Stevens (New York: Knopf, 1966); (OP) *Opus Posthumous*, ed. Samuel French Morse (New York: Knopf, 1957); and (NA) *The Necessary Angel: Essays on Reality and the Imagination* (New York: Vintage, 1951).

WALLACE STEVENS
AND POETIC THEORY

1

INTRODUCTION
Stevens and Poetic Theory

The assumption that the poems of Wallace Stevens conceal a viable theory of poetry or of the poetic imagination has guided Stevens criticism since Hi Simons first set out the aesthetic of "The Comedian as the Letter C" in 1940. This continuing project of converting the poetry to poetics or metapoetry is perhaps the inevitable consequence of attending to a poet who labored so earnestly to establish the premise that "poetry is the subject of the poem" (CP, 176). A number of years ago Northrop Frye stated the case most directly: "Wallace Stevens was a poet for whom the theory and the practice of poetry were inseparable. His poetic vision is informed by a metaphysic; his metaphysic is informed by a theory of knowledge; his theory of knowledge is informed by a poetic vision."[1] Given a poet who is of particular interest to the critical theorist because, in Frye's words, "he sees so clearly that the only ideas the poet can deal with are those directly involved with, and implied by, his own writing,"[2] it is not surprising that commentary on the body of Stevens's poetry has been devoted so extensively to a description of Stevens's theory of the poetic imagination. One version of this project goes so far as to suggest that Stevens's verse constitutes one Grand Poem, the subject of which is poetry.[3]

The issues raised by the theory (or, as the studies have multiplied, theories) seen as latent in the verse have now become the commonplaces of Stevens criticism: the subject-object duality, with its consequent emphasis on various conceptions of imagination and reality and their interrelations; the death of the gods, which leads on the one hand to the impoverishment of life and the estrangement of self and on the other to the possibility of a more sufficient myth; the supreme fiction and attendant concepts such as major man, the hero, the abstract, decreation, the first idea, resemblance, and metamorphosis; and, underlying all, a notion of the external world (and ultimately mind) as flux, change, fortuity, an

assumption that to some extent renders all theory provisional, ten-
tative. Although the list could be extended, my intent here is not to
describe the theories that have been extracted from the poems but
to raise questions about the nature of the enterprise itself.

One of Stevens's most thoughtful readers, Helen Vendler, has
recently urged a shift in the direction of commentary away from
questions of epistemology and poetic theory. She argues that Ste-
vens is a genuinely misunderstood poet; he is rarely seen as the
passionate writer, the poet of ecstatic or despairing moments that
he truly is.[4] His reputation as bloodless, dry, and abstract Vendler
traces to readers' continued engagement with Stevens as the poet of
epistemological questions: "It is popularly believed that Stevens is
a poet preoccupied by the relations between the imagination and
reality, and there is good reason for the popular belief, since Stevens
so often phrased his own preoccupation in those unrevealing words.
The formula, properly understood, is not untrue; but we must ask
what causes the imagination to be so painfully at odds with reality.
The cause setting the two at odds is usually, in Stevens' case, pas-
sionate feeling, and not merely epistemological query."[5] Vendler
reads Stevens as "our great poet of the inexhaustible and exhaust-
ing cycle of desire and despair." If he is not recognized as such, it is
because the usual, and mistaken, habit of commentators is "to take
his metaphysical or epistemological prolegomena as the real sub-
ject of the poem, when in fact they are the late plural of the subject,
whose early candor of desire reposes further down the page."[6]

Vendler's assumption that Stevens's ostensible subject is not al-
ways the one that most engages his feeling must, I think, be granted
by the attentive reader of, say, *Notes toward a Supreme Fiction* or
any number of poems that address themselves to theoretical ques-
tions. Her emphasis on Stevens as the poet of desire and despair—
set against Stevens the theorist in verse, the cold abstractionist—
should also be welcome to anyone who has surveyed the body of
commentary on the poems. This attempt to redirect the line of
critical inquiry is one sign that earlier commentary has been some-
what single-minded in its project of isolating Stevens as the theo-
rist of the poetic imagination. Vendler's correction of the current
formula for reading Stevens is instructive, and perhaps overdue, but
in its attempt to uncover the Stevens of desire and despair it quite
understandably minimizes the Stevens of the ostensible subject of
the poem. Vendler would no doubt agree that, whatever its "real"
subject, *Notes toward a Supreme Fiction* is also a poem about writ-
ing poetry and, what is more, that we cannot always locate the line

of separation between the theorist and the man of feeling. In its ardent pursuit of another, more human Stevens, Vendler's study also leaves the impression that the commentary on Stevens as theorist and epistemologist has essentially completed its task so that we are now in command of the theoretical context of the poems. "Though the conceptual bases of Stevens' poems have been ably set out, and Stevens' intellectual and poetic sources are gradually being enumerated," she remarks, "the task of conveying the poems as something other than a collection of ideas still remains incomplete."[7]

Vendler's generosity to the opposing camp (she can, of course, afford to be generous since she has reduced its significance) suggests that Stevens's ideas and their sources are now being set out with some certainty. I would argue, to the contrary, that commentary has been unable to provide an adequate description of Stevens's poetic theory and that we know very little about the intellectual sources for his conception of poetry. The commentary on Stevens's poetics has given us, in the main, not information on the sources or background of his ideas but readings of poems, readings that have been subsequently challenged by equally rigorous readings, so that we are now accustomed to a body of criticism in which every significant issue is open to question. Stevens is the poet of the imagination; he is the poet of reality. He is the doctrinal poet of ideas; he is the poet of words, less concerned with doctrine than with feeling. He is a Symbolist; he stands opposed to the Symbolist and post-Symbolist poets.[8] He belongs to an idealist tradition; he belongs to a naturalistic tradition.[9] He has shown no major change in growth, so that his late poems partake of the same sensibility and the same intellectual climate as his early verse; he exhibits a great change in sensibility and a major change in growth from the early to the late poems.[10] He works through a dialectical process from thesis to antithesis to synthesis; his poetry is not dialectical in any Hegelian sense.[11] His private symbolism is consistent throughout his poetry; his symbols such as sun and moon, blue and green, do not always mean the same thing.[12] His poet-hero is not a human individual but an abstraction who does not exist in our world; his hero is always the human individual, and he may be any man who exists among his fellows in a mythless age.[13] So it goes, through a string of oppositions that could be lengthened to a tedious survey of more than fifty years of critical controversy.

These contradictory readings are clearly more than quibbles about interpretation or emphasis; they represent differences that extend to the central issue of Stevens's conception of poetry. And such flat contradictions cannot be resolved by any fiction of interpretative progress, where early mistaken readings are corrected by later ones. Since our understanding of Stevens's theory of poetry is derived primarily from readings of poems, there has been little advance in our understanding, merely a multiplication of interpretations distinguished only by their methodologies: formalist readings have been succeeded by phenomenologist readings, which in turn have been succeeded by deconstructionist readings. A look at two of these attempts to describe Stevens's conception of the poetic imagination—and I choose studies that were published in the same year—will perhaps be sufficient to suggest how far we are from an adequate account of Stevens's poetics. Alan Perlis's *Wallace Stevens: A World of Transforming Shapes* and Helen Regueiro's *The Limits of Imagination: Wordsworth, Yeats, and Stevens* both propose to settle the issue of Stevens's view of poetry by defining his conception of the reality-imagination complex, which is regarded by both critics as the central issue of his verse. It is typical of Stevens criticism as a whole that the two, basing their findings both on previous criticism and on their own careful analyses of the body of Stevens's poetry, reach opposite conclusions, the effect of each being to negate the other.

Perlis's study attributes two important assumptions to Stevens's conception of the imagination, one having to do with reality's imperviousness to the imagination, the other with the sufficiency of the alienated imagination. Because, in Perlis's view, Stevens assumes that the "thing itself" is forever beyond the poetic imagination, the poet makes no pretense of faithfully describing objects as they exist in reality, and his imaginary constructs neither contain nor define the essence of objects themselves.[14] The relationships that Stevens's poetry establishes do not therefore exist in the world external to the imagination but are purely products of the mind.[15] Moreover, the unbridgeable separation of imagination and reality justifies the poet's impulse to transform the world willfully to the shape of his imaginary constructs.[16] The acknowledgment that the real world is beyond reach is an occasion, finally, for celebration, which derives from the recognition that "if nothing is fixed, futility can be transformed into a realization of the world's infinite possibility to inspire poetic expression."[17]

Perlis's Stevens is a poet resigned to sacrificing all else for the imagination. Helen Regueiro's Stevens, on the other hand, is able to attain the real only through the sacrifice, the annihilation, of the imagination. Stevens, in Regueiro's reading, begins with a sense of the meaninglessness of the natural world unless ordered or transformed by the imagination. Yet even in his poems of order he is aware of the inability of the imagination to approximate the "thingness" of reality, since the temptation of the imagination is constantly to transform the world, to create an intentional world separate from the real. This recognition is itself the beginning of Stevens's move toward an affirmation of the particular truth, the momentary experience, and his rejection of the total reconstruction of reality provided by the imagination.[18] In the end, Stevens denies the imagination its ordering powers in an attempt to reach the chaotic particulars of the natural world. He finally sees that reality can be experienced only by limiting the imagination, by turning its transforming power not against reality (as Perlis would have it) but against itself. Whereas for Perlis the imagination in Stevens becomes an end in itself, for Regueiro "it ceases being an end and becomes an instrument of experience, reaching the 'being' of the object in a transforming moment of awareness."[19] That is, by limiting itself, by denying the validity of its re-creation of the world, the poem becomes not a description of reality but a "vehicle of experience."[20] Reality, which was feared to have been lost to poetry, has been gained, and the imagination, which was thought to rule supreme, has silenced itself. In short, Regueiro's Stevens has shifted the imagination from its grandiose work as creator and transformer to the more modest task of becoming an instrument for the experience of being.

These two studies, taken together, suggest the dilemma faced by the reader in search of a theory underlying the verse, the recognition that the most careful scrutiny of the poems—Perlis and Regueiro are accomplished and sophisticated readers—yields results that may be contradicted at every turn. We are given at the same moment two poets who bear only the slightest resemblance. Perlis gives us the exponent of the supremacy of the imagination willfully at play in a world of resemblance and metaphor, fatally but happily sundered from the natural world. Regueiro uncovers a Stevens who rejects the metaphorical world of resemblance and who surrenders the imagination itself so that he may experience the chaotic natural world the imagination denies him. These, of course, are roughly the poles between which commentary on Stevens has been located. While Perlis and Regueiro articulate extreme positions, almost all other approaches to Stevens's poetics appear in the space between these two "unrevealing words" (as Vendler labels them), imagination and reality. This is not to suggest, however, that these are words we can easily evade, and if we wish to meet Stevens on his own ground, we must return to them repeatedly.

It is the nature of both practical and theoretical criticism to be contentious, and one of the most pervasive conventions of the critical essay is the attribution of wrong-headedness to one's colleagues. This is a normal condition which obviously accounts in some measure for the lack of consensus in the commentary on Stevens, no different from the state of affairs one encounters in the study of any major artist. Yet the case of Stevens appears variant in two important ways. First, as Vendler has suggested, the commentary on Stevens has been largely devoted not simply to the reading of poems as poems, but to the reading of Stevens's verse as a theory of poetry or an epistemology assumed to be held by the poet himself. The second and more crucial complication resides in certain generally acknowledged qualities of Stevens's poetry that appear to impede its translation into doctrine or theory. That is, the nature of Stevens's verse seems to guarantee that any formulation of a systematic or comprehensive theory derived from the verse alone will prove to be inadequate—susceptible to contradiction by elements of the poetry itself or by other equally well-grounded formulations. Why does this one area of the poetry—its status as metapoetry or self-conscious theory—resist definition? And why should Stevens's poetry present a special case?

In attempting to account for his dissatisfaction with the readings (including his own) of one of the prime sources of Stevens's poetic theory, *Notes toward a Supreme Fiction*, Harold Bloom formulates one answer. He argues that critics are so frequently wrong about Stevens's poetics because "Stevens had the uncanniness and the persistence to get about a generation ahead of his own time, and he is still quite a few touches and traces ahead of ours."[21] This is to suggest that, as theory, Stevens's poetry has so far outdistanced its commentators as to render ineffectual their efforts to describe it. In Bloom's words, Stevens's "major phase, from 1942 to his death in 1955, gave us a canon of poems themselves more advanced *as interpretation* than our criticism has gotten to be." It thus becomes the reader's task to find a critical procedure sophisticated enough to encompass the "subtle evasions" and "preternatural rhetoricity" of a poetry acutely aware "of its own status as text."[22] Bloom's emphasis on the poetry as interpretation and on its awareness of its own status as text touches on one element of the difficulty encountered in extracting Stevens's theory from his verse. While Stevens's self-conscious pursuit of the same goal sought by his critics might be thought to facilitate the task of describing his conception of the poetic imagination, the result seems to be the opposite. The poet has anticipated many of the reader's questions, but he has posed them in an obscure manner and answered them in unparaphrasable figures. A poet less self-conscious would be easier to pin down, and a poet less obsessed with the many sides of the question would not cover himself with quite so many evasions, qualifications, and paradoxes.

Helen Vendler, to whom we return as the critic who has written most perceptively on the rhetoric of Stevens's poems, has described in some detail the means by which the poet evades direct statement, qualifies assertions, introduces uncertainties.[23] She demonstrates Stevens's tendency to leave his poetic statement indeterminate by phrasing it as a hypothesis, a question, a future event, a tenseless event, or an imperative.[24] She notes the frequency with which he avoids finality by recourse to the mitigating *seems*, as well as the frequency with which he resorts to the modal auxiliaries *may, might, must, could, should*, and *would* to conclude his statement.[25] She cites the manner in which Stevens uses logical form—"not as a logician but as a sleight-of-hand man, making assertion appear in different guises and from different angles, delighting in paradoxical logic, and sometimes defying logic entirely."[26] She argues, finally, that Stevens is "unique in English poetry in the frequency with which he closes his poems on a tentative note."[27]

The results of translating the evasions, paradoxes, and disjunctions of a master rhetorician into the critics' formulations we have already observed, in one sense, in the kinds of contradictory readings cited earlier. The project may be seen in another sense as a variation of the formalists' heresy of paraphrase, but with an interesting twist. While the formalists objected to the prose translation of a poem's "meaning" because it neglected the essential art of the poem, the aesthetic dimension, theorists in quest of the poetics embedded in Stevens's poetry may well be content to leave the art behind, at least temporarily, in order to extract the ideas susceptible to prose translation. Yet if readers are sensitive to the mode in which these ideas are expressed, they must acknowledge the difficulty of a credible transposition from poetry to doctrine. It is not simply that the commentary has lost the art of the poem, a dimension it is certainly content to lose for the limited purpose of its exercise; rather, the mode of the poem, which includes the rhetorical qualifications Vendler details, has colored its theoretical content so completely that it cannot be extracted in a form that preserves its integrity as a theory attributable to the poet. To put it another way, Stevens's poetic statements of theory seem to appeal to modern theorists because of a quality inseparable from their status as poetry, a quality that does not translate well into doctrine.

The problem is further compounded when we move from the single poem to the entire body of Stevens's poetry, the so-called Grand Poem. If the single poem yields its doctrine only in a form that debilitates it, then we may project this exercise repeated over more than five hundred pages of collected poems written over several decades by a poet who kept changing his mind (or who believed at one juncture that an essential quality of the supreme fiction is that "It Must Change"). Denis Donoghue has noted in this regard that "the philosophic positions registered in Stevens's poems are severally in contradiction. If we were to list every variant reading in the argument of epistemology, for instance, we could quote a poem by Stevens in favor of each."[28] J. Hillis Miller, observing the same phenomenon, has stated, "The critic can develop radically different notions of Stevens's aims as a poet, and for each of these it is easy to find apposite passages from the text."[29]

Donoghue and Miller, interestingly enough, have offered explanations for this circumstance that are themselves at odds, confirming in a way they had not intended the justice of their observations that Stevens's poetry is capable of sustaining antithetical positions. Donoghue has suggested that the contradictions in Stevens matter only if we regard him as a philosopher, but he "did not play with philosophic ideas." His poems are in apparent conflict because "moment by moment, poem by poem, he committed himself to the 'mental state' of the occasion." Stevens was not distressed that these states were contradictory; "he trusted that the work would conform to the nature of the worker, and no other conformity was required."[30] Miller, on the other hand, has found the source of the contradictions in the poems' conformity to the state of reality that the poet seeks to capture. For Miller (the pre-deconstructionist Miller, it should be noted), Stevens was clearly engaged in a philosophic enterprise comparable to that of a phenomenologist such as Heidegger or Husserl. This enterprise involved the perception of being, and the phenomenologist Miller attributed the impossibility of finding "a one-dimensional theory of poetry and life in Stevens"[31] not to the shifts in his mental state but to the contradictions inherent in the reality to which he was so faithful. Miller's consequent shift in theoretical allegiance from Poulet to Derrida has, however, prompted a corresponding change in his view of Stevens's theory of poetry. He now holds that three theories of poetry may be identified in Stevens's poems, but that it is impossible to adopt any one of these "without being led, willy-nilly, to encounter the ambiguous inherence within it of the other two."[32] This ambiguity is now traced not to the nature of reality but to the nature of language, within the fabric of which these three theories are entangled.

We have, then, a number of explanations for the inaccessibility of Stevens's theory of poetry as exhibited in his verse, and they have been proposed by the most distinguished of Stevens's commentators. My aim is not to serve as arbiter on this question, but to point up the implications of such conclusions for the failed project of extracting a theory of poetry from Stevens's poems. My own conclusion is not, however, that we should cease reading the poetry in quest of its theoretical grounding. Despite Vendler's timely argument for a shift in emphasis to a less theoretical Stevens, I am convinced that much remains to be learned about Stevens's changing views of poetry. Although Vendler's poet of desire may be ultimately of more value to us than the poet of theory, we are sufficiently engaged by the latter to attempt to recover him. And, curiously enough, it may be that the passionate Stevens is, in the end, more accessible to us than the theoretical one. *Notes toward a Supreme Fiction* has been enjoyed and commented on, sometimes brilliantly, by readers who have been unable or unwilling to follow its argument about the nature and origin of poetry. Reading the commentary, one could compile a catalog of readers' skillful evasions of the theoretical problems the poem raises. (Frank Kermode's opening gambit is typical: "I will not disgrace Stevens' greatest poem by plodding commentary."[33])

My argument has to do not with the direction of Stevens criticism but with the method that has been employed in describing Stevens's poetics, the assumption that close reading of the verse is sufficient to disclose its theoretical base. While we may perhaps approach Stevens's poetry as verse with the same hope of success enjoyed in employing our critical methodologies on any body of literature, we should recognize the pitfalls of translating his poetry into a theory of poetry that retains the integrity it exhibits as poetic statement. These difficulties arise not simply because of the self-consciously interpretative nature of the poetry, or because of its rhetorical mastery, which evades definition and renders every doctrine problematical, but finally because of the many self-negating perspectives assumed in the body of the verse as a whole. Whether these contradictions are due to the shifting imagination, to the nature of reality, or to the nature of language is not crucial to my argument, but I would not like to surrender any of these alternatives. Given the disjunctive quality of Stevens's poetry, it is possible to conceive of a body of commentary in which critics such as Perlis, Regueiro, Donoghue, and Miller offer us conflicting interpretations that are yet faithful to their selective texts, if in no way definitive. This means not that particular versions of Stevens's poetics cannot be shown to be mistaken for various reasons; only that, in the absence of a critical methodology as subtle and resourceful as Stevens's own poetic art, we shall continue to see intelligent studies of his poetics, derived from the poems, which are at variance with one another.

The alternative is not, however, a "definitive" study of Stevens's poetic theory based on sources other than his poetry. Poststructuralist criticism has denied us the possibility of a definitive reading of any aspect of literature, and no more than other readers would I be willing to surrender Stevens's poetry as one source for conceiving his supreme fiction. Yet I have tried to suggest that the poetry in itself is not a sufficient base for constructing theory and, furthermore, that the formulation of aesthetic theory is not the same as *explication de texte*, since readers engaged in ferreting out Stevens's view of the imagination, for example, are using the poems to argue a theory or an epistemology that they attribute to the poet. Acknowledging the goal of a great deal of commentary on Stevens to be the recovery of the conceptions of poetry that Stevens held when he composed his poems, and granting as well the generally inaccessible nature of the poetry as theory, it would seem inevitable that criticism would turn elsewhere for help, and I have attempted in this study to broaden the base of the search. William York Tindall in a clever essay asserts that the subject of poems such as *Notes toward a Supreme Fiction* is not the formulation of an aesthetic itself but "the experience of trying to formulate it." "When he wanted to announce his aesthetic," Tindall says, "he wrote an essay or made a speech."[34] One need not agree with this division of the poetry from the prose to concur with its implication that the aesthetic concerns of the poetry differ in crucial ways from those of the essays, addresses, letters, and journals.

Stevens himself makes a similar distinction in his introduction to *The Necessary Angel*. "One function of the poet at any time," he begins, "is to discover by his own thought and feeling what seems

to him to be poetry at that time." Yet the poet exercises this func-
tion without being conscious of it, "so that the disclosures in his
poetry, while they define what seems to be poetry, are disclosures of
poetry, not disclosures of definitions of poetry." The essays, on the
other hand, "are intended to disclose definitions of poetry." They
are, he states flatly, "intended to be contributions to the theory of
poetry" (NA, vii). We do, in fact, have two large bodies of work by
Stevens that are concerned with aesthetic issues. While one has
generated a great deal of excitement, it has not readily disclosed the
definitions of poetry that its readers have sought. The other, con-
sisting of the essays of *The Necessary Angel* and *Opus Posthumous*,
the letters, and the journals, is indeed susceptible to direct treat-
ment in theoretical terms, but it has created little interest among
theorists for its intrinsic worth as theory, having been valued pri-
marily for the light it throws on the poems.[35]

While I have used Stevens's prose extensively in the chapters that
follow, I would not claim a high place for the essays and letters in
the theoretical literature of modernism. The letters, which contain
numerous paraphrases and explanations of difficult passages and
ideas, are frequently as equivocal as the poems themselves, per-
haps because Stevens recognized that "it is not possible to tell what
one's own poems mean, or were intended to mean" (L, 354). The
essays, usually delivered as lectures, also lack any sense of finality
as theory. Stevens never mastered the rhetoric of the essay the way
he mastered the rhetoric of the poem, and, typically, the effect of
the prose is a profusion of ideas, many of them borrowed from his
reading, which are never quite assimilated or brought to a focus.
There is, additionally, the problem, as Stevens concedes in *The
Necessary Angel*, that the prose works were never intended to be
"the carefully organized notes of systematic study" (NA, vii). They
are occasional pieces, most of them written to be spoken to small
audiences of academics, with whom Stevens was always ill at ease
and consequently at his most evasive.

Although it does not disclose the definition of poetry promised in
the introduction to *The Necessary Angel*, Stevens's critical prose is
helpful in a number of marginal ways. The essays offer what Ste-
vens labeled a "portent" of his subject. They contain hints of his
shifting interests, a sketchy guide to the development of his think-
ing about poetry from 1936, when he delivered "The Irrational Ele-
ment in Poetry" at Harvard, almost to the time of his death in 1955.
The prose pieces of *The Necessary Angel* and *Opus Posthumous*
also perform another valuable service for anyone interested in Ste-

vens's search for a theory of poetry: they leave a clear trail of his reading in contemporary aesthetic theory and, consequently, of the sources of much of his speculation on poetry. Stevens's reading in critical theory is of no more ultimate authority as a gauge of his poetics than the other sources that have been investigated, but it is the one source that remains largely untapped. It is of significance also because of Stevens's readiness to employ, in both his prose and his verse, the theories and conceptions he encountered in his reading.

As I have argued at greater length in Chapter Four, Stevens's attitude toward influence was complex, amounting almost to a double standard in regard to poetry and prose. His infamous denials of the influence of other poets and his claims that he did not read contemporary poets for fear of absorbing their manner suggest, even if they are unconvincing, a state of mind intent on remaining untainted by outside influences. His prose pieces, on the other hand, are filled with allusions to contemporary theorists and critics, his debts to whom he does not attempt to conceal. That is, Stevens's uneasiness about influence seems to have been restricted to the realm of manner or style. He feared the appropriation of another poet's manner of expression; he was not so uneasy in employing another theorist's ideas.[36] It may be, in fact, that the dread of contamination by other poets led him increasingly to theoretical prose as a source for inspiration. It is certainly true that the composition of his most intensely theoretical poems—those published between 1942 and 1950—coincides with the period in which he was engaged in the reading reflected in the essays and lectures. (The first of the lectures collected in *The Necessary Angel* was read in 1941, the last in 1951.)

In March 1941, during his intensive preparation for "The Noble Rider and the Sound of Words," Stevens mentions in a letter to Henry Church the great number of books he has been scrutinizing in search of material for his subject (L, 388). Judging from the references in the published lecture, these books included I. A. Richards's *Coleridge on Imagination*, H. P. Adams's *The Life and Writings of Giambattista Vico*, and Charles Mauron's *Aesthetics and Psychology*. Sometime the following year he read Henri Focillon's *The Life of Forms in Art*, which was a major source for the second lecture in *The Necessary Angel*, "The Figure of the Youth as Virile Poet." Stevens's copies of these theoretical works reveal the care with which he followed their arguments. His underlining and bracketing of passages and his marginal notations are extensive, and for each work he has prepared his own index to key statements or discussions. The marked passages and entries in his indexes are quite revealing as a guide to the use Stevens made of his readings, for many of these are later echoed in both essays and poems.

It should be noted that these four volumes are not unique among the books in Stevens's personal library. Among other studies that were heavily marked and indexed, apparently as a part of his preparation for lectures, are F. W. Bateson's *English Poetry and the English Language: An Experiment in Literary History*, Benedetto Croce's *The Defence of Poetry: Variations on the Theme of Shelley*, Freud's *The Future of an Illusion*, Jakob Burckhardt's *Reflections on History*, F. L. Lucas's *The Criticism of Poetry*, and Leon Roth's *Descartes' Discourse on Method*.[37] The books in this latter group do not, however, appear to have contributed to Stevens's formulation of an aesthetic to the same degree as the first four studies, although all of them find a place in the first two lectures of *The Necessary Angel*.

It was Henry Church who persuaded him to undertake the first of these lectures, "The Noble Rider and the Sound of Words,"[38] and his dedication to Church of *Notes toward a Supreme Fiction* is, I suspect, a sign of Stevens's recognition that the poem was one result of the immersion in poetic theory to which Church's invitation had led him. The presence in the poem of Richards, Vico, Mauron, and, to a lesser degree, Focillon is also a sign that these critics survived their limited roles as sources for the early lectures. Stevens's report to Church a month before he was to deliver "The Noble Rider" is this: "Everything is going well with the paper. I shall have to eliminate a great deal of the reading. The truth is that, if you want to work your way through your library, the simplest way to go about it is to have a definite subject and then look for something pertinent to it. I find something pertinent everywhere; I must have two or three dozen books on my table that I have never looked at before. After reading a great many of them, I have concluded to say my say on my own account, with the least possible reference to others" (L, 388). He was not able to hold to this resolve. Richards and Mauron dominate the finished lecture; among contemporaries, he also makes use of his reading of H. P. Adams, Bertrand Russell, F. W. Bateson, Virginia Woolf, C. E. M. Joad, F. L. Lucas, Sigmund Freud, and Benedetto Croce. Typically, Stevens saw a number of disparate points of view as pertinent to his subject and found it difficult to avoid appropriating them.

Some of the critics Stevens encountered in his reading were, of course, more pertinent than others to the larger project that transcended the composition of a lecture—that is, his continuing preoccupation with a viable conception of the poetic imagination, what was shortly to become the supreme fiction. He discovered in I. A. Richards, for example, not simply an account of the romantic imagination but an attempt to resolve the epistemological issue that formed the basis for a great deal of his poetry. Because one of Richards's aims in *Coleridge on Imagination* was to adjust Coleridgean theory to contemporary psychology and, in so doing, to settle the mind-world quandary on which romantic theory rests, his "solution" applied as well to Stevens's own imagination-reality complex. Stevens also found a sanction for his supreme fiction in Richards's search for an all-inclusive myth that would include the imagination and that would supplant the insufficient myths of science, religion, and politics. Finally, Stevens discovered in Richards a conception of abstraction that he found useful for the first section of *Notes toward a Supreme Fiction*.

The attractiveness for Stevens of another psychological study, Charles Mauron's *Aesthetics and Psychology*, may have been due initially to Mauron's anti-utilitarian conception of art, a view Stevens held against the attack of the social critics in the thirties and restated at some length in "The Noble Rider." Mauron's attempts to define the aesthetic attitude and to find a line of separation between the emotions of art and those of ordinary life were entirely in keeping with Stevens's privileging of the imagination at the time of "The Noble Rider" and *Notes toward a Supreme Fiction*. He was attracted as well by Mauron's effort to provide a psychology of creativity, an account of the inner dynamics of a mind contemplating a world that "has expelled us and our images" (CP, 381). Since, for Mauron, the function of art is to give pleasure, and the consequences of the aesthetic attitude are described as various classes of pleasure, Stevens found his psychology germane to the overall scheme of *Notes toward a Supreme Fiction*, although Mauron's presence in Stevens's verse is by no means confined to *Notes*. Equally useful was Mauron's justification for poetry's necessary resistance to the intellect, his vindication of obscurity in terms Stevens himself employs in poems of *Parts of a World* and *Transport to Summer*.

Stevens's reading in aesthetic theory was clearly unsystematic, even haphazard. The only discernible link between many of the sources he alludes to in the essays, one feels, is that they happened to be on his table at the same moment. Yet a mind that found something pertinent everywhere was also open to the fortuity of circumstance. It is odd to find Adams's early study of Vico side by side with Mauron's psychology of pleasure, yet Stevens found in them almost identical notions of the conditions necessary for the creation of poetry. Vico's account of the origin of poetry in ignorance and poverty of language reinforces Mauron's prescription for disavowing the familiar and rational as a preliminary for achieving the aesthetic attitude, and Stevens was able to draw on both of them for the first section of *Notes*. Adams's version of Vico's philosophy, as it happened, was also pertinent to several other of Stevens's concerns. Vico's notion of history as a progression of mental states parallels Stevens's account of the history of the imagination in "The Noble Rider." Vichian conceptions of the role of the imagination and of poetry in the evolution of human culture, of the hero, and of human culture ultimately as a product of the creative mind of man may all be located in Stevens.

Coleridge on Imagination, *Aesthetics and Psychology*, and *The Life and Writings of Giambattista Vico* were all read or reread for "The Noble Rider," and their greatest influence was in the prose and verse of the early forties. Focillon's *The Life of Forms in Art* makes its appearance a bit later. Although Stevens alludes to it briefly in *Notes*, its chief effect was on the poems of *Transport to Summer* and *The Auroras of Autumn* which followed *Notes* in composition. The title poem of *The Auroras of Autumn* is particularly indebted to Focillon's theories of form and metamorphosis, as well as to the language and imagery of *The Life of Forms in Art*. Stevens used the book freely as a source for images and figures, but he was also intrigued with Focillon's conception of a changing world of aesthetic forms that exist independent of the ideas, feelings, and skills of the individual artist. It is an approach to art that runs counter to the view of the individual imagination Stevens held at the time he first read the work, a view that tends to magnify the sensibility and the individuality of the artist. Yet Stevens drew on Focillon extensively for "The Figure of the Youth as Virile Poet," and the theory of *The Life of Forms in Art* is increasingly evident in the prose and verse between 1943 and 1950. In the theoretical prose that follows "The Noble Rider," as in the verse of this period, Stevens attempts in various ways to escape the tyranny of the imagination, to locate a place for a reality outside the mind. Focillon was of immense help to this effort because he offered a theory of art that shifts the activity of creation from the imagination of the artist to an external world of form, a world that, like the enthroned imagination of "The Auroras of Autumn," obeys its own laws of change and transcends the momentary and ultimately illusory rule of the individual imagination.

The degree to which Stevens's poetry and theory were shaped by Focillon and his other sources is, of course, open to question. In the following chapters I have attempted to trace the effect of his reading in these theorists as it reappears in his prose and verse. The search centers on two of Stevens's most important long poems, *Notes toward a Supreme Fiction* and "The Auroras of Autumn," but it also includes a great deal of the poetry and prose written during the last fifteen years of his life. My aim is not to identify sources—that Stevens drew on these works is, I think, beyond dispute—but to gauge the extent of their influence and to point out the implications of their presence in Stevens's work. There are without question other important sources for Stevens's poetic theory, many of them yet to be identified. The studies I have considered are, however, the most significant of those I have located in surveying the material remaining in Stevens's library. I am concerned here not with the whole of Stevens's intellectual background or his place in a philosophic tradition, but with a collection of contemporary texts read at about the same time that affected his work in immediate and specific ways.

The study has, of necessity, been structured by the topics addressed in these texts, but they encompass many of the central issues of Stevens's aesthetic—conceptions of abstraction, decreation, and the first idea; versions of literary history and of the relation of the new poet to tradition; descriptions of the nature and origin of poetry, of "ignorance," the death of the gods, and the cycles of ennui and desire; notions of the hero, major man, and the supreme fiction; psychologies of creativity; assumptions about interpretation, misreading, obscurity, nonsense, and irrationality; and, finally, quests for a solid reality beyond the incalculable imagination. I have considered these issues and others in the context provided by the theoretical sources that appear to have been the most compelling for Stevens, and I have offered readings of a great number of passages that I believe are clarified in the light of this context. My conclusions are in no way definitive, and they do not escape the realm of interpretation. They are, however, attempts of the sort Stevens made in his late poems to discover a solid body of fact that does not wholly dissolve itself into the play of the mind, or, more properly in this instance, a substantial body of material in which the play of the mind may be grounded.

2

WHY IT MUST BE ABSTRACT
Stevens, Coleridge, and I. A. Richards

Of the three predicates for Stevens's ultimate human fiction, only the first, the quality of abstraction, produces uneasiness in readers of *Notes toward a Supreme Fiction* and the other theoretical poems that allude to this requisite. "It Must Be Abstract," the title of the first section of *Notes* states flatly and unequivocally. The further requirements that the supreme fiction must change and that it must give pleasure might easily have been anticipated from the poet of "Sunday Morning"; yet if, as we assume (and as Stevens sometimes assumed in his own statements on *Notes*[1]), the fiction is to be identified in some way with poetry, the requirement that it be abstract seems odd, whimsical. Not only does it fly in the face of twentieth-century poetics from Ezra Pound on, but it also appears initially to go against one tendency in Stevens's own poetry—his rejection of "the thought of heaven," the abstraction, in favor of "pungent fruit and bright, green wings" (CP, 67), the sensuous particulars of the physical world. Clearly, if we are to read *Notes* well, and indeed the bulk of Stevens's later poetry, some adjustment is called for either in our notion of what abstraction entails or in our understanding of the manner in which Stevens is using the term as a base for his conception of poetry.

Some sort of accommodation with traditional conceptions of poetic abstraction has, in fact, been the task of the body of commentary on *Notes* and on the poetic theory in which the poem plays a part. The resulting conceptions of abstraction attributed to Stevens since the appearance of *Notes* in 1942, although they cover almost the entire spectrum of possibilities, have tended to fall on one side or the other of the mind-world duality from which the bulk of Stevens criticism issues. Consequently, the reader who wishes to learn why "It Must Be Abstract" from those who have written best on Stevens discovers two conflicting notions of abstraction, depending in part on whether he is viewed as the Poet of Imagination or the Poet of Reality.

That is, however, to state it somewhat too simply, for other considerations have also influenced judgments of the abstract in Stevens and have resulted in numerous variations within the two larger categories of interpretation. These complications include Stevens's shifting use of the term in his prose, the "abstract" style that began in earnest with *Parts of a World* in 1942, the interpretations provided for the term by poems such as *Notes* and "The Ultimate Poem Is Abstract," the possible sources for Stevens's use of the concept, and the nuances of definition of the term itself. Yet, because these considerations are ambiguous and malleable enough to be made to fit almost any larger view of the poet's imagination-reality construct, it is essentially true that, allowing for differences in emphasis, discussions of the supreme fiction most frequently settle the troublesome issue of abstraction in one of two ways. Either abstraction is defined in a conventional sense as something disassociated from the concrete, the specific, the sensuous—that is, abstraction as artifice, idea, concept, generalization—or it is argued that Stevens is employing the term in a manner that runs counter to normal usage so that it comes to mean, for him, almost the opposite of what Pound meant when he warned the poet to "Go in fear of abstractions."[2]

Since any attempt to elucidate Stevens's notion of abstraction must take into account these two diverse categories of explanation, I want to look more closely at each in turn before introducing material that casts some new light on the continuing debate about Stevens's conception of the poetic imagination. This excursion into Stevens criticism is made necessary not simply because every important Stevens scholar has addressed the issue but, more important, because what seems at first to be a quibble about the slippery term *abstraction* turns out to have somewhat larger implications.

What may be called the conventional readings of abstraction in Stevens, taking the term at face value, have generally emphasized the "poetry of thought," Stevens's "push toward a higher level of generalization," or his "habit of philosophizing in poetry." These views—of Frank Doggett, Denis Donoghue, and Randall Jarrell[3]—reflect the early trend of critics to equate Stevens's statements on the necessity of abstraction with a similar tendency toward an aphoristic and generalizing style. Here is Jarrell:

When the first thing that Stevens can find to say of the Supreme Fiction is that "it must be *abstract*," the reader protests, "Why, even Hegel called it a *concrete* universal"; the poet's medium, words, is abstract to begin with, and it is only his unique organization of the words that forces the poem, generalizations and all, over into the concreteness and singularity that it exists for. But Stevens has the weakness—a terrible one for a poet, a steadily increasing one in Stevens—of thinking of particulars as primarily illustrations of general truths, or else as aesthetic, abstracted objects, simply there to be contemplated; he often treats things or lives so that they seem no more than generalizations of an unprecedentedly low order.[4]

Similarly, Doggett implies throughout *Stevens' Poetry of Thought* that abstraction may be equated with the use of quasi-philosophical ideas or concepts. He finds, for example, that Stevens's habit is "to use an abstraction as an over-all expository scheme and then within that scheme to move from one idea to another."[5] In a more recent study Doggett suggests that Stevens's theory of abstraction was a result of and a rationalization for his growing habit of employing ideas in his verse: "This realization of his tendency toward abstraction was accompanied by an awareness of a change in his idea of the nature of poetry."[6]

Doggett and Jarrell leave us with the impression that the title of the first section of *Notes* means something like "it must use ideas" or "it must state general truths," and Denis Donoghue's view of abstraction in Stevens produces the same sense. In one of the first essays to address this issue Donoghue finds that abstraction arises in Stevens's "habit of forming concepts."[7] Setting himself against readers like Jarrell, who viewed the later poems as a falling off from the more accessible satisfactions of *Harmonium*, he argues that the advance of the later poems is due primarily to Stevens's recognition of the importance of abstraction—for Donoghue, "a higher level of generalization."[8] The burden of his approach is to clear Stevens of violations against the common notion that poets should avoid abstractions by demonstrating that "there is no point in making abstractions dirty words if they can be kept or made clean."[9] To accomplish this, Donoghue offers a description of Stevens's procedures in deploying abstraction, the intent of which is to show that Stevens's method of rehabilitating the "abstract order" is not only "an escape from the Symbolist impasse" but, finally, the "best method" for modern poetry.[10]

Donoghue's notion of abstraction as an escape from established modes is not, however, widely shared. Daniel Tompkins, in a study of Stevens's abstract diction, concludes that the practice results in "the death of the imagination,"[11] and Helen Regueiro argues that "the abstractive imagination, which sought to humanize reality . . . found that abstraction and conceptualization are alienating processes."[12] For Regueiro, Stevens's flirtation with abstraction was merely a phase that he passed through on his way to becoming the complete poet of reality. Indeed, the critics I have grouped here—and others who could be included[13]—would disagree about the implications of the abstract in Stevens. What holds them together is their common assumption that Stevens meant by abstraction very nearly what we mean when we refer to a poet's diction as "abstract," use the term to describe the practice of generalizing or conceptualizing in verse, or equate it with the ideal, the purely mental.

There is, however, a second set of readings for which this traditional usage will not serve. For those readers who have placed Stevens's poetry on the reality side of the imagination-reality conflict, the title of the opening section of *Notes* and Stevens's other references to the necessity of abstraction present an obstacle that can be surmounted only through a revision of the conception itself. Curiously, the definitions resulting from this revision posit a meaning that is closer to *concrete* or *real* than to any accepted usage. Louis Martz, for example, argues that in *Notes* Stevens does not use *abstract* "in the usual sense of a philosophical abstraction." His use represents a return to the root meaning—*abstrahere*, to draw away: "By 'abstract' Stevens seems rather to imply a quality of being taken out, abstracted in the root sense, from that world we call the outer universe: something concrete taken out of this and taken into the mind through a process of full, exact realization."[14] Thus, in a strange turnabout, the abstract is associated with the concrete, the fully realized.

This method of redefining the term to avoid the unfortunate implications of standard usage is also employed by Harold Bloom, who has offered several different explanations of why it must be abstract. In an early reading of *Notes* Bloom equates abstraction with "fabrication," which turns out to mean something very close to Martz's root sense of *abstract*, that is, to withdraw the concrete, the real, from existing conceptions of reality. For Bloom, as for Martz, the abstract in Stevens constitutes a disassociation not from the real, but from false conceptions of the real. Bloom speaks of the "poet's first abstraction, or saving withdrawal of the real from the unreal," of major man as "abstracted into reality," and of the "separation or withdrawal of the imagination from its worn coverings and reality from its stale disguises."[15] Although he changes his mind about some aspects of *Notes* in his later study *The Poems of our Climate* (where *abstract* is defined as "antithetical," on the model of Yeats's usage of *primary* and *antithetical* in *A Vision*), his insistence on linking the abstract with the real remains unchanged. Finding a possible source for Stevens's use of the term in Valéry, he maintains that " 'abstract,' for Stevens, as for Valéry, is not opposed to 'concrete' but means 'to separate out from.' "[16]

This endeavor to permit the poet full access to the concrete, the real through a recasting of the process of abstraction achieves its most complete expression in J. Hillis Miller's brilliant essay on Stevens in *Poets of Reality*.[17] Perhaps the single most influential reading of Stevens yet to appear—no approach after the mid-sixties could afford to ignore its implications—the essay sanctioned the tendency already present to claim for Stevens's poetry the victory over reality implied by the title of the volume in which it appeared. Basing his interpretation on the now-fashionable notion of "decreation" in Stevens—a term from Simone Weil that the poet used in "The Relations between Poetry and Painting"[18]—and on the *act* of decreation achieved in the first section of *Notes*, Miller finds a warrant for adjusting the requirement of abstraction to his thesis that Stevens attempts "to annihilate mental fictions and reach the uncreated rock of reality behind."[19] "Armed with a passion for decreation," Miller states, "and convinced that it is the only way in 'these days of disinheritance' (CP, 227), the poet cries: 'Let's see the very thing and nothing else. / Let's see it with the hottest fire of sight' (CP, 373)."[20]

But how is the poet able to see the "very thing" if the supreme fiction itself must be abstract and if the poet's original seeing is called the "first idea"? Miller's answer acknowledges the "curious" terms Stevens employs for achieving the thing in itself:

> Curiously enough, one of Stevens' terms for this cauterizing is "abstraction," and to see the very thing is, strangely, to "see it clearly in the idea of it" (CP, 380). These unexpected uses of the terms "abstraction" and "idea" hold out a possibility that imagination and reality may be united after all. Apparently Stevens means by "abstraction" the power man has to separate himself from reality. . . . To place reality in the imagination by abstracting it does not mean, however, twisting it into some unreal mental fiction. It means the power to carry the

image of the very thing alive and undistorted into the mind. The phrase which gives a name to the first part of "Notes toward a Supreme Fiction" is "It Must Be Abstract" (CP, 380). This means that the poet should abstract himself from the layers of interpretation which have piled up over the years on objects of the external world. He must throw out, for example, what science, mythology, theology, and philosophy tell him about the sun and see the sun as a blazing gold disk in the sky. The sun in itself is "inconceivable." It cannot be transcribed into mental conceptions, but it can be perceived, and this is enough.[21]

Miller's conception of abstraction in Stevens, on examination, turns out to be that of the majority of readers who agree with his assumption that Stevens's poetry seeks the "uncreated rock of reality." These commentators—and they include Bloom, Frank Kermode, Roy Harvey Pearce, and Joseph Riddel (with some reservations)—equate the meaning of Stevens's section title "It Must Be Abstract" with the process of decreation described at the beginning of the section. Although each defines the abstract in his own way, all are united in opposing it to conventional conceptions and in appropriating the language and imagery of the first part of *Notes* as confirmation of their definitions. Thus Kermode argues that, in using the term, "Stevens does not mean falsifications of intellect. . . . Blake's 'minute particulars' are of the essence of his 'abstract.' They have to be abstracted from all the dead formulae that obscure them, to be looked on as a reality free of imaginative . . . accretions."[22] For Pearce, "It Must Be Abstract" means "We must begin with perceived reality, and argue from it to the *Ding an sich*."[23] Riddel, with some hesitancy, also leans toward a realist explanation of the abstract: "Abstraction is a way to pure reality, a stripping away of the husk of things; yet abstraction also denies the reality of process. . . . We abstract by merely being conscious, abstraction being the given of experience."[24] Although he sees the dangers in committing Stevens to a materialist epistemology, Riddel, like the other critics of this group, is persuaded by his assumptions that Stevens equates abstraction and decreation—the cleansing of the thing itself from the accretions that obscure it—and that decreation is a way to bare reality.

But did Stevens identify abstraction with the process of decreation or the real, as this set of readings would have it? Did he identify it with an "abstract" mode or style, a higher level of generalization, as Doggett, Donoghue, Jarrell, and other readers have assumed? Stevens's own statements on *Notes*, which followed closely the publication of the poem, indicate that he did not himself hold either view. Stevens, of course, cannot tell us how to read his poem, but the issue here, as these critics keep reminding us, is what he *meant* by abstraction and the other ambiguous concepts (such as the "first idea") associated with it. The evidence of the *Letters* is that Stevens did not share the view of abstraction held by either side in the divided commentary. Since it is Stevens's use of these curious terms that is in question, it seems proper to consult him, although one must keep in mind that his commentary on his verse is frequently as elusive as the poems themselves.

The practice of identifying Stevens's notion of abstraction with stylistic elements is, as has been noted, characteristic of readers of the "mind" or "imagination" school, who see no essential contradiction in the fact that the fiction must be abstract but who must instead justify the poet's "abstract" style. If poetry is confined to the realm of the mind or imagination, then abstraction presents no real obstacle apart from its unfortunate connotations. Alan Perlis states one assumption underlying this view when he argues that Stevens's thesis that the ideal poetry must be abstract originates from his fundamental belief in the impossibility of apprehending nature as a stable realm of forms.[25] Perlis is perhaps more explicit than other critics of his persuasion in denying Stevens access to the real world, but even critics (like Donoghue) who do not share his extreme epistemology have seen the task of accommodation as a problem not of adjusting Stevens's theory of abstraction but of explaining his practice.

It could perhaps be argued that Stevens's theory of an abstract fiction was influenced by his own rhetorical mode, as Doggett has suggested. But to identify one of the requisites of this fiction with a particular poetic style is inconsistent with Stevens's repeated admonitions that the fiction could never be named explicitly, embodied in a concrete form, or equated with one particular mode. Speaking directly to this point in a letter to Henry Church shortly after *Notes* was published, Stevens remarked: "I have no idea of the form that a supreme fiction would take. The *Notes* start out with the idea that it would not take any form: that it would be abstract" (L, 430). Here the term *abstract* is used in one of its many legitimate senses—that is, having only intrinsic form with no attempt at actual representation, or, more accurately, expressing a quality apart from an object or embodiment of that quality. Stevens used the term in his letters and theoretical prose in a number of different ways; the letter to Church, however, obviously refers to the use of the term in *Notes* and indicates that Stevens's own conception of abstraction in the poem cannot be equated with an "abstract" or aphoristic style. Indeed, by the very fact of *being* abstract, Stevens suggests, the fiction resists representation in any one manner. One feels, to put it another way, that even if Stevens had evolved a completely different style after 1942, or if he had continued the more sensuous diction of *Harmonium*, abstraction would have yet remained the first condition of the supreme fiction.

The realist explanations avoid this problem of equating the abstract with stylistic tendencies by perceiving abstraction not in terms of a mode of representation but in terms of a process—the process by which the poet "must become an ignorant man again" (CP, 380). There is no question that Stevens describes this process in the opening verses of *Notes*, and that some nine years later he borrowed the term *decreation* to label it. But there remains the question of whether either this process or the bare reality that has been seen as its result is the reference of the title "It Must Be Abstract."

Miller's assumption is that abstraction, through decreation, strips the object of perception of its accumulated interpretations and allows the poet to carry the image of the "very thing" into the mind, thus producing the "first idea." Stevens's explanation of the "first idea" to Henry Church is this: "If you take the varnish and dirt of generations off a picture, you see it in its first idea. If you think about the world without its varnish and dirt, you are a thinker of the first idea" (L, 426–27). Two points about this statement are significant. In one example the object reduced to the first idea is not the "very thing" but an artistic representation of the thing, a picture. That is, the painting is itself an "idea" of reality. The second example, which does refer to the real world, emphasizes not direct perception but thinking about the world, and to refer to a "thinker of the first idea" leaves us closer to Doggett's "mental construction" than to Miller's "direct sense image."[26]

Stevens also reveals in a letter to Church that the first poem in Section I originally "bore the caption REFACIMENTO" (L, 431), a term (more often, *rifacimento*) associated with the practice of rewriting or recasting established works of literature. Had he retained this caption, speculation on the "first idea" might have taken a different turn, since the practice of *refacimento* simply replaces one artist's representation of reality with another's, rather than exchanging some unreal fiction for the "very thing." Stevens implies this interpretation in the same passage: "The first step toward a supreme fiction would be to get rid of all existing fictions. A thing stands out in clear air better than it does in soot" (L, 431). The "thing" here would seem to be the supreme fiction, which can be seen more clearly after the existing fictions are removed. To put it another way, it could be argued that the implication of Stevens's comment here is that the result of decreation produces something that must yet be abstract in the traditional sense of the word, that is, an idea or concept rather than the "very thing alive and undistorted." Furthermore, nothing in Stevens's statements on *Notes* indicates that he tended to equate decreation and abstraction. In his letters he speaks as if the process of removing the old fictions and thus seeing the world afresh were merely the first step in formulating a supreme fiction, which "must be abstract" in perhaps another sense than that we see in the commentary.

In his paraphrases of passages of *Notes* Stevens is quite explicit in opposing the abstract fiction to reality, the "thing seen" (L, 444); and the "first idea," in opposition to Miller's "direct sense image" or Kermode's "reality free from imaginative accretions," is identified with the pathetic fallacy: "The first idea . . . was not our own. It is not the individual alone that indulges himself in the pathetic fallacy. It is the race. God is the centre of the pathetic fallacy" (L, 444). Stevens frequently uses the idea of God as an illustration of the ontological status of the supreme fiction, as he does in a letter to Simons, commenting on canto vi of "It Must Be Abstract": "The abstract does not exist, but it is certainly as immanent: that is to say, the fictive abstract is as immanent in the mind of the poet, as the idea of God is immanent in the mind of the theologian. The poem is a struggle with the inaccessibility of the abstract. First I make the effort; then I turn to the weather that is not inaccessible and is not abstract. The weather as described is the weather that was about me when I wrote this. There is a constant reference from the abstract to the real, to and fro" (L, 434). This is perhaps the closest Stevens ever came to defining the term *abstract* as he uses it in *Notes*, although his theological analogy may be misleading to readers unfamiliar with his view of the gods as creations of the imagination. By comparing the supreme fiction to the idea of God in the mind of the theologian, Stevens appears to reserve abstraction to a form of content and to leave out its relation to style. However, as is made clear in the essay "Two or Three Ideas," his interest in the gods is as "aesthetic projections" (OP, 209), and it is their style that chiefly concerns him: "What matters is their manner, their style. . . . It is their style that makes them gods" (OP, 212). More than that, the "style of the gods is derived from men" (OP, 213). The fictive abstract in the mind of the poet and the idea of God in the mind of the theologian are thus not so far apart, since "the creative faculties operate alike on poems, gods and men up to a point. They are always the same faculties" (OP, 211).

In regard to the traditional opposition between the abstract and the real, Stevens's conception of abstraction in the letter to Simons is not foreign to customary usage. By suggesting that the supreme fiction is abstract in the same sense that the idea of God is abstract for the theologian, Stevens clearly means that it does not exist as a real thing capable of being perceived concretely. It is only immanent, existing in the consciousness or the mind. As such, it is inaccessible in a way that the weather, for example, is not inaccessible and therefore not abstract. Although Stevens's use of the term in his prose is frequently ambiguous or evasive, there is no mistaking here the opposition in his own mind between the abstract and the real.

It could be argued that such statements by Stevens merely demonstrate that he did not read *Notes* in the same way that his commentators have read it, and certainly Stevens was wary of committing what has come to be called the intentional fallacy.[27] But even if one accepts, as Stevens apparently did, the principle that the critic's reading of a poem may legitimately go against the poet's intention, that is not quite the situation we face in determining the meaning of *abstract*. Commentators who have interpreted *Notes* in such a way as to support their views of abstraction have not been engaged merely in *explication de texte* but in employing the poem to argue a theory of the imagination that they attribute to Stevens himself (i.e., "Stevens means by 'abstraction' . . ." or "by 'abstract' Stevens seems rather to imply . . ."). The common practice of those engaged in explaining the theory of abstraction, moreover, is to comb the poet's prose for uses of the term that support their explanations. Clearly the issue is the conception of abstraction that Stevens himself held when he wrote *Notes*. It is relatively easy to see the problems inherent in the views of that conception offered thus far. The more difficult task is to demonstrate the assumptions about the abstract that led Stevens to choose the term as the first of the three essential qualities of the supreme fiction.

Stevens has stated that he wrote *Notes toward a Supreme Fiction* during March and April 1942 (L, 443). That may be substantially true, but the April date for its conclusion is almost certainly wrong, for on May 14 he writes to the Cummington Press that he has completed the first two sections and is at work on the third (L, 406). It is more difficult to say when any poem actually begins. Stevens mentions the project first in January 1942, but the poem had its real beginnings, I want to suggest, a few months earlier, in his intensive preparation for the Princeton lecture "The Noble Rider and the Sound of Words." In March 1941 he gives Church, who had solicited the lecture, a progress report and mentions in passing the "two or three dozen books" he has been scrutinizing for "something pertinent" on the subject of the lecture (L, 388). One of these books, I. A. Richards's *Coleridge on Imagination*,[28] he found extraordinarily pertinent not only to "The Noble Rider" but also to the final shaping of the poem he had been edging toward for more than twenty years. It was Richards's attempt to reconcile two romantic conceptions of the imagination, I hope to show, that provided the theoretical basis for the notion of abstraction with which *Notes* begins.

There can be no question as to the care with which Stevens followed Richards's argument. His copy of *Coleridge on Imagination*, now in the Wallace Stevens Archive at the Huntington Library, is more heavily marked and annotated than was Stevens's usual practice. Beginning on page 5 and continuing almost to the last page, a great number of passages have been marked or bracketed, and on the back flyleaf and the back inside cover Stevens has added this index:

14 affinities of the feelings with words and ideas
24 Longinus
26 imagination & values in nature
57 imagination & fancy
108 words as living, inexhaustible meanings
137 the general disparagement of intellectual . . effort
149 Plato's "dear, gorgeous nonsense"
152 "The colours of Nature are a suffusion from the light of
    the mind" Doctrine 2 on p. 145
157 The chief senses of Nature
171 Mythologies
220 a general drift . . in the West
230 Poetry is the supreme use of language[29]

The index was apparently prepared expressly for "The Noble Rider," since most of these references, including Longinus, turn up in the lecture. Stevens begins "The Noble Rider" with an allusion to "Plato's dear, gorgeous nonsense" (NA, 3). He borrows Richards's definition of the language of poetry as "something inexhaustible to meditation" (NA, 9) and his distinction between imagination and fancy. He cites Richards by name four times in the lecture and includes his statement that "poetry is the supreme use of language" (NA, 19). In a more general way, Richards's ideas and methodology pervade "The Noble Rider." Stevens is partly indebted to *Coleridge on Imagination* for his references to "new and local mythologies" and the contemporary "disparagement of reason" (NA, 17), and for his definition of reality. Both Stevens's copy of *Coleridge on Imagination* and the lecture for which it was read (or reread) testify to the influence on Stevens of Richards's discussion of the Coleridgean imagination.

As to the nature of the discussion of Coleridge and imagination that Stevens encountered in Richards, a distinction must be made between the customary scholarly or historical account of romantic theory and Richards's own rather creative reconstruction. *Coleridge on Imagination* has now achieved the rank of a minor classic of romantic criticism. In her foreword to the third edition, Kathleen Coburn lists it as one of two books (the other is Lowes's *Road to Xanadu*) that changed the face of Coleridge studies in the thirties. It was not, however, Richards's principal intent to contribute to Coleridge studies, but to employ Coleridge's theoretical distinctions, updated and rephrased, as a basis for a "scientific" study of language and literature. As a materialist trying to reconstruct the theory of an extreme idealist, Richards is frequently forced to restate Coleridge's arguments in terms more acceptable to modern psychology, and he is quite frank in admitting that his purpose is "to use Coleridge's metaphysical machinery as machinery, disregarding the undeniable fact that Coleridge himself so often took it to be much more" (p. 21).[30] What Richards has produced, then, could aptly be classified as *refacimento*, the term Stevens considered for the first poem of *Notes*. Richards so completely recasts the Coleridgean theory of imagination that the resulting conception is almost as much his own as it is Coleridge's.

Crucial to Richards's *refacimento* is the difficult task of redefining both mind and nature in such a way as to violate neither Coleridge's intent nor a contemporary materialist's more skeptical epistemology. *Coleridge on Imagination* thus has some of the qualities of works that attempt to show that there is no essential conflict between biblical miracles and the laws of science. What must have interested Stevens most in his close reading of the work was that, in the process of adjusting romantic theory to contemporary thought, Richards claims to have solved the epistemological dilemma that had provided Stevens with one of his principal poetic themes, that is, the opposition of two seemingly irreconcilable views of the relation between mind and world. Further, Richards's solution depends on our acknowledging, as Stevens does in *Notes*, that "it must be abstract." Richards concludes his account of the imagination with the notion of abstraction with which Stevens begins his poem.

Richards introduces the epistemological problem central to romantic theory first in Chapter 2, in the process of listing several pre-Coleridgean conceptions of imagination. He notes that "comparison between the versions well brings out one deep opposition which haunts the whole subject: that between a *projective* outlook, which treats imagination's products as figment, and a *realist* outlook, which takes the imagination to be a means of apprehending reality" (p. 26). Like Stevens, Richards recognizes that the projective-realist quandary—Stevens's "imagination-reality complex"—is not simply a problem of the material to be interpreted, but a consideration that affects as well the mode of interpretation, since the interpreter will have to choose a language that seems to force him into one camp or the other: "The choice between the doctrine that we project values into nature and the doctrine that we discover them in her should be noticed as likely to show itself in *our* interpretations of several accounts of Imagination; but a discussion of it is best postponed . . . until the assumptions behind both views have been separated and examined" (p. 26). Beside this passage Stevens has noted the page number in Chapter 7 on which Richards begins the discussion in earnest.

In Chapter 7, "The Wind Harp," and Chapter 8, "The Boundaries of the Mythical," Richards attempts to show that both the projective and realist doctrines derive from Coleridge's conception of imagination, that they are both true, and that they are not, after all, contradictory. His argument for the last conclusion depends in part on an earlier distinction between our *description* of a process or experience and the experience itself, that is, between the artificiality of our doctrines of experience and what he calls the "facts of mind" from which these doctrines originate. "Fact of mind" is the phrase used throughout *Coleridge on Imagination* to allow the materialist to escape the idealist implications of Coleridge's theory of consciousness. By referring Coleridge's doctrines back to the "fact of mind" from which they are derived, Richards is able to translate metaphysics into psychology or semantics, as he does with the projective-realist doctrines:

> Which of these doctrines, the realist or the projective, did either Coleridge or Wordsworth hold? . . . I hope, by examining them, to make more acceptable to some the position that the realist and the projective doctrines are—in the only interpretations in which either is true—both true. As currently formulated they undoubtedly seem to conflict, to be exclusive alternatives. I shall suggest that this appearance is the result of systematic linguistic illusions, arising in the course of the translation *from* the fact of mind *into* philosophic terminologies; that in the form in which they conflict they are both false; and that in the forms in which they are true they combine to be a description of the fact of mind which is their ground and origin. [pp. 146–47]

This is a very large claim indeed. If, as Richards states, these doctrines represent "the central problem of philosophy" (p. 192), then his success in harmonizing them would certainly have consequences beyond romantic theory. One consequence for Stevens would be to reveal that the implicit subject of much of his own poetry is based on a false dilemma resulting from "systematic linguistic illusions." Given the attention that Stevens himself had devoted to this subject—most recently in *The Man with the Blue Guitar*—the scrutiny with which he pursued Richards's argument is not surprising.

He may, however, have been somewhat disappointed with Richards's demonstration of his solution, which loses its focus in a long and diffuse discussion of the various meanings of the term *nature*. The ambiguities inherent in our use of the term, Richards holds, is one source of the "linguistic illusions" that have led to the imagination-reality dilemma. In this discussion, which Stevens noted in his flyleaf index, Richards lists four chief senses of nature that often become blurred in romantic epistemology. Richards attempts to show that, in terms of his multiple definitions of nature, the conflict between the two doctrines of mind and world becomes "an artificial product of a shifting of the senses of *Nature, mind* and *see*." The conflict, that is, resides in the artificial distinctions forced on us by the use of language, and a "fuller description of the 'facts of mind' from which the poet and the philosopher alike set out carries both doctrines as accordant functions, as uncontradictory interpretations." In order to escape contradiction, one must avoid "the transformations that inevitably occur in deriving the doctrines from the 'facts of mind.' " Since any prose description will seem to choose one doctrine over the other, it "is better to say, with Coleridge, that our concern is with the fact of mind itself, the immediate self-consciousness in the imaginative moment which is the source of the doctrines" (p. 162). Richards's "solution" to the problem of the romantic imagination, then, depends on our recognition of the gap between the experience itself and any description of the experience, which must be abstract and therefore artificial.

It is, I believe, from Richards's more extensive treatment of abstraction in Chapter 8, "The Boundaries of the Mythical," that Stevens derives his use of the term in *Notes*. Chapter 8 of *Coleridge on Imagination* constitutes Richards's own *Notes toward a Supreme Fiction*, a statement of his belief that "with more self-knowledge we could live in a world which was both a transcription of our practical needs for exact prediction and accommodation, *and* a mythology adequate to the whole of our spiritual life" (p. 177). Beginning with the assumption that all of our conceptions of nature, including those of science, are myths, Richards works toward the "bounding, all-inclusive myth," which includes "the human imagination" and in which " 'the whole soul of man' is reflected" (p. 181). The myths of science "result in a Nature, over which our power of control is increasing with embarrassing leaps and bounds," but "wisdom requires . . . another Nature for us to live in—a Nature in which our hopes and fears and desires, by projection, can come to terms with one another" (pp. 169–70). Richards's "all-inclusive myth" would provide the kind of nature "that the religions in the past have attempted to provide for man" and that the "political mythologizing" of the twentieth century is attempting unsuccessfully to provide (p. 170).

Although Richards prefers the term *myth* to *fiction*, there is little difference between his formulation of the conception and Stevens's, and he sanctions the term Stevens had employed as early as *Harmonium* with a quotation from F. H. Bradley.[31] Richards's "all-inclusive myth"—Bradley's "fiction"—contains, however, one important quality which has to be acknowledged; it must be "abstractly conceived": "As the inclusive myth, if it could not be abstractly conceived but concretely imagined, it would contain all meanings. Nature, in Sense I [that is, nature independent of the mind], on the other hand, contains the minimum of meaning. It is the other boundary of the mythical. We can say nothing of it and think nothing of it without producing a myth. It is the whatever it is in which we live: and there we have to leave it; for to say more of it is not to speak of it, but of the modes of our life in it. For us, it *can* be only—but it also *must* be—such that *all* the modes of our life are supported by it" (p. 181). Stevens marked a portion of this passage, and he seems to have drawn on it for his definition of reality in "The Noble Rider" when he states that "reality is not that external scene but the life that is lived in it" (NA, 25).

To acknowledge, as Richards does, that the world external to the mind has no meaning in itself, and that any formulation of it in thought or language is a myth, is to acknowledge as well that the "all-inclusive myth" would of necessity be an abstraction. Because he is aware of the pejorative associations of the word *abstraction*, he attempts to place the whole notion of abstraction in a more favorable light. Quoting an attack on the "hypostasy of abstractions" as a "defect and weakness of the human mind," Richards responds:

> That is a stage at which the matter is too often left. For what is there, of which we can think or speak, which is not a hypostatized abstraction? To eliminate this "defect and weakness of the human mind" would be to eliminate the mind itself and all its universes. We may grant that there are vicious as well as virtuous abstractions—abstractions which, in their independent being, are of better or worse service to their fellows. As Coleridge points out, things and notions—like the words to which he compares them—may be living or dead, responsive to the rest of things or not. The word in itself comes to us as a mere undulation; it becomes "a living word" in and with our interpretation of it; and without this it must be "as sounds in an unknown language, or as the vision of heaven and earth expanded by the rising sun, which falls but as warmth upon the eyelids of the blind."   [p. 183]

There are, then, living abstractions as well as dead ones, and the difference lies in our interpretation of the term. Some of the reasons for its pejorative interpretations may be traced to the confusions surrounding the projective-realist doctrines. When we say, for example, that the mind produces images, we imply that these are insubstantial or unreal, "mere copies of actualities other than themselves—figments" (p. 165). This, however, is the kind of "linguistic illusion" that leads to false notions of reality: "*figment* and *real* and *substantial* are themselves words with no meaning that is not drawn from our experience. To say of anything that it is a figment seems to presuppose things more real than these images. To say that anything is an image suggests that there is something else to which it corresponds; but here all correspondence is between images. In short, the notion of reality derives from comparison between images, and to apply it as between images and things that are not images is an illegitimate extension which makes nonsense of it" (p. 165). In Richards's interpretation, all of our universes as well as our descriptions of them are abstract. Using the term in a more inclusive sense than can be found in Stevens, Richards would include under the category of abstraction the products of myth, science, religion, and literature. Whether or not we are happy with this conclusion, the fact remains that any human utterance, from the most elementary description to the loftiest poetry, *must* be abstract.

It is interesting to note, moreover, that Richards's discussion of abstraction is coupled with his examination of another troublesome term, *idea*, that Stevens employs in *Notes*. Richards concludes "The Boundaries of the Mythical" with a statement from Coleridge supporting his contention that abstraction, far from being a "defect and weakness of the human mind," represents the necessary condition of all intercourse with the external world. Coleridge, in a passage from *The Statesman's Manual*, had placed *idea* at the top of his hierarchy of aspects of the mind's activities:

> "That which is neither a sensation nor a perception, that which is neither individual (that is a sensible intuition) nor general (that is a conception) which neither refers to outward facts, nor yet is abstracted from the forms of perception contained in the understanding, but which is an educt of the imagination actuated by the pure reason, to which there neither is nor can be an adequate correspondent in the world of the senses,—this and this alone is—an Idea. Whether ideas are regulative only, according to Aristotle and Kant; or likewise constitutive, and one with the power and life of nature, according to Plato and Plotinus . . . is the highest problem of philosophy, and not part of its nomenclature."   [pp. 183–84]

This conception of ideas, which identifies them as products of the imagination "actuated by the pure reason," is quite close to Stevens's use of "idea" and "first idea" in *Notes*, where "the first idea is an imagined thing" (CP, 387) and "the idea of man," the "major abstraction," "comes . . . from reason" (CP, 387–88). Coleridge's notion that there cannot be an adequate correspondent to the idea in the world of the senses is echoed by Stevens's "inconceivable idea of the sun" (CP, 380). In fact, Richards had earlier included a quotation from Coleridge that employs the same language: " 'This is the test of a truth so affirmed (a truth of the reason, an Idea) that in its own proper form it is *inconceivable*' " (p. 166). Furthermore, Coleridge's attempt to differentiate the idea as "an educt of the imagination" from both "outward facts" and "the forms of perception contained in the understanding" parallels Stevens's effort to allow the idea to mediate between the object of perception, on the one hand, and our traditional understanding of it on the other. That is, Stevens's "idea" appears to be neither the thing itself nor a conventional image of it:

> You must become an ignorant man again
> And see the sun again with an ignorant eye
> And see it clearly in the idea of it. . . .
>
> How clean the sun when seen in its idea,
> Washed in the remotest cleanliness of a heaven
> That has expelled us and our images. . . .   [CP, 380–81]

A more detailed analysis of the first section of *Notes* would be required to match Stevens's use of *idea* with Coleridge's, and there is no reason to suppose that the two conceptions match in every respect. But even a cursory examination suggests that Stevens's choice of the term to describe what Richards calls a "realizing intuition" could very well have been prompted by his reading of *Coleridge on Imagination*.

It is even more likely that his choice of the title "It Must Be Abstract" for the first section of *Notes* and his conception of abstraction in the poem were inspired by Richards. What argues most forcefully for this link is the context in which Richards's discussion of abstraction appears. "The Boundaries of the Mythical" not only maintains the necessity of something very much like Stevens's supreme fiction; it also shows that a recognition of the inevitability of abstraction enables the imagination to free itself from the dilemma of the mind-world duality and thus to begin the "inexhaustible inquiry" that would lead to the creation of a sustaining mythology. Richards ends his own notes toward this myth with a comment on Coleridge's definition of *idea*:

"The imagination actuated by the pure reason" is "the whole soul of man in activity." What by and in it we know is certainly not a part of philosophy's nomenclature. But what we *say* about it—whether we say that it is the mode of all our knowledge (ideas are regulative); or that it is what we know (ideas are constitutive)—must be said (thus abstractly) in a vocabulary. And I have tried to make the position acceptable that these rival doctrines here derive from different arrangements of our vocabularies and are only seeming alternatives, that each pressed far enough includes the other, and that the Ultimate Unabstracted and Unrepresentable View that thus results is something we are familiar and at home with in the concrete fact of mind.   [p. 184]

Once these rival doctrines are harmonized through the conception of abstraction, the artificial notion of "reality" is no longer a stumbling block for the imagination. The "unabstracted and unrepresentable" view is indeed present in the "concrete fact of mind." However, recognizing the fictive nature of all efforts to articulate it, the imagination is unconstrained in its pursuit of the myth that, to revert to Stevens's terms, "gives to life the supreme fictions without which we are unable to conceive of it" (NA, 31). If this approach were generally accepted, Richards says, "the problems of criticism would no longer abut, as they so often did for Coleridge, on this problem of Reality; they would be freed for the inexhaustible inquiry into the modes of mythology and their integration 'according to their relative worth and dignity' in the growth of our lives" (p. 184).

To frame Richards's whole argument in terms that apply to Stevens in 1941: once he accepts the premise that "it must be abstract," he is able to shift his focus from the relationship *between* reality and imagination (i.e., *The Man with the Blue Guitar*) to the preliminary considerations of the sustaining fiction that includes both imagination and reality as equals. Richards has provided an epistemology for resolving the problem of the endlessly elaborated conflict. And Stevens apparently finds, as he puts it in "The Noble Rider" speaking of the "possible poet," that it is "imperative for him to make a choice, to come to a decision regarding the imagination and reality; and he will find that it is not a choice of one over the other and not a decision that divides them, but something subtler, a recognition that here, too, as between these poles, the universal interdependence exists, and hence his choice and his decision must be that they are equal and inseparable" (NA, 24). *Notes* transposes this passage into one of the most important moments of the poem, at the conclusion of the Canon Aspirin episode:

> He had to choose. But it was not a choice
> Between excluding things. It was not a choice
>
> Between, but of. He chose to include the things
> That in each other are included, the whole,
> The complicate, the amassing harmony.   [CP, 403]

The choice *of* and not *between* is made possible by the acceptance of abstraction as a necessary predicate of the supreme fiction and the consequent dissolution of the imagination-reality conflict. In 1935 Stevens had stated, in response to the charge of didacticism, that "my real danger is not didacticism, but abstraction" (L, 302). Following his reading of Richards, however, he makes the power of abstraction the "measure" of the poet. Constructing the future poet in "The Noble Rider," he says of him: "He will consider that although he has himself witnessed, during the long period of his life, a general transition to reality, his own measure as a poet, in spite of all the passions of all the lovers of the truth, is the measure of his power to abstract himself, and to withdraw with him into his abstraction the reality on which the lovers of truth insist. He must be able to abstract himself and also to abstract reality, which he does by placing it in his imagination" (NA, 23). This passage has been quoted in support of almost every definition of the abstract in Stevens as put forward by his commentators, and it is obviously susceptible to varying interpretations, mostly because of Stevens's use of the phrase "to abstract himself." However, three points in particular argue for a reading of abstraction here that is in line with Richards's use. First, the poet's abstraction is set against both "a general transition to reality" and "the passions of all the lovers of the truth" in the same manner in which Richards upholds abstractions against illusory notions of reality and false claims that science is somehow more "true" than the myths of the poet. Second, such a use of the term preserves the abstraction as a product of imagination without sacrificing reality, which is placed *in* the imagination. (Richards preserves what is commonly thought of as reality in the "concrete fact of mind.") Finally, the passage appears in the paragraph with—and leads to—Stevens's assertion that the poet must not choose between imagination and reality but must regard them as equal and inseparable. As in *Notes* and *Coleridge on*

Imagination, the reconciliation of imagination and reality follows directly from the poet's realization of his abstractive powers.

One further indication that Stevens's abstract is essentially Richards's is that *Notes* appears to echo several other passages in *Coleridge on Imagination*. Although most of these echoes are rather faint, the cumulative effect is to suggest that Richards's work was very much in Stevens's thought as he composed the poem. It may be, in fact, that the first line of *Notes* was suggested by Richards's discussion of Coleridge's Secondary Imagination. Richards states that the "Secondary Imagination, re-forming this world, gives us not only poetry" but "all objects for which we can feel love" (p. 58). Stevens's opening address to the imagination begins, "And for what, except for you, do I feel love?" (CP, 380). Phoebus as a type of the outworn images for the sun may also be traced to Richards's extended discussion of Phoebus in connection with Coleridge's attack on Gray's line "And reddening Phoebus lifts his golden fire." Coleridge's objection is the same as Stevens's—that the poet has confounded "the real *thing* with the personified *representative* of the thing" (p. 124). More than that, the underlying thesis of the persona's instructions to the ephebe in the first section of *Notes*—to reject the stale image of the thing and thus to see it in its *idea*—parallels Coleridge's analysis of the "life in the idea" quoted by Richards: " 'This elevation of the spirit above the semblances of custom and the senses to a world of spirit, this life in the idea, even in the supreme and Godlike, which alone merits the name of life, and without which our organic life is but a state of somnambulism; this it is which affords the sole anchorage in the storm, and at the same time the substantiating principle of all true wisdom, the satisfactory solution of all the contradictions of human nature, of the whole riddle of the world. This alone belongs to and speaks intelligibly to all alike, the learned and the ignorant, if but the heart listens' " (p. 167). Stevens later returned to this passage for a poem entitled "Somnambulisma," which is more obviously based on the Coleridgean distinction between the state of somnambulism and the world of a "man feeling everything" (CP, 304).[32]

Cantos iv and v of "It Must Be Abstract" may also owe something to Richards. Canto iv develops the notion of the "muddy centre" that preceded us:

The first idea was not our own. Adam
In Eden was the father of Descartes
And Eve made air the mirror of herself. . . .

There was a muddy centre before we breathed.
There was a myth before the myth began,
Venerable and articulate and complete.   [CP, 383]

In his analysis of the different senses of nature, Richards notes
that in one sense man "makes of her, as with a mirror, a trans-
formed image of his own being" (p. 145). He stresses, however,
that this does not deny the existence of something like Stevens's
"muddy centre"—something of which we cannot speak without
creating a myth—prior to the "projection of our sensibility." Nature
is "shaped by certain of our needs," but "our needs do not originate
in us. They come from our relations to Nature in Sense I. We do not
create the food that we eat, or the air that we breathe . . . we do
create, from our relations to them, every image we have 'of' them"
(p. 164). Or, as he puts it in a similar context, our perceptions of
nature are "responses . . . whose form has a prehuman origin" (p.
161). Neither Richards nor Stevens wants to surrender the external
world for a purely idealist epistemology, but both are resigned to
the fact that it can be spoken of only as "the whatever it is in which
we live" or the "muddy centre."

Canto v, which follows from this condition that "we live in a
place / That is not our own and, much more, not ourselves" (CP,
383), develops an idea that Richards employs in the final chapter of
his study of Coleridge. The chapter deals with the shifts in human
consciousness during the last four hundred years and asserts the
impossibility of returning "to any mythological structures prevail-
ing before the seventeenth century" (p. 225). The waning of older
modes of order is not, however, the loss of all possibilities of order,
and Richards places the burden of creating a new order on contem-
porary poetry. The poet must become "the necessary channel for
the reconstitution of order" (p. 228) for two reasons. First, if we
grant that all is myth, poetry is the mythmaking that most engages
the whole man. Beyond that, "poetry is the supreme use of lan-
guage, man's chief coordinating instrument, in the service of the
most integral purposes of life," and it is only through man's search
for meaning in language that "our world and our life have grown
and taken what order they have for us" (p. 230).[33] The sage may
avoid words, and animals may live harmoniously in a world devoid
of them, but the "meanings sufficient for the dumb creatures are
not enough for man" (p. 231). The poet's sense of his insufficiency
as a natural creature, coupled with his mastery of language, gives
him the importance he attains in Richards's mythmaking process.

Canto v develops this contrast between the self-sufficiency of lion, elephant, and bear, whose sounds are inseparable from nature itself and not "about" it, and the young poet, alienated from nature, who struggles to articulate the "first idea" that would bring him into harmony with his world. The lion's roar "Reddens the sand with his red-colored noise"; the elephant's blare is merely one element of his locale; the bear "snarls in his mountain / At summer thunder and sleeps through winter snow" (CP, 384). The violence of the ephebe, however, produces a "bitter utterance," the function of which is not simply to exist as a part of nature but to impose a human order on it—"to lash the lion, / Caparison elephants, teach bears to juggle" (CP, 385). It is the poet's violent response to his alienation from which the poem springs, and from which Richards's new order of the mind will arise "if man is to become again a noble animal" (p. 226).

Other parts of "It Must Be Abstract" could be examined with Richards in mind,[34] but the issue of direct influence on specific passages is secondary to the larger question of whether the whole conception of the first third of Notes owes its genesis in part to Richards's redactions of Coleridge's theory of the imagination. The sources for Stevens's conceptions of abstraction and the "first idea" have been traced variously to Paul Valéry, Alfred North Whitehead, F. H. Bradley, Charles Ives, and Charles Peirce.[35] Without discounting the possibility of more than one influence, it seems more likely that Richards was Stevens's principal source not only for the conception of abstraction but also for an epistemology that makes the poem possible.

If this assumption is correct, then some views of the poem may need to be revised. It would appear, for example, that both groups of critics surveyed earlier have mistaken Stevens's conception of abstraction. If, as it appears, Stevens was influenced by Richards's use of the term, then he means both less and more than the meanings previously attributed to him. He means less than Miller and the realist school have assumed, because he uses the term not in an eccentric manner, to suggest the power of the poet to capture the "very thing" alive and undistorted, but in a conventional manner, to suggest the inability of the poet's fiction to escape the artificial and therefore abstract nature of language. The *must* of "It Must Be Abstract" is not prescriptive—i.e., "it should be abstract"—but a sign of the necessary condition of the symbolizing process of any fiction or myth. Contrary to the more widely accepted reading of Notes, the title of the first section says, then, exactly what it appears to say on one level, what, in fact, the persona asks the ephebe to recognize—that his world is of necessity an invented world:

Begin, ephebe, by perceiving the idea
Of this invention, this invented world,
The inconceivable idea of the sun.   [CP, 380]

On the other hand, Stevens means more by *abstract* than critics like Doggett and Donoghue have seen, since he is not making a distinction between levels of language (i.e., abstract versus concrete) or levels of thought (concepts or ideas versus particular details) but stating the premise of an epistemology by which even the most sensuous detail remains radically a product of abstraction. He is, finally, implying more than either group has acknowledged by using the notion of abstraction as the basis for a dissolution of the imagination-reality conflict, a conflict that itself separates the two groups of readers of the poem.

However, a further lesson to be gained from Richards's analysis of abstraction is that, even if the poem does succeed in removing the opposition between the two contrary views of imagination, the critics' doctrines will no doubt succeed in reinstating it, since the language employed in interpretation will appear to reveal Stevens as either the Poet of Imagination or the Poet of Reality. Both Richards and Stevens were wary of the paradoxes associated with the doctrine of the romantic imagination, and *Coleridge on Imagination* and *Notes toward a Supreme Fiction* both recognize the dilemma contained in their description of the acts of imagination—the dilemma by which the mode of description itself, since it must be abstract, will push the "unabstracted and unrepresentable view" into one doctrine or another.

In a recent essay on Stevens, J. Hillis Miller notes this quandary of interpretation. He now finds not one but three theories of poetry present in Stevens's poems, and he states that the conflict among these three theories "is woven into the fabric of our language" so that it is "impossible to adopt one theory of poetry without being led, willy-nilly, to encounter the ambiguous inherence within it of the other two."[36] Based on his study of Richards, Stevens was of course aware of this problem before he wrote *Notes*, and his attempt to escape it led directly to such ambiguous consequences as the notion of abstraction, the "first idea," and the numerous other paradoxes (i.e., "the sun / Must bear no name, gold flourisher" [CP, 381]) that make *Notes* the "unrepresentable" poem that it is. Miller's conclusion is that, whatever theories are detected in Stevens, his poetry cannot be explained by its theories or sources, since "the authentic voice of Stevens as a poet is not touched by such explanations."[37] No one could argue with this principle; the qualities that make *Notes toward a Supreme Fiction* one of the triumphs of modern poetry cannot be traced to Richards or Coleridge or any other source. To understand the intellectual tradition within which the poem was conceived can, however, aid us in correcting mistaken views of it and provide a context in which we can come closer to appreciating the task the poem undertakes. It can also help to remind us, as Miller does, that it is only in the language and structure of the poem itself, impervious to the critics' doctrines, that the poet's triumph exists. Stevens was struck by a statement with which Richards ends his chapter on the rival doctrines of the imagination, and on page 163 of his copy of *Coleridge on Imagination* he marked this portion of a passage in which the critic warns of the treacheries of abstract language: "It is the privilege of poetry to preserve us from mistaking our notions either for things or for ourselves. Poetry is the completest mode of utterance."

3

WHY IT MUST CHANGE
Stevens, Vico, and Harold Bloom

The second of the notes toward Stevens's supreme fiction, "It Must Change," involves assumptions less problematic than the principle of abstraction and more pervasive in his poetry and theory. As the ground of Stevens's epistemology, change, a property of both mind and world, denies him any final resting place in a formulation of reality that will suffice. As the basis of his psychology, it determines the cycles of ennui and desire from which the poem springs. As a component of his conception of literary history, it helps to explain what Stevens takes to be our diffidence to much of the poetry of the past and leads ultimately to his view of the tradition of poetry as "a cemetery of nobilities" (NA, 35). It is this last conception, change as a determining principle of Stevens's account of literary history, that I am chiefly concerned with here. Stevens's assumptions about what he calls the "history of the imagination" (NA, 21) are crucial to the theoretical works published in the early forties, especially *Notes toward a Supreme Fiction* and the first two lectures of *The Necessary Angel*. *Notes*, for example, begins with the relationship of the young poet, the ephebe, to the tradition that he has inherited and that he must renounce to "become an ignorant man again" (CP, 380). The attitude of sons to poetic fathers also pervades the lecture "The Figure of the Youth as Virile Poet," which follows a notion of literary history articulated earlier in "The Noble Rider and the Sound of Words."

Stevens's version of literary history, and especially of the relationship of new poets to their precursors, has been dismissed by Harold Bloom as unconvincing,[1] and Bloom has gone further to say that "Stevens, as a theorist of poetry is little more than a self-deceiver" (PR, 281). Because of Bloom's attack on Stevens as a theorist and because of his appropriation of Stevens for his own theory of influence, I want to examine some links between the two theories. In addition, I shall look at Stevens's theory of literary kinships in connection with a much earlier theory of poetic origins that had some influence on it—Vico's account of the invention of poetry, which Stevens read in H. P. Adams's *The Life and Writings of Giambattista Vico*.[2] These three versions of the history of poetry I take up in an order roughly analogous to Vico's three ages of gods, heroes, and men—first Vico, then Stevens, and finally Bloom.

To suggest a Vichian element in Stevens's theory of poetry would be merely whimsical were there not evidence for it in two works completed shortly after Stevens read *The Life and Writings of Giambattista Vico*. *Notes* picks up some of Vico's (or Adams's) language in describing the origin of poetry, and "The Noble Rider and the Sound of Words" cites a Vichian principle in support of its argument that progressive mental states in the race are responsible for changes in response to poetic figures such as Plato's figure for the soul. The clearest evidence for Stevens's interest in Vico's theories may be seen, however, in his copy of Adams's work.[3] Stevens apparently returned to the book for a second reading, for he prepared two overlapping indexes, one on the inside back flap of the dust cover and the other on a small memo sheet, headed "From the desk of Wallace Stevens," laid into the book. In all likelihood the memo-sheet index represents Stevens's rereading of the book in preparation for "The Noble Rider," since some of its entries point to ideas developed in the lecture. Here it is in full:

120 morphology of human culture
122 The Invention of Poetry
    The invention of language
126 The poet's strong turn for . . the sublime
    (exaggeration)
    The truth of science has destroyed . . great poetry
152 *The true history of the human race is a history of its
    progressive mental states.*
153 psychology as the basis of philology
166 Wings of Pegasus
169 Ages of language
201 Dante—fount of the most beautiful Tuscan speech and as
    an example of sublime poetry

Stevens's dust-cover index, probably compiled during an earlier reading, indicates his concern with the main line of Vico's argument rather than a search for material to support his own:

70 sapienza riposta
  sapienza volgare
72 Scienza Nuova a great liberation of creative power
85 the divine character of the human mind
87 geometry
89 language of poetry
90 early poets
212 philosophy of history
214 The individual is only to be understood through the
    history of society
217 his dominant idea
218 The creative mind which produces the world of
    institutions is the mind of man
219 "the sublime imaginings of Homer and of Dante"
221 humanity is its own work

What Stevens sees as Vico's dominant idea—Adams calls it the "central proposition of the new science" (LWV, 218)—is suggested in the notations for pages 218 and 221, where Adams makes clear that, in Vico's view, human history is never the result of an arbitrary divine will but the product of the creative mind of man. Stevens found this idea congenial to his own view of the creative imagination, and it is echoed in a later poem, "Conversation with Three Women of New England" (OP, 109): "The author of man's canons is man, / Not some outer patron and imaginer."

Taken as a whole, Adams's exposition of Vico's philosophy addresses a number of issues with which Stevens was concerned when he read the work.[4] Among these are Vico's theories of the place of imagination and of poetry in the development of human culture, his reaction against Cartesianism, his epistemological doctrine that we can know only what we ourselves create, his account of the origins of poetry, his conception of the hero, and his view of human history and of language as the progression of mental states. The more than two dozen passages Stevens marked in the text are typically discussions either of the role of creative mind in history or of the nature and origin of poetry, two areas in which Stevens's own thinking most resembles Vico's.

Given a number of parallels between the two theorists, it would be tempting to argue that Stevens's conception of poetry in the early forties reflects a Vichian tradition. But this is to assume that a Vichian tradition existed outside Italy in 1940. When Stevens read Adams, no English translation of Vico's work was available, and

Adams represents his own book as the first full-length study of Vico in English.[5] Vico's philosophy thus went almost without notice outside Italy until the late forties, when the first English translations of his *Autobiografia* and the *Scienza Nuova* appeared and sparked a renewed interest in Vico's philosophy of history. Donald Verene has recently argued that Vico's thought had "no serious effect on the development of modern thought" or, more generally, "on the course of Western thought and life in the two and one-half centuries since the publication of his definitive version of the New Science."[6] Although that may appear a slight exaggeration, it is reasonable to assume that any Vichian traces found in Stevens's poetry and critical prose came primarily from his reading of Adams's study. As is the case with Stevens's use of *Coleridge on Imagination*, which gives us Coleridge filtered through Richards, Stevens's Vico is thus Vico as read (or misread) by Adams. Adams's study is in no way a rigorous philosophical analysis, and contemporary Vico scholarship would perhaps have difficulty with the implications of some of its conclusions. Taking into account, then, Adams's popularizing of Vico's philosophy and Stevens's creative use of Adams, what we find in Stevens's work are Vichian conceptions twice removed from their source.

The absence of first-hand knowledge of Vico does not, however, reduce Stevens's debt to the Vichian principles he found in Adams and made use of in the theory articulated initially in "The Noble Rider" and later in the verse of *Notes*. To consider the poem first, it is clear that the opening cantos of *Notes* owe a great deal to Adams's account of Vico's theory of the origin of language in poetic speech. In a section headed "The Invention of Poetry" Adams traces Vico's solution to the problem of primitive speech in the discovery that it was essentially poetic: "The questions he asked himself were how men, such as he conceived them long ago to have lived and felt, could or rather must have invented these forms of language. . . . It was, therefore, a question of invention; the faculty of invention he called *ingenium*. Early men having the mentality of boys, the questions of how invention occurred in the childhood of the race can be answered from the study of boys endowed with *ingenium*, 'ingenious boys' " (LWV, 123–24).

Vico assumes that the first words were monosyllabic, nothing more than exclamations, and that the development of language depended on the extended use of a small number of expressions to suggest new thoughts. The development thus required the use of figures of speech: "In a poverty of words the necessity of new uses became the mother of invention, not so often the invention of new words as of devices for making the old word serve a new purpose" (LWV, 124). Language was thus born in poetry. Its invention was made possible by ignorance, by the poverty of resources, and by the circumstance that imagination preceded reason. Here is the relevant passage from Adams (which Stevens marked with an arrow in the margin):

> All these tropes, exaggerations, sublimities, personifications and fables of the poets depend for their origin upon genuine ignorance and simplicity, and on the fact that imagination had to do the work later done by reason. Their invention required the spur of overwhelming necessity. So far as they had progressed in an age of ignorance they were available for later poets who used them with professed artifice. The truth of science has destroyed the conditions that favour great poetry. Vico propounds a new art of poetry. Whoever would be a poet must forget the wealth of words that enables him to describe an event as it actually happened. He must confine himself to language that is sensuous and impassioned, and find out the means of saying in such language all that he has to say, as primitive men were forced to do. He must disown the scientific and philosophical approach to life, must learn to think and feel as boys and rustics think and feel, and must know what tropes and pictures will reduce modern readers to a corresponding degree of credulity. He will work with as much art as a rhetorician, giving the lie to the maxim that poets are born and orators are made. He must work, above all, with his imagination, must become a supreme phantast.   [LWV, 126]

One coincidence of Stevens's reading for "The Noble Rider" (reading which, I have suggested, was later reflected in the theory of *Notes*) is that two of his sources offered him the same general description of the necessary grounds for the creation of poetry. Charles Mauron's *Aesthetics and Psychology* proposes a theory of the aesthetic moment that is in essential agreement with Adams's summary of Vico above, and I shall discuss it at greater length in Chapter Four. Both conceptions assume that the creation of poetry depends on the act of disowning or forgetting a utilitarian, scientific, or philosophical view of life in favor of what Mauron calls "the aesthetic attitude." The key term employed by Stevens is, I think, taken from the passage above, the argument that the basic elements of poetic language "depend for their origin upon genuine ignorance." Stevens begins *Notes* with the notions of invention and ignorance:

Begin, ephebe, by perceiving the idea
Of this invention, this invented world,
The inconceivable idea of the sun.

You must become an ignorant man again
And see the sun again with an ignorant eye
And see it clearly in the idea of it.   [CP, 380]

Although Stevens's "first idea" is not derived from Vico, it contains some of the qualities of the idea of Vico's first poets, who saw the world in a perfect ignorance that later poets can only approach in an artificial manner. In a passage referred to in Stevens's index, Adams notes that, in the early stages of his philosophy, "Vico is already facing the problem of the superiority of the poets of early and barbarous times." His explanation for this superiority is found in "the tendency of later writers to imitate their predecessors. The only way to excel these is for the poet or artist to study life and nature for himself" (LWV, 90). That is, rather than imitating the style of their precursors, new poets must imitate the mental state under which the first poets created their poetry. They must attempt to recover a "first idea," a way of seeing that depends on genuine ignorance. This in itself is a supreme act of imagination, Adams notes; Vico himself performed such an imaginative act to recover the conditions of the first poets, and readers of the *Scienza Nuova* must themselves perform it. Since the knowledge possessed by the first men "was a knowledge of a humanity immersed in sense, it could only be expressed in the poetic, heroic language, in concrete, imaginative, symbolic fashion" (LWV, 214). To recover it, "we must again create it in ourselves, must divest ourselves of our rational nature so far as to embody with our imagination the conditions of the men immersed in sense" (LWV, 215). When, in *Notes*, the ephebe is instructed to "become an ignorant man again," he is thus being directed to return not merely to a former state in himself but, imaginatively, to a former state in the race, to the ignorance of the first poets. It is significant that neither *ignorant* nor *ignorance* appears in Stevens's poetry prior to his reading of Adams, and his conversion of ignorance from a description of the first poets to a prescription for the condition of the new poet is sanctioned by a statement he underlined in Adams: "The investigation into the origin of poetry leads to a revolution in the conception of its nature" (LWV, 128).

The difficulty of imagining the conditions of the first poets is related to Vico's theory of progressive mental states. He separates human history into three ages—the age of gods, in which humanity thought and ordered its world in terms of gods; the age of heroes, in which humanity conceived its world in terms of heroic figures; and the age of men, in which humanity recognized an equality in human nature and established the forms of human government.[7] Adams notes that what, in Vico, is far ahead of his time "is the way in which the stage of mental development determines for each successive period the character of every manifestation of human thought" (LWV, 135). For Vico, Adams notes, the gods of the first poets never existed, and the fables of the first poets were not interpretations of the physical universe but attempts to make sentences: "In forming this concatenation of symbolical objects the primitive poets were simply putting together into an intelligible sequence what to them were the equivalents of words; they were making sentences" (LWV, 134). The gods were attempts to name that which was without a name: "The names of anthropomorphic gods were a very early vocabulary. Saturn, for instance, was the harvest" (LWV, 169). In attempting to recover the conditions of the first poets, then, a poet from the age of men would have to recognize that "Phoebus was / A name for something that never could be named" (CP, 381). More than that, "The death of one god is the death of all," since his death represents the end of one era of the imagination and the beginning of another: "Let purple Phoebus lie in umber harvest, / Let Phoebus slumber and die in autumn umber" (CP, 381). The first canto of *Notes* combines the Vichian instruction on the recovery of ignorance, the condition of the first poets, with the Vichian principle of successive mental states. The poet of the third age cannot conceive the sun in terms of Phoebus as the first poets did, but Phoebus was only a name, an aesthetic project for the sun which is yet to be completed: "There was a project for the sun and is" (CP, 381).

In "Two or Three Ideas" Stevens speaks of the death of the gods in Vichian terms. He refers to them, he says, not in any religious aspect, "but as creations of the imagination." To speak of them "is to speak of the origin and end of eras of human belief" (OP, 205). In an age that is "largely humanistic . . . it is for the poet to supply the satisfactions of belief, in his measure and in his style" (OP, 206). One way of thinking of the gods of classical mythology is that they "were merely aesthetic projections. They were not the objects of belief. They were expressions of delight" (OP, 207). "When the time came for them to go, it was a time when their aesthetic had become invalid in the presence not of a greater aesthetic of the same kind, but of a different aesthetic, of which from the point of view of greatness, the difference was that of an intenser humanity. The style of the gods is derived from men. The style of the gods is derived from the style of men" (OP, 212–13). The assumption here is that the aesthetic projections of successive ages are determined by progressive mental states, and Stevens notes that "the creative faculties operate alike on poems, gods and men up to a point. They are always the same faculties" (OP, 211). In *Notes* the ephebe is instructed to employ the same creative faculties with which the first poets imagined the gods. Since he is living in a humanistic age, his ignorance will produce not gods but an equivalent first idea that is left unnamed. To give the sun a proper name, to personify it in the manner of the first poets, is to return to an age of the imagination that has ended:

> The sun
> Must bear no name, gold flourisher, but be
> In the difficulty of what it is to be. [CP, 381]

In canto iv Stevens suggests that the first idea is an invention of the race, not of the individual poet. Imagination preceded reason, and the first inhabitants found themselves strangers in a world that they peopled with gods made as mirrors of themselves. They did not create the physical world that preceded them, only the myths that made it their own:

> The first idea was not our own. Adam
> In Eden was the father of Descartes
> And Eve made air the mirror of herself,
>
> Of her sons and her daughters. They found themselves
> In heaven as in a glass; a second earth;
> And in the earth itself they found a green—
>
> The inhabitants of a very varnished green.
> But the first idea was not to shape the clouds
> In imitation. The clouds preceded us
>
> There was a muddy centre before we breathed.
> There was a myth before the myth began,
> Venerable and articulate and complete.
>
> From this the poem springs: that we live in a place
> That is not our own and, much more, not ourselves
> And hard it is in spite of blazoned days. [CP, 383]

For Stevens, Eden is the imaginative state prior to reason, the state of ignorance that is his secular equivalent for innocence, and Descartes is the "later reason" (CP, 399) into which we fall from imagination. Descartes's presence in the poem may have resulted from Adams's discussion of Vico's attack on Cartesianism, which Stevens acknowledged in one of his few marginal notations (p. 89). One defect of Cartesianism for Vico is its exclusive reliance on analytic and deductive reasoning and its consequent neglect of imagination and memory, which are weakened by the application of the Cartesian methodology (LWV, 89). Descartes's "I think, therefore I am" does not give us knowledge of our own existence, Vico argues, but merely indicates a consciousness of it. In Vico's *verum-factum* doctrine we can know only what we make ourselves, and therefore to "have true knowledge of my own being I must have created myself" (LWV, 95). We did not create ourselves, but we did, in Vico's system, create the language and myths by which we know human history, just as "Eve made air the mirror of herself." For Vico, as for Stevens, poetry and mythology derive from an intense need to make the world our own. In a passage underlined by Stevens, Adams notes: "Poetry, because it is the earliest form of utterance, belongs to the category of what is necessary. It is prior historically to the merely convenient or ornamental. It was early man's only way of speaking of the highest things" (LWV, 128). Here is a portion of Stevens's gloss on canto iv, which argues that the racial first idea was God, and that it resulted from the same sense of alienation from which the poem springs: "If 'I am a stranger in the land,' it follows that the whole race is a stranger. We live in a place that is not our own and, much more, not ourselves. The first idea, then, was not our own. It is not the individual alone that indulges himself in the pathetic fallacy. It is the race. God is the centre of the pathetic fallacy" (L, 444). The poem, then, is the result of the same conditions and the same imaginative faculty by which the first poets produced their gods.

In Vico, the age of heroes intervenes between the age of gods and the age of men. Stevens does not follow this order in *Notes*, but he does depict his hero or major man in terms that parallel Vico's conception of the hero. Adams points out that the most important figure of speech for Vico is *autonomasia*, "the giving of the same name to a number of individuals having like qualities, so that every hero becomes Hercules" (LWV, 125). That is, in the age of heroes Hercules is not one hero but the inclusive name for heroic action in any man. It is as if the heroic self is something apart from man's common self, a separate mind that descends on him at moments of heroic action. Vico, according to Adams, detected this example of primitive thinking in Homer, "who wrote, as if men's minds were something apart from them and unknown to them, 'the sacred strength of Antinous understood,' and 'the sacred force of Telemachus spoke.' Here the chief characteristic of the hero, his strength, is used to denominate his mind, a something, however, separate from his common, visible self" (LWV, 127). Vico entertained a similar conception of Homer, who, he conjectured, was not a single poet but " 'an idea or a heroic character of Grecian men in so far as they told their history in song' " (LWV, 191). Homer was the name for men as creators of poetry, just as Hercules was the name for men as heroic actors. "All the doers of the time were Hercules, all utterers of the poetic speech were Homer" (LWV, 191).

Stevens's conception of the figure whom he calls both the hero and, in *Notes*, major man is quite similar to this. Hercules and Homer have become diminished to MacCullough, the common man, but at moments such as the one depicted in canto viii of "It Must Be Abstract" MacCullough becomes *the* MacCullough, major man or hero. The MacCullough is the heroic self set apart from MacCullough's "common, visible self." At moments of extraordinary clairvoyance, imaginative moments, MacCullough experiences "a leaner being, moving in on him, / Of greater aptitude and apprehension" (CP, 387). MacCullough becomes at such moments the MacCullough in the way that Vico's doers become Hercules and his utterers of poetic speech become Homer. In Vico's second age, the manner of conceiving gods has been transferred to men so that the heroic self is still viewed as separate from the common self. In suggesting the possibility of a humanistic transcendent self, man as hero, Stevens retains this fiction, as he suggests in his comment on the canto: "the MacCullough is MacCullough; MacCullough is any name, any man. The trouble with humanism is that man as God remains man, but there is an extension of man, the leaner being, in fiction, a possibly more than human human, a composite human. The act of recognizing him is the act of this leaner being moving in on us" (L, 434). In the primitive poets the first idea produced God, but in a humanistic age "The major abstraction is the idea of man / And major man is its exponent" (CP, 388). Man as God remains man, "part, / Though an heroic part, of the commonal."

It might be argued that Stevens reorders Vico's three ages to those of gods, men, and heroes, reserving the final age, not yet achieved, for one in which "Man must become the hero of his world" (CP, 261). This is the implication of *Notes* and of other poems from *Transport to Summer*, such as "Montrachet-le-Jardin," which is more explicit in anticipating a "world / In which man is the hero" (CP, 261). In *Notes* this project is outlined in the final three cantos of "It Must Be Abstract," devoted to the "pensive giant" (CP, 386), major man. For Vico, the first men were literally giants (LWV, 159–60); for Stevens, the giant is, metaphorically, "A thinker of the first idea" (CP, 386). One aim of *Notes* is to suggest the environment in which man, as major man, may indeed become the hero of his world:

> Can we compose a castle-fortress-home,
> Even with the help of Viollet-le-Duc,
> And set the MacCullough there as major man?
>
> The first idea is an imagined thing.
> The pensive giant prone in violet space
> May be the MacCullough. . . .   [CP, 386–87]

Such a project assumes that the fiction appropriate to a humanistic age is that of major man, "man as God . . . a possibly more than human human," as Stevens puts it in his gloss on the MacCullough passage. At a deeper level, Stevens's anticipation of a supreme fiction that includes man as hero assumes the Vichian interpretation of human history as a history of the progressive mental states of the race, the doctrine that sanctions Stevens's reading of literary history in "The Noble Rider" as one version of the principle "It Must Change."

We return, then, to the second of the three predicates for the supreme fiction. A great deal of Stevens's theorizing on poetry is made up of elaborations on the principle of change, especially as it applies to the poet's response to tradition. Why is change one of the three essential qualities of poetry? The answers for Stevens are multiple, but they depend on his assumption that one of the chief factors in poets' reactions to the poetry of the past is an attitude that he labels variously "diffidence," "monotony," and "ennui." One problem of literary history that "The Noble Rider" addresses is why certain traditional poetry is unaffecting, dead to our sensibilities—why, in short, "poetry is a cemetery of nobilities" (NA, 35). The argument of the essay follows from an instance of such diffidence. Quoting a passage from Plato's *Phaedrus*, which involves the soul figured as a charioteer drawn by winged horses, Stevens asks what happens in a contemporary reading of this passage. Why has it become "gorgeous nonsense," the figure "antiquated and rustic" (NA, 4)? "The figure does not lose its vitality because of any failure of feeling on Plato's part. He does not communicate nobility coldly. . . . The result is that we recognize, even if we cannot realize, the feelings of the robust poet clearly and fluently noting the images in his mind and by means of his robustness, clearness and fluency communicating much more than the images themselves. Yet we do not quite yield. We cannot" (NA, 5). While we may be moved by Plato's figure, "we are moved as observers." We recognize it, but we "do not realize it"; we cannot "participate in it" (NA, 6–7).

The conceptions of reality and imagination, of poetry and the function of the poet that follow in the essay are based in part on Stevens's answer as to the cause of our diffidence here. That cause, it turns out, has to do with readers not so much as individuals but "as representatives of a state of mind" (NA, 6). Stevens has here converted Vico's philosophy of history to a principle of reader response: "Adams in his work on Vico makes the remark that the true history of the human race is a history of its progressive mental states. It is a remark of interest in this relation. We may assume that in the history of Plato's figure there have been incessant changes of response; that these changes have been psychological changes, and that our own diffidence is simply one more state of mind due to such a change" (NA, 6). Stevens was clearly intrigued with Adams's claim that one of Vico's great discoveries in the field of historical interpretation was the "positing of psychology as the basis of history and philology" so that their "explanation is to be sought in the mind of man" (LWV, 153). He marked this discussion in Adams and noted it in his index. His use of it in "The Noble Rider" quite obviously represents a much broader application of the principle than is found in Vico. Whereas this assumption for Vico results in only three distinct phases of history, for Stevens these psychological changes occur at a much faster rate, between generations even, producing a great number of "ages" of the imagination.

Stevens's loose reading of the Vichian principle of progressive mental states is, however, a focus for his conception of literary history in "The Noble Rider," viewed as a succession of new eras of reality and imagination in which the old imaginations have come to an end of their vitality because they no longer suffice. He develops at some length an account of what he calls "the pressure of reality," by which he means the effect of external events great enough to engage the mind in "what is direct and immediate," and which "involve the concepts and sanctions that are the order of our lives" (NA, 22). This pressure is "great enough and prolonged enough to bring about the end of one era in the history of the imagination and, if so, then great enough to bring about the beginning of another." Since his history of the imagination unfolds at a much more accelerated pace than Vico's, for Stevens "the imagination . . . is always at the end of an era. What happens is that it is always attaching itself to a new reality, and adhering to it. It is not that there is a new imagination but that there is a new reality."

Because the pressure of reality is, for Stevens, "the determining factor in the artistic character of an era and . . . of an individual" (NA, 22–23), it is now clear why the poet's response to the great figures of the past may be one of diffidence. He will be moved by their greatness and will recognize it without, however, desiring to emulate achievements that belong to another era of the imagination. Constructing a "possible poet" in "The Noble Rider," Stevens says of him: "He must have lived all of the last two thousand years, and longer, and he must have instructed himself, as best he could, as he went along. He will have thought that Virgil, Dante, Shakespeare, Milton placed themselves in remote lands and in remote ages; that their men and women were the dead—and not the dead lying in the earth, but the dead still living in their remote lands and in their remote ages, and living in the earth or under it, or in the heavens—and he will wonder at those huge imaginations, in which what is remote becomes near, and what is dead lives with an intensity beyond any experience of life" (NA, 23).

In the version of literary history set forth by Harold Bloom, to which we will turn presently, the new poet's attitude toward his precursors is one of envy and despair, since they have already filled all imaginative space. In Stevens's version the possible poet instructs himself in his precursors; their huge imaginations induce neither envy nor despair, however, because their reality is remote and their men and women the living dead. The poet will not fear that they have filled all imaginative space, because the progression of mental states is incessantly creating new imaginative space. It is true that they are able to make what is dead live "with an intensity beyond any experience of life," but it is this very quality of the incredible—beyond any experience of life—that distances them. "The Noble Rider" develops one version of "It Must Change" in its Vichian account of literary history as a series of psychological

states in which the credible quickly becomes incredible, just as
Plato's figure for the soul has become "gorgeous nonsense."

In "The Figure of the Youth as Virile Poet" Stevens enlarges on
his concept of the ephebe confronting his poetic father, here "the
Miltonic image of a poet, severe and determined" (NA, 52). Assum-
ing the principle of change that dictates the conception of literary
history in "The Noble Rider," Stevens reverts again to a dichotomy
of the incredible and the credible. "When we look back at the face
of the seventeenth century," he states, "what we are remembering
is the rather haggard background of the incredible, the imagina-
tion without intelligence, from which a younger figure is emerging,
stepping forward in the company of a muse of its own. . . . This
younger figure is the intelligence that endures. It is the imagination
of the son still bearing the antique imagination of the father. It is
the clear intelligence of the younger man still bearing the burden of
the obscurities of the intelligence of the old. It is the spirit out of its
own self, not out of some surrounding myth, delineating with accu-
rate speech the complications of which it is composed. For this
Aeneas, it is the past that is Anchises" (NA, 52–53). The world of
the fathers is the world of the incredible, of the "antique imagina-
tion," of the "obscurities of the intelligence of the old." It is the
world of the poems of heaven and hell, and the task of the son is "a
moment of victory over the incredible, a moment of purity that
does not become any less pure because, as what was incredible
is eliminated, something newly credible takes its place" (NA, 53).
The victory is momentary: the imagination is always at the end of
an era, and what is credible will in time become incredible. All of
this is a way of saying that "the great poems of heaven and hell
have been written and the great poem of the earth remains to be
written" (NA, 142). Because the great poem of the earth, the su-
preme fiction, always lies ahead, proper work remains for the new
poet to perform. The realization that "It Must Change"—that the
imagination is always attaching itself to a new reality—posits an
infinity of imaginative space for the poet.

The conception of literary history implicit in these two theoreti-
cal essays is reflected in the three divisions of Notes. As I have
suggested, "It Must Be Abstract" is concerned with the process—
the return to the first idea—by which the ephebe, the new poet,
divests himself of the dead names that are the inheritance of past
eras of the imagination. By assuming the manner of instruction,
the passing on of knowledge or craft, Notes informs us immedi-
ately that it is to be concerned with poetic relationships—master

poet and ephebe, poetic fathers and sons, poetry past and present. The ephebe of *Notes* is the figure who appears in the essays written during this period as the "possible poet" and "The Figure of the Youth as Virile Poet." By splitting himself into instructor and student, master and ephebe, Stevens represents both the "antique imagination of the father" and "the imagination of the son," the "obscurities of the intelligence of the old" and the "clear intelligence of the young man." In one sense, the first section of *Notes* gives us the poet talking to himself or at least one aspect of the poet—that part of himself that has "lived all of the last two thousand years"—addressing another, "a younger figure . . . stepping forward in the company of a muse of its own."

Stevens's initial strategy of adopting the persona of the tutor helps to soften the didactic character of his pronouncements on poetry, but it also leads him to a paradox, which is addressed at the conclusion of the first canto. The ephebe is instructed to return to a state of ignorance, to experience the sun directly without a name or history. In effect, he is required to experience the sun as if no prior poet has intervened in his seeing of it, so that he might attain a first idea, an "immaculate beginning" (CP, 382). He is told that the sun "Must bear no name, gold flourisher, but be / In the difficulty of what it is to be" (CP, 381). "Gold flourisher" is the master poet's secular substitution for Phoebus, the sun as god, but it remains the instructor's name for the sun that the student is required to ignore, suggesting indeed that the master poet's instructions constitute a violation of the conception of poetry being passed on to the new poet. It is as if the instructor, in the course of the lecture, exposes the paradox of his instruction. He is counseling the ephebe to wipe clean all he has inherited from the past—whatever stands between him and the first idea—of which the instructor, his view of poetry, and his metaphor for the sun are a part. More than that, his instruction appears in a form that the poet-lecturer has borrowed from one of his earlier poems, so that even his mode of presentation here is a relic of the past. This final paradox may be lost on the ephebe, but not on the reader who recalls a passage from "Add This to Rhetoric":

To-morrow when the sun,
For all your images,
Comes up as the sun, bull fire,
Your images will have left
No shadow of themselves.   [CP, 198]

It is doubly ironic that the master should warn the ephebe of the stale projections of the past in a conceit which has itself grown stale in its reuse. Stevens can never quite evade this paradox, for it is implicit in his notion of change, which renders obsolete all naming such as "gold flourisher" or "bull fire" the moment it is named.

The voice of instruction with which *Notes* begins is not consistently maintained, and the ephebe is not always present, even in "It Must Be Abstract." He is dropped altogether after the first section, and "It Must Change" moves to an investigation of "the distaste we feel" for what "has not changed enough" (CP, 390). Two instances of this distaste recall the conception of literary history developed in the essays. The great statue of the General Du Puy from canto iii reminds us of the noble riders of the first essay, to whom we have become diffident, since they represent imaginations of a past era. The General has become "a bit absurd," a part of the incredible. To a modern sensibility it is as if "There never had been, never could be, such / A man" (CP, 391). As was the case with Plato's figure, our response to the statue has been dictated by incessant psychological changes, and it now belongs "Among our more vestigial states of mind." Because he represents a state of the imagination that is remote, "the General was rubbish in the end" (CP, 392). The archaic "bethous" of the "idiot minstrelsy" in canto vi suffer a similar fate. Unable to change their song, the birds are depicted as if they were poets of a past age frozen in a poetic diction to which we can no longer respond, and their static chorus forms "A single text, granite monotony" (CP, 394). The birds' chorus suggests, that is, the monotony of an antithetical poetic tradition devoid of change, "Of an earth in which the first leaf is the tale / Of leaves, in which the sparrow is a bird / Of stone, that never changes" (CP, 394).

"It Must Give Pleasure" opens with a canto that distinguishes between the "facile exercise" of singing while "borne on / The shoulders of joyous men" and the "difficultest rigor" of catching from the "irrational moment its unreasoning" (CP, 398)—the difference, that is, between the "exact, accustomed" occasions of singing derived from the past and the "irrational" songs that are the products of a reality not yet made customary by the later reason that follows the first idea. Throughout *Notes* Stevens celebrates the irrational, life's nonsense, the "ever-early candor" experienced only in an "immaculate beginning" (CP, 382). The theory of poetry articulated in *Notes* demands both the imaginative ignorance of Vico's early poets and a conception of poetic history in which the products of earlier imaginations no longer suffice.

"Somnambulisma," from *Transport to Summer*, is one of Stevens's most explicit figurations of the concept of change as it governs the poet's response to his poetic past. Here change is figured as the perpetual roll of the ocean, "resembling a thin bird / That thinks of settling, yet never settles, on a nest":

> The generations of the bird are all
> By water washed away. They follow after.
> They follow, follow, follow, in water washed away.   [CP, 304]

This state of flux makes new creation possible and prevents the world of the new poet from becoming a "geography of the dead," a perpetuation of those huge imaginations that placed themselves in remote lands. Stevens in fact picks up some of the phrasing here from the passage in "The Noble Rider" where the concept was first treated:

> Without this bird that never settles, without
> Its generations that follow in their universe,
> The ocean, falling and falling on the hollow shore,
>
> Would be a geography of the dead: not of that land
> To which they may have gone, but of the place in which
> They lived, in which they lacked a pervasive being,
>
> In which no scholar, separately dwelling,
> Poured forth the fine fins, the gawky beaks, the personalia,
> Which, as a man feeling everything, were his.   [CP, 304]

Only the conditional manner of Stevens's construction obscures the argument. We may paraphrase the sense of it: Were it not for change, the principle by which the imagination is always adhering to a new environment, successive generations would live in the dead world of their precursors, a world of the incredible whose inhabitants, from a present perspective, lacked a pervasive being. The scholar, the man of imagination "separately dwelling," must, on the contrary, feel everything for himself if he is to discover the personalia uniquely his. To phrase this in terms of Stevens's version of the history of the imagination, we may say that if succeeding generations of poets feed only on the past, ignoring the principle of flux that is the life of the imagination, they produce only diminished versions of the geography of the dead and bring about the death of poetry.

Although Stevens found confirmation for this view in Vico's account of the origin of poetry and the development of human culture, it is an assumption that antedates his reading of Adams. It is, for example, the motive behind his interest in the thirties in a "new romanticism" in which "the romantic of poetry must be something constantly new and, therefore, just the opposite of what is spoken of as the romantic" (L, 277). His most thoughtful statement of this early version of reading literary tradition occurs in the first of his essay-reviews on the poetry of Marianne Moore, whom he sees as the model for the new poet's relation to the precursors. He characterizes her as a romantic but is careful to distinguish between two senses of the term. The pejorative sense is one in which the romantic is "a relic of the imagination" (OP, 251), the romantic of an imaginative era that has ended. In this sense, the term "merely connotes obsolescence"; it "is rot" (OP, 251, 254): "the romantic in its other sense, meaning always the living and at the same time the imaginative, the youthful, the delicate and a variety of things which it is not necessary to try to particularize at the moment, constitutes the vital element in poetry" (OP, 252). Here the assumption that "the imagination does not often delight in the same thing twice" is an anticipation of the later theory, in "The Noble Rider," that the imagination is always confronting a new situation, which is what revitalizes the romantic: "It must also be living. It must always be living. It is in the sense of living intensity, living singularity that it is the vital element in poetry" (OP, 252).

Stevens called his new romanticism a "temporary theory" (L, 277), but only the label was temporary. The conception of literary history that informs it may be detected everywhere in Stevens, and we discover a phrase from the 1935 Moore essay in "Of Modern Poetry" from *Parts of a World* in 1942. "It has to be living," he says of contemporary poetry, "to learn the speech of the place. / It has to face the men of the time and to meet / The women of the time" (CP, 240). These as opposed to the men and women of the last two thousand years "still living in their remote lands and in their remote ages." "Of Modern Poetry" is essentially a summary of the view of literary history that I have described in Stevens. Its thesis—that the theater of poetry changes so that one cannot repeat "what / Was in the script" (CP, 239)—is unmistakable. Perhaps it is for this reason that Bloom calls it a "weak poem, inaccurate about past poetry and mistaken about itself" (PC, 149).

Although Bloom does not discuss in any detail the conception of literary history contained in the theoretical essays, he has collected a number of Stevens's statements on influence, principally those found in the letters, as a basis for his judgment that Stevens represents a classic case of the anxiety of influence. Bloom is able to dismiss the version of literary history outlined above, since it represents for him merely a symptom of the anxiety that marks the strong poet's denial of an obligation that severely compromises his priority as an artist. Stevens, who figures so prominently in Bloom's own theory of influence, is denied the least insight into the whole issue: "poetic influence was hardly a subject where Stevens's insights could center" (AI, 7). But he does not rest here; he depicts Stevens the theorist as a weak, emotionally crippled figure. Stevens exhibits a "contemptuous attitude toward poetic influence" (PR, 277); he could not bear "to think about his indebtedness" (PC, 94). Blinded by his anxiety, Stevens can give us only lies while concealing the purpose of the poems: "we cannot trust his asserted aim any more than we can trust his asserted freedom from poetic origins" (PC, 175). It is "almost always the case with Stevens's comments upon *Notes* [that] his remarks give us a weak misreading" (PC, 186); "a Stevensian denial of influence, whether Nietzschian or Whitmanian, is merely confirmation of how unconvincing Stevens's notions of influence are" (PC, 289). Finally, and most drastically, "Stevens as a theorist of poetry, is little more than a self-deceiver"; he "does not begin to match Valéry in subtlety of mind or clarity of consciousness"; he has "an inadequate sense of vocation, and a fearful poverty of invention" (PR, 281).

This description of the writer who has profoundly influenced the way Bloom and his generation of critics now read poems may prompt us to wonder at the heat with which the critic characterizes his subject. I want to pursue Bloom's account of Stevens as theorist not simply because of what it tells us about Stevens but because of what it reveals about Bloom's use of Stevens in his own criticism. Any serious student of Stevens must recognize an odd circumstance in current Stevens criticism: as one of the strongest of contemporary critics in his own sense of *strong* (most given to creative readings or misreadings), Bloom has so brilliantly appropriated Stevens for his own uses and so successfully revised Stevens's attitude toward poetic influence that an ante-Bloom Stevens is difficult to recover. Although my principal interest is in Stevens's view of literary history as a part of his larger conception of poetry, this view has now become thoroughly entangled in Bloom's own theory of literary history. Given the sophistication of Bloom's rhetoric and the built-in defenses of his system, it may be impossible to extricate Stevens's conceptions from Bloom's revisionary formulations, but I shall make the attempt by examining the manner in which Bloom reads certain of Stevens's prose statements on poetry. This task is facilitated by the fact that Bloom has provided a detailed account of the way he reads texts. The models for misreading set out in *The Anxiety of Influence* and applied in his later studies furnish a guide to his use or misuse of a prior writer's insights. Bloom assumes that all strong writers read their precursors in the same way that he does, but that is a different matter altogether. To extend Bloom's psychology of reading to all readers raises serious questions beyond the scope of this discussion, not the least of which is the outrageously reductive tendency of his theory. Thus to assume that all strong readers read in a manner identical to Bloom is certainly problematic; he has, however, demonstrated again and again how well his theory applies in his own case.

We may take, for example, the revisionary tactic that Bloom labels *tessera*, defined as "completion and antithesis." A poet (or critic)[8] "antithetically 'completes' his precursor, by so reading the parent-poem as to retain its terms but to mean them in another sense, as though the precursor had failed to go far enough" (AI, 14). The writer, finding "all space filled with his precursor's visions, resorts to the language of taboo, so as to clear a mental space for himself," the language of taboo being the "antithetical use of the precursor's primal words" (AI, 66). The new writer persuades himself that the precursor is an "over-idealizer," that he is "tougher-minded" than his precursor, as Bloom does when he suggests that no other poet of Stevens's achievement has written as "blindly" or "self-deceivingly" about the relation of the poet to his ancestors (PR, 277). By retaining the precursor's language but employing it in a new context and so meaning it in a new sense, the writer denies the influence of the precursor and persuades himself that he is declaring what the blind and self-deceived precursor was incapable of saying: "the *tessera* represents any later poet's attempt to persuade himself (and us) that the precursor's Word would be worn out if not redeemed as a newly fulfilled and enlarged Word of the ephebe" (AI, 67).

The use of the term *ephebe* here, taken from Stevens, would seem an instance of the revisionary strategy Bloom describes. By redefining Stevens's "idealized" ephebe, Bloom apparently sees himself fulfilling and enlarging a concept that Stevens was not tough-minded enough to realize. The same could be said of the great number of other examples of his antithetical use of Stevens's primal language—"figures of capable imagination," "poverty" or "imaginative need," "the hero as poet," "what will suffice," "the pure good of theory," "the motive for metaphor," "abstraction." From *The Anxiety of Influence* in 1973 to *The Poems of Our Climate* and beyond, Bloom's approach to Stevens and his theory of poetic influence have been inextricable. The theoretical books at times seem to be thinly disguised studies of Stevens, and the Stevens study becomes, in the last chapter, the purely theoretical treatise it had been approaching all along. Bloom incorporates Stevens's phrasing and terminology so frequently in his writing on whatever subject that the poet is everywhere present in the critic.

By freely exhibiting Stevens's language Bloom relieves himself of any covert indebtedness, and by shifting the context and meaning of the language (i.e., Stevens's "It Must Give Pleasure" shifted to a criterion for criticism) he redeems it, which is to say he removes his obligation by converting it into something of value. Bloom's figures of capable imagination are, he clearly assumes, more complicated and interesting poets than Stevens's, just as his motive for metaphor is a more severe concept than Stevens could bear to think about. Yet such an "advance" on the precursor cannot be made, Bloom admits, without the kind of literary treason he calls misprision: "In the *tessera*, the later poet provides what his imagination tells him could complete the otherwise 'truncated' precursor poem and poet, a 'completion' that is as much misprision as a revisionary swerve is" (AI, 66). On the basis of his method of reading texts, Bloom can "complete" Stevens only by severely misrepresenting him, although he will perhaps not admit to himself the severity of his misrepresentation.

The most advanced form of this type of revision, in which the later writer seems to open his work to the earlier one, rather than concealing him, is what Bloom calls *apophrades*. He does not state exactly what revisionary techniques are employed in *apophrades*, but one could think of it (Bloom apparently does not) as an extension of *tessera*. That is, through the appropriation and shifting of the prior writer's language and concepts the new writer achieves "a style that captures and oddly retains priority" over the precursor, so that one could almost believe that the new writer is being imitated by the older one (AI, 141). Rather than analyzing the means by which the writer achieves this style, Bloom prefers to speak of *apophrades* as an effect a reader experiences in comparing the disciple and the precursor. The final triumph of *apophrades* is "the triumph of having so stationed the precursor, in one's own work, that particular passages in *his* work seem to be not presages of one's own advent, but rather to be indebted to one's own achievement, and even (necessarily) to be lessened by one's greater splendor" (AI, 141).

Bloom could well be describing here his own revision of Stevens. In the most successful instances of this type of revision, he notes, one cannot read the earlier writer without hearing the voice of the later one; this is, it seems to me, the effect a reader well versed in Bloom will experience on examining certain of Stevens's passages on poetic influence. One may not feel that Stevens is imitating Bloom so much as *responding* to him, since Bloom has been successful in reversing priority. A part of the intent and effect of this technique of misreading is to make us read the precursor differently (AI, 147). In the case of Stevens, it may now be impossible for a reader familiar with Bloom's criticism to see certain of Stevens's passages as anything more than the poet's weak response to the stronger theorist.

This fiction—that Bloom is actually the prior theorist on influence—is strengthened by Bloom's manner of reading Stevens's observations on influence, which we are now in a position to examine. It is a fiction, however, that may be usefully sustained in this examination. That is, it is illuminating to examine Stevens's statements as if he were the latecomer on influence whose views threatened the established theory. This method at least helps to account for the heat in Bloom's commentary on Stevens as a poetic theorist. His tendency is to caricature or misrepresent the tone of Stevens's remarks or, if they are pertinent enough to pose a threat to his priority, simply to conceal them. He labels as "revealingly vehement" (AI, 6) Stevens's admission that of course he comes down from the past, but one that is not "marked Coleridge, Wordsworth, etc." (L, 792), and Bloom offers a second passage from the letters as evidence that "[t]oward the end, his denials became rather violent, and oddly humored" (AI, 7). Stevens is writing to Richard Eberhart: "I sympathize with your denial of any influence on my part. This sort of thing always jars me because, in my own case, I am not conscious of having been influenced by anybody and have purposely held off from reading highly mannered people like Eliot and Pound so that I should not absorb anything, even unconsciously. But there is a kind of critic who spends his time dissecting what he reads for echoes, imitations, influences, as if no one was ever simply himself but is always compounded of a lot of other people" (L, 813).

One might well doubt Stevens's lack of awareness of any influence without, however, characterizing his denial as "violent."

Bloom reads this passage as evidence of Stevens's affliction by "a variety of melancholy" brought on by the anxiety of influence (AI, 7), but the symptoms of melancholy are also difficult to detect here. The phrase with which Bloom introduces the quotation ("toward the end") implies, moreover, that the poet was in the violent terminal stage of his affliction when he wrote it. Why, we might ask, does Bloom so egregiously misread the tone of the passage? From the point of view of Bloom's psychology of literary relations, when the ephebe turns so aggressively against the master, it can only be because he resents the master's priority, which represents a threat to his position. In fact, Stevens's observation on critics like Bloom does present a threat.

Stevens notes that there is "a kind of critic who spends his time dissecting what he reads for echoes, imitations, influences," and Bloom must recognize himself in the description, since he has devoted his career to establishing a theory of influence. He does not, however, wish to admit to that kind of characterization of his criticism, and he has sought to distance himself from those who deal in traditional studies of sources and influence, whom he terms the "carrion-eaters of scholarship" (MM, 17). Although his claim is that source study is wholly irrelevant to his concerns, that is a bit misleading, since he has simply evolved a more elaborate system of source study that does not depend on authenticating sources. His system, moreover, devours dead writers more readily by proposing that a prior poem may be brought forward as an influence "even if the ephebe never read that poem" (AI, 70). If Stevens's charge, in our fiction of reversed priority, appears at first an exaggeration— surely no critic spends *all* of his time dissecting poems for influence—Bloom alone would guarantee its accuracy. And when he remarks, in his defense, that the "profundities of poetic influence cannot be reduced to source study" (AI, 7), we note that this does not answer Stevens's objection to his theory.

Stevens's objection—that conceptions such as Bloom's propose a literary history in which "no one was ever simply himself but is always compounded of a lot of other people"—uncovers a troubling feature of Bloom's theory, its reductiveness. Stevens asks, in effect, whether everything that interests us in a writer is simply a revision of an earlier writer or, on the other hand, whether there are qualities in a writer that make their appeal because he is unlike earlier writers, in some sense unique, "simply himself." In *The Breaking of the Vessels* Bloom describes his discovery, as a seventeen year old, of the poetry of Stevens: "I still remember the pleasurable shock of first reading *Notes toward a Supreme Fiction, Esthé-tique du Mal* and *Credences of Summer*. I read them over and over, memorizing them until I could hear myself chanting them in my sleep. What I made of them I could hardly tell. . . . These days I cannot read Stevens without also reading Whitman . . ." (BV, 7–8). Is it a loss or a gain to be unable to read Stevens without also read-ing Whitman? Bloom evidently regards it as both, if we can trust the note of nostalgia here. As a pre-anxiety-of-influence reader, he found something in Stevens so compelling that it created a lifelong obsession. It is difficult to believe that what he found was a buried Whitman, although that is what we are told. Bloom now realizes that, even at seventeen, "one was reading Whitman, whether one knew it or not" (BV, 8). This extreme position would seem to result from a reductiveness that haunts Bloom's theory of reading and that Stevens's remark perceptively uncovers.

Stevens's contrary position is, of course, equally extreme. To look at the aspect of a poet that is compounded of a lot of other people, he suggests, is necessarily to ignore the part of him that Stevens values: what is unique to him, what is capable of capturing the imagination of a young reader who wishes not to construct theory but to read poems. Stevens's advice to his ephebe in this instance would presumably be that offered the ephebe in *Notes*: "You must become an ignorant man again" (CP, 380). Bloom's theory will not, however, allow him to read one poet without also reading another, and he must reject Stevens's assumption that the poem "satisfies / Belief in an immaculate beginning" (CP, 382). Bloom would no doubt seize on this notion as an example of Stevens's (and our) tendency to idealize poetry and poets; yet, if he cannot now read Stevens without reading Whitman, and if he suggests that he was reading Whitman in Stevens as a seventeen year old, has he not idealized theory and theorists at the expense of poets?

Another circumstance of Stevens's letter to Eberhart, however, may help to account for the force of Bloom's reaction to it. Stevens extended the view of influence expressed there in another letter to Eberhart written five days later ("I have a habit of thinking of some-thing I should like to have said in a letter after I have posted it" [L, 815]). What is perhaps most significant about the second note on influence, which appears in the *Letters* two pages after the first, is that Bloom omits any notice of it in his discussion, although it asks and answers the question that forms the basis of his own theory: "Why do poets in particular resent the attribution of the influence of other poets? The customary answer to this is that it gives them the appearance of being second-hand. That may be one of the aspects of what seems to me the true answer. It seems to me that the true answer is that with a true poet his poetry is the same thing as his vital self. It is not possible for anyone else to touch it" (L, 815). Bloom asks Stevens's question this way: "Why is influence, which might be a health, more generally an anxiety where strong poets are concerned?" (AI, 88). His answer, of course, is an endlessly elaborated version of what Stevens regards as an incomplete explanation—the fear of looking second-hand. The true answer for Stevens is one that makes the writing of poetry more than the adoption of a literary stance, and his formulation of the issue relegates Bloom's answer to the periphery of criticism. More than that—it denies Bloom's priority as a theorist by suggesting that his answer is the "customary" one.

But what does it mean to say that poetry is the same thing as the poet's vital self? Stevens's view here is consistent with his repeated refusals to separate the poetry-making faculty from other aspects of the poet's personality. In "Two or Three Ideas" he argues that "we use the same faculties when we write poetry that we use when we create gods or when we fix the bearing of men in reality" (OP, 216). In direct contrast to Bloom, Stevens notes in the letter to Eberhart that "poetry is not a literary activity: it is a vital activity" (L, 815), and in "The Figure of the Youth as Virile Poet" Stevens characterizes poetry as "a process of the personality of the poet." He states, "This is the element, the force, that keeps poetry a living thing, the modernizing and ever-modern influence" (NA, 45).

One consequence of equating poetry with the vital self of the poet is thus to allow for an element of change in the continuing production of poems. It is another version of Stevens's view of poetic tradition as a progression of mental states. In "The Figure of the Youth as Virile Poet" he observes, "Just as the nature of truth changes, perhaps for no more significant reason than that philosophers live and die, so the nature of poetry changes, perhaps for no more significant reason than that poets come and go. It is so easy to say in a universe of life and death that the reason itself lives and dies and, if so, that the imagination lives and dies no less" (NA, 40). Stevens's conception of literary history, with its emphasis on successive ages of the imagination and the individual poet's vital self as a force to maintain the life of poetry, is in part an attempt to forestall one implication of Bloom's theory of influence. Since Bloom reduces the creation of poetry to a purely literary activity, one that takes place only in response to prior works (without which no truly "strong" poem could be written), his conclusion is that poetry must diminish as each poet rewrites the precursors' poems in the absence of any other source of power: "From his start as a poet he quests for an impossible object, as his precursor quested before him. That this quest encompasses necessarily the diminishment of poetry seems to me an inevitable realization, one that accurate literary history must sustain. . . . The death of poetry will not be hastened by any reader's broodings, yet it seems just to assume that poetry in our tradition, when it dies, will be self-slain, murdered by its own past strength" (AI, 10).

Stevens, to the contrary, projects the great poem of earth into the future so that even the strongest contemporary poets can compose no more than notes *toward* the supreme fiction, which lies always beyond us. What makes the continued life of the supreme fiction possible for Stevens is the realization that "It Must Change"; change, in turn, is dependent on a conception of history as a progression of psychological states and on "the personality of the poet, his individuality, as an element in the creative process" (NA, 48). In Bloom's conception of the creative process, all strong poets operate from only one drive, as if there were only one case study available for the critic. If this were true for the poet or the reader, Stevens notes in another uncanny response to Bloom, then one poet would be sufficient:

> If we were all alike; if we were millions of people saying do, re, mi in unison, one poet would be enough and Hesiod himself would do very well. Everything he said would be in no need of expounding or would have been expounded long ago. But we are not all alike and everything needs expounding all the time because, as people live and die, each one perceiving life and death for himself, and mostly by and in himself, there develops a curiosity about the perceptions of others. This is what makes it possible to go on saying new things about old things. The fact is that the saying of new things in new ways is grateful to us. If a bootblack says that he was so tired that he lay down like a dog under a tree, he is saying a new thing about an old thing, in a new way. His new way is not a literary novelty; it is an unaffected statement of his perception of the thing.   [OP, 267]

By offering as an example of a novel manner of expression the statement of an unlettered bootblack, Stevens is suggesting that the force that keeps poetry living is not a literary activity, but

a product of an individual mode of perception. This observation
(which Bloom, to his credit, does not evade) produces the most spir-
ited of Bloom's responses to Stevens on influence. "Was there ever
another poet of his achievement," he asks, "who could write this
blindly and self-deceivingly about the relation of a new poet to
anteriority?" (PR, 277). His answer to the implicit charge of reduc-
tivism in his own theory is that Stevens, "insisting upon the per-
ceptiveness of his fictive bootblack, is representing his own anxi-
eties about anteriority,"[9] and that "his own rhetoric belies the fact
of a belated poet's deepest fear, which is that increasingly we do
become all too much alike" (PR, 278). One could perhaps as easily
argue that Bloom's strong rhetoric here represents his fear that po-
ets are not as much alike as his reading of them would indicate.
The more telling response, however, is to note that Bloom's impli-
cation (that Stevens's melancholy obviates the necessity for an
answer) does not touch the issue Stevens has raised: in Bloom's
theory all poets are one poet—and, one might add, they all meet in
Stevens.

Bloom cannot allow the implications of this point of view to
stand, but his argument is weak and uncharacteristically muddled:
"Stevens can say, pugnaciously and effectively, that 'one poet would
be enough and Hesiod himself would do very well,' but how would
it have seemed, to Stevens or to us, if he had said that 'one poet
would be enough and Whitman himself would do very well,' let
alone a contemporary rival like Eliot or Pound or Williams?" (PR,
278). This misses the mark because Bloom seems obstinately con-
fused about who is arguing what. Since Stevens believes that we are
not all alike, then for him one poet is *not* enough, whether it be
Whitman, Pound, or Williams. The one-poet argument is a charge
that Bloom, not Stevens, must answer, since his concept of the
strong poet has the effect of drastically shrinking the traditional
canon. Indeed, from his point of view modernism has managed to
produce only two strong poets—Stevens and Hardy—and Hardy is
scarcely heard from in Bloom. Stevens, it would appear, is closer
to the mark in uncovering the severely reductive element of ap-
proaches like that of Bloom, who resorts here finally to an assault
on Stevens's standing as a literary spokesman.

This assault is offered as a final example of Bloom's represen-
tation of Stevens as theorist. Reacting to the one-poet argument,
Bloom states: "In the same introduction to a new poet that I have
just cited, Stevens proceeded to obfuscate American Transcenden-
talism, with the same zest for misprision that he frequently mani-

fested toward Romanticism" (PR, 278). Stevens, that is, could not
bear to read accurately either tradition that strongly influenced him
(although it is difficult to know how any faithful reading could oc-
cur in a system in which all reading is misreading). Bloom gives us
only a few words of the passage in question. Here is what Stevens
says of the poet (Samuel French Morse) whose first book of poems
he is describing:

> But what is his exact character as a poet? One of his poems,
> "The Track into the Swamp," relates to one of the abandoned
> roads, the lost roads, of which New England is so full. We
> have been accustomed to think that at the far end of such
> roads the ghosts of the Transcendentalists still live. Obviously
> they do not live at this end. Mr. Morse is not the ghost of a
> Transcendentalist. If he has any use at all for Kant, it is to
> keep up the window in which the cord is broken. He is anti-
> transcendental. His subject is the particulars of experience. He
> is a realist; he tries to get at New England experience, at New
> England past and present, at New England foxes and snow and
> thunderheads. When he generalizes, as in "End of a Year," his
> synthesis is essentially a New England synthesis. He writes
> about his own people and his own objects as closely as possi-
> ble according to his own perception.   [OP, 268]

This account Bloom calls an "uninteresting falsification," and
while he is accurate in the first regard, the degree to which it is a
falsification deserves closer scrutiny.

Bloom is alarmed by the phrases "anti-transcendental" and "par-
ticulars of experience," no doubt because their implications violate
his own reading of Transcendentalism. He cites Emerson in rebut-
tal in a passage that, curiously, strengthens Stevens's distinction.
" 'The idealist,' " Bloom quotes Emerson as saying, " 'in speaking of
events, sees them as spirits. He does not deny the sensuous fact; by
no means; but he will not see that alone.' " Emerson's definition of
the idealist position concludes, " 'This manner of looking at things
transfers every object in nature from an independent and anoma-
lous position without there, into the consciousness' " (PR, 278).
Presumably the poet whom Stevens describes is content with the
sensuous fact and is not concerned with speaking of events as spir-
its. Stevens therefore labels him a realist, which leads Bloom to
charge him with a blatant falsehood. While Stevens's is by no
means a rigorous examination of Transcendentalism, to brand it a
deliberate misrepresentation seems inappropriate. The realist-ideal-

ist antithesis Stevens employs is not unknown in intellectual history, and it is one that Emerson's own definition of idealism appears to invite. If the idealist speaks of events as spirits, the label of realist for a poet who stops at foxes, snows, and thunderheads seems fairly enough applied.

The pertinent question is, Why turn this bland and entirely conventional conception of Transcendentalism into an instance of obfuscation and falsification? The answers I have implied are, by this point, no doubt obvious. First, Bloom's reading of Stevens's statements on poetic tradition rests on the assumption that any strong poet's response to his ancestors can be nothing other than envy, despair, and deep-seated anxiety. Since they have already written his poems, "no proper work remains for him to perform" (AI, 148). It is in part because of this assumption that a poet like Stevens must be seen as falsifying Transcendentalism and Romanticism and must be denied any insight into the question of indebtedness. If either assertion is misapplied—if Stevens does not falsify his tradition; if he understands how one poet responds to another—then the assumption is weakened and the theory threatened.

Beyond that, however, is the curious position Stevens occupies in Bloom's writing. Bloom's stylistic appropriation of Stevens—his lifting of Stevens's terms and concepts to be used in a new context —is a sign that his attitude toward this poet is more ambivalent than that exhibited toward other poets and theorists he employs. Stevens is, for Bloom, not simply an example of the consequences of the anxiety of influence or a strong poet upon whose verse the theory can be tested, but the object of a life-long obsession, in Bloom's terminology, the precursor whose influence is so disturbing as to produce the sort of willful misreading to which I have called attention. Bloom has argued that, although all of our readings are misreadings, it is only the true precursors that the writer must willfully deny, distort, or caricature. Stevens, for example, may freely acknowledge his debt to the French Symbolists, but "French colorings in Stevens, in *Harmonium* and after, invariably are evasions of more embarrassing obligations to Anglo-American literary tradition" (PC, 51). Presumably, Bloom's misreadings of writers for whom his feelings are not so strong may be of a different character from his misreading of one who engages him so obsessively. If we accept, then, Bloom's account of his own manner of reading, we are justified in our impression that his version of Stevens on poetic influence is hardly to be trusted.

I am, of course, concerned here not with the general validity of

Bloom's theory, but only with some of its practical results as a description of the way he reads Stevens. The degree to which Stevens or Bloom is accurate about the relation of the poet to earlier poetic tradition is thus not the question addressed. I have attempted, rather, to confront Bloom's claim that Stevens's notion of literary history is a product of his anxiety of influence and hence evidence of the validity of Bloom's theory. "I take the resistance shown to the theory by many poets in particular," he says, "to be likely evidence for its validity, for poets rightly idealize their activity; and all poets, weak and strong, agree in denying any share in the anxiety of influence" (MM, 10). Such a circular argument is of no consequence. If Bloom is not himself accurate in his assumptions about the operation of poets' psyches, then any argument based on his assumptions (such as his interpretation of poets' responses to his theory) is equally mistaken. And whether or not he is accurate in the first regard would have to be determined, if that is possible, by means other than his appeal to the theory itself.

Bloom has stated that "whether the theory is correct or not may be irrelevant to its usefulness for practical criticism" (MM, 10), and it may well be that only on the basis of their usefulness to readers and poets can these two conceptions of literary tradition be evaluated. The practical value of Bloom's theory for criticism as a rhetoric of misreading has been immense, and Bloom's account of literary history is obviously more sophisticated and more engaging as theory than is Stevens's. The strength of Stevens's conception lies in its usefulness for the poet, himself included, rather than for the critic—its ability to justify the continued creation of great poems after all the great poems have been written, its recognition of multiplicity and the value it attributes to change:

And out of what one sees and hears and out
Of what one feels, who could have thought to make
So many selves, so many sensuous worlds,
As if the air, the mid-day air, was swarming
With the metaphysical changes that occur,
Merely in living as and where we live.   [CP, 326]

4

THE PSYCHOLOGY OF
PLEASURE
Charles Mauron and
Notes toward a Supreme Fiction

Of the works of critical theory that Stevens reviewed in
preparation for "The Noble Rider and the Sound of Words," Charles
Mauron's *Aesthetics and Psychology*[1] perhaps exerted the deepest
influence on his conception of poetry in the early forties. Stevens's
copy preserves the evidence of his scrutiny. In addition to the great
number of passages marked throughout, the volume includes nota-
tions on the front and back flyleaves and a running paraphrase of
Mauron's discussion in the margins.[2] Noting the care with which
Stevens followed the argument of *Aesthetics and Psychology*, it
is not surprising to discover references to Mauron in "The Noble
Rider" and in "The Irrational Element in Poetry," Stevens's first
serious attempt at poetic theory. Mauron's force appears to have
extended beyond the lectures; indeed, a large number of the po-
ems written during the period in which *Aesthetics and Psychology*
dominated Stevens's thinking on poetry may profitably be read in
the light of Mauron's psychology. Several of the poems that best
reveal Mauron's attractiveness for Stevens—those dealing with the
two theorists' parallel notions of obscurity in poetry—will be dis-
cussed in Chapter Five. Here I want to concentrate on the manner
in which *Aesthetics and Psychology* helped to shape *Notes toward
a Supreme Fiction*, although some preliminary discussion of Mau-
ron's conception of art is necessary before arriving at Stevens's most
ambitious theoretical poem.

Mauron's initial attraction for Stevens may have owed something
to both men's rather tentative attitude toward poetic theory. At a
time when Stevens was being forced somewhat against his will into

the role of lecturer and aesthetician, he discovered a young French critic who emphasized the contribution to aesthetics of the gifted amateur, a role Stevens apparently found congenial.[3] Stevens's marginal notation in Chapter 2 of *Aesthetics and Psychology* aptly summarizes the point of view that Mauron adopts. "The role of amateurs," Stevens wrote, "is to make known our reactions and our generalizations therefrom stated without any other respect than that for fact."[4]

Ultimately more important for Stevens, however, was the substance of Mauron's argument, his formulation of a concept of the mind in its encounter with the utilitarian world that became for a time the pivotal doctrine of Stevens's verse. In *Aesthetics and Psychology* Mauron attempts, through the ordering of his own impressions, to define the boundary between what he terms the "aesthetic emotion" and the emotions of ordinary life. His aim, in brief, is to define art in psychological terms, to fix a line between two kinds of emotional response to the external world. Following Roger Fry, whom he regards as his master, he discovers this line in a distinction between two fundamentally different attitudes of mind, the active and the contemplative. The difference between life and art, for Mauron, is that in the former the mind is constantly anticipating future action, while in the latter it is absorbed in the present. Assuming that the function of art is to give pleasure, he argues that the work of art, in contrast to our experience in active life, stimulates us without requiring a corresponding reflex. Since we do not have to act on it, our interest lies solely in what we feel. And because the artist offers us something of which we can make no use, he gives potential pleasures every possible opportunity; the mind is suspended just at the point where pleasure becomes manifest, between the stimulus and the response. The artist, Mauron states in a sentence Stevens borrowed for "The Noble Rider," thus transforms us into epicures. Stevens, in a marginal comment, puts the case in his own words: "A work of art is inactive and useless and constitutes a stimulus, which we enjoy for its own sake, since it entails no reaching beyond the enjoyment of the sensation it provokes. Thus the basis of the aesthetic emotion is the aesthetic attitude; contemplation without any idea of making use of the object of contemplation."[5]

Aesthetics and Psychology develops a number of implications from this equation of the contemplative state of mind with the aesthetic emotion, and Stevens was intrigued by most of them, as his running commentary testifies. Bits and pieces of Mauron's discussion begin to appear in his poetry and prose in 1936, when he apparently first read *Aesthetics and Psychology*. Although my interest here is in describing the impact of Mauron's writing on Stevens's conception of poetry, rather than in finding echoes in scattered passages of verse, a few examples of the latter will indicate the degree to which, for a period in the late thirties and early forties, *Aesthetics and Psychology* was infused into Stevens's imagination.

Here is, I think, a typical instance of the manner in which Stevens, perhaps not altogether consciously, employed details and images from *Aesthetics and Psychology* in his poetry. Although his borrowing is almost never obvious, it is persistent, and at times a particularly striking argument by Mauron may be reflected in several poems. In his first two chapters Mauron rejects the notion of aesthetics as based on a universal concept of beauty—that is, a metaphysical aesthetic—and proposes to replace it with the idea of aesthetics as a branch of psychology. This would produce, he argues, an aesthetic of relativity in which there would be no universal truth and in which we would have no need to concern ourselves with apparent contradictions in our aesthetic judgments, since our divergences would be seen as arising from psychological differences in our natures. This discussion, which occupies less than ten pages, is echoed in various forms in at least three passages in Stevens—in "A Postcard from the Volcano" (CP, 158), "On the Road Home" (CP, 203), and the final canto of the third section of *Notes toward a Supreme Fiction* (CP, 406).[6] Taken separately, these passages would show little evidence of Mauron's presence; read together, they are more revealing.

"A Postcard from the Volcano" appears to have been conceived from the chance association of two or three details on pp. 7–11 of *Aesthetics and Psychology*. Mauron's image for the fall of metaphysics is a "ruin haunted by the melancholy sighing of the four or five winds of the spirit" (AP, 7–8). To replace this ruined mansion, Mauron foresees a new aesthetic that would be constructed as a "science of our emotions":[7] "We amateurs have our rôle in the edification of this science—I mean the rôle of stones and other materials. When future treatises speak of aesthetic emotions it will be our emotions that are in question" (AP, 11). Mauron's discredited past as a ruin blown by the winds and haunted by the spirit of another time becomes Stevens's "shuttered mansion-house," over which the "spring clouds blow" and of which the children of the future will say that "he that lived there left behind / A spirit storming in blank walls" (CP, 159). Mauron's conception of future generations constructing theories on the records of our present feelings and conceptions—as if the part of us that survives were to become the artifacts, the "stones and other materials" of archeologists—Stevens renders in this way:

Children picking up our bones
Will never know that these were once
As quick as foxes on the hill

And that in autumn, when the grapes
Made sharp air sharper by their smell
These had a being, breathing frost;

And least will guess that with our bones
We left much more, left what still is
The look of things, left what we felt

At what we saw.   [CP, 158–59]

Stevens had no interest in preserving the exact meaning Mauron assigned to his images and conceits. The ruin of a "dirty house in a gutted world" (CP, 159) is for Stevens something more than metaphysics; it has been broadened to include the notion of the past itself, gutted by time. Mauron's conceit of our present emotions as the artifacts for future study Stevens also broadens considerably to a conception of life imitating art, each generation unwittingly seeing the world through the artistic sensibility of the preceding generation:

We knew for long the mansion's look
And what we said of it became

A part of what it is . . . Children,
Still weaving budded aureoles,
Will speak our speech and never know. . . .   [CP, 159]

What in Mauron is quite clearly a practical suggestion for amassing the data for a psychology of art has become, for Stevens, a figure for the manner in which the poet "creates the world to which we turn incessantly and without knowing it" (NA, 31).

Apparently inspired by the same argument, "On the Road Home" reveals another curious kinship with "A Postcard from the Volcano" in its Aesop-like association of foxes and grapes:[8]

It was when I said,
"There is no such thing as the truth,"
That the grapes seemed fatter.
The fox ran out of his hole.   [CP, 203]

The poem is based loosely on the conclusion Mauron draws in his shift from a metaphysical aesthetic to a new aesthetic that accepts apparent contradictions and disagreements in judgment by denying "a standard of beauty." He argues that it is not the theorist's task to construct such a standard: "If all those who discuss aesthetics would understand that, I believe their consciences would be the lighter. They would say simply what gives them pleasure, without seeking . . . to be in agreement with Mr. X or Mr. Y or with the generality" (AP, 14). Having rejected the notion of absolutes or universal truths, Mauron argues, we would be freed from doctrines by which our response to experience is categorized and labeled: "One of the great benefits of science in these and analogous cases (for example, sexuality) is to replace the notions of superior and inferior or of normal and abnormal by that of facts more or less common, but in any case equally respectable. Apart from the fanatics, all the world would profit by this exchange. As a patient of the psychologist a man can consent to be what he is, he finds himself freer and happier" (AP, 15).

In "On the Road Home" Stevens reduces all this to its essence —"'There are many truths, / But they are not parts of a truth'" (CP, 203)—with the same result as Mauron. The last stanza describes the moment when one consents to a world without absolutes, when one says, "'There is no such thing as the truth'" (CP, 203):

It was at that time, that the silence was largest
And longest, the night was roundest,
The fragrance of the autumn warmest,
Closest and strongest.   [CP, 204]

"On the Road Home" is a relatively straightforward account of Mauron's notion that the absence of universal doctrines, the acceptance of things as they are, offers us access to the pleasures of the haphazard and the fortuitous, a theme of great importance in the poems of *Parts of a World* (1942), where "On the Road Home" appears.

Mauron begins *Aesthetics and Psychology*, then, by denying the importance of what he calls the "feverish research . . . for a standard of beauty" (AP, 14), laying the groundwork for a theory that places great emphasis on the originality of the artist and the individuality of the aesthetic response. Speaking of a future science of aesthetics, he notes, "And if it were, one day, to establish the fact that all men are agreed about such and such aesthetic pleasures, and that in consequence there is an objective definition of beauty, so much the better; but if not, it can't be helped. There is no reason, after all, why we all should have the same pleasures. Reduced to a question of fact, this unanimity has no real importance" (AP, 15). Stevens's version of this possible unanimity—the discovery of a universal principle by which aesthetic pleasure is made rational— occurs at the conclusion of *Notes toward a Supreme Fiction*, and is handled with the same light skepticism as Mauron's:

> They will get it straight one day at the Sorbonne.
> We shall return at twilight from the lecture
> Pleased that the irrational is rational,
>
> Until flicked by feeling, in a gildered street,
> I call you by name, my green, my fluent mundo.
> You will have stopped revolving except in crystal. [CP, 406–7]

The tone of the passages makes it apparent that Stevens, like Mauron, is ironic in his speculation that they "will get it straight one day at the Sorbonne." As Harold Bloom has noted in a gloss on this passage, the poem ends on a moment that recognizes that "the pleasure of art ensues from a willing error, a more than rational distortion, an evasion of the truth, because truth either is or becomes death."[9] To "get it straight," to fix the world in any formula or doctrine, is of course to deny one of the requisites of the supreme fiction—that it must change.

As is the case with Richards's *Coleridge on Imagination*, the accumulation of verbal echoes such as those above is more compelling than any particular instance in arguing for the influence of Mauron's aesthetics on Stevens's later poetry. More than that, the passages in Stevens that seem to have gotten their start in Mauron take on a life of their own, so that their origins, simply as sources, become relatively unimportant. A particularly interesting example occurs in *Esthétique du Mal*. In Chapter 8, discussing the misunderstandings between artist and audience, Mauron offers the example of an audience listening to Beethoven: "Actually, when a thousand persons are listening to Beethoven, each one probably flatters himself that he is feeling over again more or less what Beethoven once felt. But what reason have we to agree with them? If we could, at that moment, read all hearts, what a confusion, what a chaos we should find! Certainly *something* passes from artist to auditor; but that the transmission must needs be bad who can deny? Happily a veil of illusion softens what would be too shocking in the admission of misunderstanding; each hearer accepts his own reactions, and leaves the concert hall equally satisfied with himself and Beethoven" (AP, 60). Here is Stevens's more ambiguous version from canto iv of *Esthétique du Mal*:

When B. sat down at the piano and made
A transparence in which we heard music, made music,
In which we heard transparent sounds, did he play
All sorts of notes? Or did he play only one
In an ecstasy of its associates,
Variations in the tones of a single sound,
The last, or sounds so single they seemed one?   [CP, 316]

Stevens's questions here are based on Mauron's conception of the problem in transmission between Beethoven and his audience, but he transforms what is a rather simple notion in Mauron—the lack of unanimity in audience response—into something else entirely. It is possible to read the passage as a version of the issue Mauron raises—the epistemological dilemma Stevens had himself dealt with earlier in "Metaphors of a Magnifico" (CP, 19). That is, would "Twenty men crossing a bridge, / Into a village" (CP, 19) see "all sorts of" bridges and villages or only one bridge and village? Or would they see variations so "single that they seemed one?" Put in these terms, Stevens's poem could be read simply as a versification of Mauron's Beethoven example. Stevens's passage is, however, more ambitious, and its context provides a quite different reading. Canto iv of *Esthétique du Mal* is concerned with the "genius of misfortune" (CP, 316) and the sentimentalist: "All sorts of flowers. That's the sentimentalist." Listening to Beethoven's "transparent sounds," the sentimentalist would hear "All sorts of notes." The genius of misfortune, "that evil in the self, from which / In desperate hallow, rugged gesture, fault / Falls out on everything," would hear only one note, which would color all its associates until they became "variations . . . of a single sound." The genius of misfortune, the poem says, is "the genius of / The mind, which is our being, wrong and wrong" (CP, 316–17). The mind, that is, wrongly reads Beethoven's transparence to reflect its own one-note view of an evil world, and the canto ends as an instance of "the genius of the body, which is our world, / Spent in the false engagements of the mind" (CP, 317). Stevens is interested here not so much in the problems of misreading per se as in the opposition between two motives for misreading—those of the "genius of misfortune" and the sentimentalist. Mauron's use of Beethoven's transparent music and auditors with a tendency to confuse their own feelings with Beethoven's has become something richer and more elusive in Stevens. From Mauron's example Stevens has produced a passage of verse approaching his ideal of an art that almost defies paraphrase.

Scrutiny of *Aesthetics and Psychology* by readers familiar with the poetry Stevens published between 1942 and 1950 will turn up a number of strangely familiar passages. It appears that Stevens's scrupulous avoidance of influence from contemporary poets did not extend with equal intensity to critical prose. Although his denials of any indebtedness to other poets are now notorious, his indebtedness to critics and theorists he apparently regarded in a different light. The essays and lectures provide an ample index of the names he feels obliged to acknowledge for the substance of his arguments. A fastidiousness about originality permeates his remarks on his own poetry but is curiously absent in his theoretical prose. For example, more than thirty references to theorists and critics appear in the first two essays of *The Necessary Angel*, and the opening paragraph of "About One of Marianne Moore's Poems" acknowledges that the substance of the essay is taken almost entirely from a paper by H. D. Lewis that had recently appeared in a philosophical journal.[10]

Perhaps the key to the distinction Stevens draws between his obsession with originality in the poems and his almost slavish adherence to contemporary thought in the prose is present in the letter to Eberhart, in his use of the term "mannered." It is the *manner* he does not wish to absorb, even unconsciously. For Stevens the *manner* of expression, the distinct voice of the poet, is essential and can never be compromised; ideas, conceptions, theories, on the other hand, have the status of "isolated fact" (NA, 95). The difference is perhaps that between the *Encyclopædia Britannica*'s description of the ostrich and Marianne Moore's, set in opposition in the essay mentioned above. The reality of the poem is an "individual reality," while that "of the *Encyclopædia* is the reality of isolated fact" (NA, 94–95). The "interest of the poem," he argues, "is not in its meaning but in this, that it illustrates the achieving of an individual reality" (NA, 98). Apparently paraphrasing Lewis (but ironically, in this context, quoting him verbatim), he concludes:

"The 'something said' is important, but it is important for the poem only in so far as the saying of that particular something in a special way is a revelation of reality" (NA, 99). In combing theorists like Lewis and Mauron for the "something said" in both his prose and poetry, Stevens, then, felt no betrayal of his resolve to remain poetically pure. As long as his own saying of the idea or theory retained his manner, the "individual reality" imparted by the "distinct tongue" (L, 873) of the authentic poet, its source was of little consequence. It is perhaps assumptions such as these that allowed Stevens to employ Mauron's psychology so freely in constructing *Notes toward a Supreme Fiction*. Whatever his assumptions, there seems little doubt that Mauron contributed substantially to the "something said" in the poem, which is on the whole quite faithful to the conception of poetry articulated in *Aesthetics and Psychology*.

Aesthetics and Psychology is not, in any conventional sense, the "source" for *Notes toward a Supreme Fiction*. Few of the qualities that make it a great poem (as opposed to an argument about the nature of poetry) can be traced to Mauron. To put it another way, a poem something like *Notes* could doubtless have been written if Stevens had never discovered Mauron. Yet, comparing the two works, one feels that the form of the argument in *Notes* would not have taken its final shape without Mauron, and that it was principally in providing a structure for the personal observations of a practicing poet that he was most useful to Stevens. The use for Stevens's readers in recognizing Mauron's contribution is not to identify a source but to be aware of certain assumptions about the reading and writing of poetry that are present obliquely in the poem but spelled out quite clearly in the prose work. Reading *Notes* in the light of *Aesthetics and Psychology* is of less help in explicating passages of the poem as poetry than in grasping the context of the poem's submerged aesthetic, an aesthetic that has proven to be quite elusive to commentary. To read the poem *as if* it were written in response to Mauron's reflections on art—and recognizing, simultaneously, that this is an exaggeration—has the advantages at least of providing an approach to several of the poem's toughest issues and of avoiding, at the same time, the imagination-reality terminology that has plagued Stevens criticism for decades.

To read *Notes* as if it were modeled after the argument of *Aesthetics and Psychology* is to recognize, first of all, that its overall aim is identical with that of Mauron's study. By adopting in the title a stance that suggests that the poem is merely a preliminary set of notes for a future treatise, Stevens echoes Mauron's conception of the ends of his own study: "It does not propose to add one more aesthetic theory to so many others, but rather to furnish the psychologists with a document; the ordered exposition of certain personal pleasures" (AP, 16). Or, as he puts it in the statement quoted earlier, "When future treatises speak of aesthetic emotions it will be our emotions that are in question" (AP, 11). His mention of the psychologists for whom his study is directed and the "personal pleasures" that form its substance also reminds us that it is equally a *psychology* of art toward which Stevens drifts both in "The Noble Rider" and in *Notes*, the two works most directly in the theoretical line charted in *Aesthetics and Psychology*. In "The Noble Rider," for example, the aesthetic problem Stevens first poses has to do with our psychological response to a passage from Plato, and his explanation for our inability to "realize" the passage—which comprises the ostensible motive for the lecture—is a psychological explanation: "We may assume that in the history of Plato's figure there have been incessant changes of response; that these changes have been psychological changes, and that our own diffidence is simply one more state of mind due to such a change" (NA, 6).

Notes, of course, opens with the same psychological problem—the ephebe's instruction in "realizing" the object, the psychology of creativity that follows from the speaker's assumptions about what happens in the mind in contemplating a world that has been stripped of its utilitarian components, a world, as Stevens put it, that has "expelled us and our images" (CP, 381). The psychology of the aesthetic moment in *Notes* is much too complex for a short summary, and I shall examine it in more detail later. It is, however, primarily a psychology of art—a description of the dynamics of emotional response in the artist, of the cycles of ennui and desire that provide the psychological motive for the poem, of the effects of the shared poem on the reader, for example—that intrigues Stevens in *Notes* and that Mauron's study sets out to provide.

More to the point is the specific nature of the aesthetic experience assumed in both "The Noble Rider" and *Notes*. Stevens never questions Mauron's premise that the key to this experience is the contemplative attitude that directs our attention to the pleasures of the moment with no thought of past or future action; that is, we become artists when our experience is sheared of the trappings of the active world and we are intent on the object of our meditation for its own sake: "In ordinary life we sometimes pause in this way before a tree, a landscape, a piece of furniture, a sentence, or the face of a friend—or at table even, with a mouthful of wine, our attention concentrated wholly on the delicate black savour which we are rolling between the palate and the tongue. In such moments, I think, we are all artists, because instead of putting an end to the stimulus by a prompt reaction, we keep it in suspense" (AP, 32).

It is important to recognize also that this aesthetic attitude is identified both with the auditor's response to the work of art and with the artist's response to the world which provides the impetus for the work. The two are not different in essence, although they may differ in intensity:

> The same oddly fascinating glance which the creator makes us cast on his work, he must himself have cast, in the first place, on the world around. If I may trust my own experience, there is no essential difference between the two attitudes. Obviously the artist's task is much heavier: he has to discover the possible work of art in the real world, then to extract it, when he does not compose it entirely, while the amateur has only to recognize a beauty ready-made. But from our point of view that is of small importance, for all the efforts of the artist are directed to giving the spectator *his own vision*. Therefore I think we may speak of an aesthetic attitude in general. [AP, 39]

Stevens underlined a portion of this passage, refers to it in his fly-leaf index to *Aesthetics and Psychology*, and paraphrases it in "The Noble Rider" in a series of statements borrowed from Mauron that emphasize the contemplative nature of poetry assumed in the lecture.

Mauron's observations, Stevens notes, tell us how poets help people to live their lives. They aid as well in a defense of the poet against the charge of escapism: "They are: that the artist transforms us into epicures; that he has to discover the possible work of art in the real world, then to extract it, when he does not himself compose it entirely; that he is *un amoureux perpétuel* of the world that he contemplates and thereby enriches; that art sets out to express the human soul; and finally that everything like a firm grasp of reality is eliminated from the aesthetic field" (NA, 30). Stevens was no doubt attracted to Mauron's psychological account of poetry as contemplation, partly because it reinforced a view of art's lack of utility that he had maintained in the thirties against the pressures of the social critics and Marxist-inspired reviewers such as Stanley

Burnshaw, who had attacked *Ideas of Order* for its social irresponsibility. Referring to Mauron's observations on the non-utilitarian nature of the aesthetic experience, Stevens observes in "The Noble Rider": "With these aphorisms in mind, how is it possible to condemn escapism? The poetic process is psychologically an escapist process. The chatter about escapism is, to my way of thinking, merely common cant. My own remarks about resisting or evading the pressure of reality means escapism, if analyzed" (NA, 30).

Stevens's definition of nobility in "The Noble Rider" as "the imagination pressing back against the pressure of reality" (NA, 36) is, in fact, his own version of Mauron's theory of "inactive" contemplation. Mauron's utilitarian world of past and future, of science, politics, and events with consequences, Stevens labels "the pressure of reality." The pressure of reality includes "a set of events, not only beyond our power to tranquillize them in the mind, beyond our power to reduce them and metamorphose them, but events that stir the emotions to violence, that engage us in what is direct and immediate and real, and events that involve the concepts and sanctions that are the order of our lives" (NA, 22). From a psychological point of view, Stevens argues, the "possible poet," the individual "of extraordinary imagination," cancels the pressure of reality by resisting it or evading it (NA, 23). That is, the poet must be able to resist the pressure for active response to events "that engage us in what is direct and immediate," countering such pressure with the internal pressure of a contemplative view that seeks only the present moment for its own sake. The measure of the poet, he suggests, is a power of contemplation and abstraction greater than the utilitarian world's mastery through action and reaction. The poet's power of abstraction, what Mauron describes as the poet's ability "to discover the *possible* work of art in the real world, then to extract it" (AP, 39), Stevens describes in a passage clearly indebted to Mauron. The measure of the poet, Stevens says, "is the measure of his power to abstract himself, and to withdraw with him into his abstraction the reality on which the lovers of truth insist. He must be able to abstract himself and also to abstract reality, which he does by placing it in his imagination" (NA, 23). For Stevens, as we have seen, "abstracting" reality is simply turning it into "the fiction that results from feeling" (CP, 406), transforming feeling into abstract language to extract the potential work of art from the real world. In doing so, he "gives to life the supreme fictions without which we are unable to conceive of it" (NA, 31). The mind, he notes in the conclusion of "The Noble

Rider," is "a violence from within that protects us from a violence without. It is the imagination pressing back against the pressure of reality" (NA, 36). In the course of the lecture Stevens borrows I. A. Richards's definition of art as "something inexhaustible to meditation" (NA, 9), and he quotes Croce's statement that "Poetry . . . is the triumph of contemplation" (NA, 16). But it was Mauron, rather than Richards or Croce, who suggested the particulars of this conception of poetry in "The Noble Rider."

Stevens begins his 1943 lecture "The Figure of the Youth as Virile Poet" by noting that "what is central to philosophy is its least valuable part" (NA, 39). A variation of this observation might easily be applied to his own lectures and essays. The ostensible concerns of these prose works are most frequently their least engaging aspects. What appears to be Stevens's central concern in "The Noble Rider," the history of the idea of nobility, is of less consequence to him than a conception of poetry that operates in the lecture only as a set of assumptions never fully articulated. One might also observe that a poet's unstated assumptions about poetry—beliefs so unconsciously held that they do not appear to the poet to require justification—form the most valuable part of his observations on his craft. Central to "The Noble Rider" is Stevens's assumption that poetry is the "triumph of contemplation." This assumption, for which Mauron provided the theory, is equally central to the argument of the poem that transformed the unstated aesthetic of "The Noble Rider" into something even less susceptible to statement.

From the point of view of Mauron's psychology of art, *Notes toward a Supreme Fiction* is a description of the moment of something very like his "aesthetic emotion"—or, rather, of many such moments, with special emphasis on the consequences of this attitude for the poet. "It Must Be Abstract" begins, in fact, with the ephebe's instruction in adopting the purely contemplative attitude, penetrating "this invented world" to "see it clearly in the idea of it" (CP, 380). At times such moments occur naturally, without prompting:

A composing as the body tires, a stop
To see hepatica, a stop to watch
A definition growing certain and

A wait within that certainty, a rest
In the sways of pine-trees bordering the lake.   [CP, 386]

These are times of "inherent excellence," when the pressure of reality is balanced by the internal pressure of contemplation strong enough to resist it, "incalculable balances, / At which a kind of Swiss perfection comes." Yet the speaker is aware that these are "not balances / That we achieve but balances that happen" (CP, 386). All of us are artists at fortuitous moments, as Mauron observed: "In ordinary life we sometimes pause in this way before a tree, a landscape" (AP, 32). Such "moments of awakening" are "Extreme, fortuitous, personal" (CP, 386). The speculation of the poem concerns the possibility of deliberately creating the circumstances for these moments, of cultivating the "leaner being" who is "Of greater aptitude and apprehension" (CP, 387), and whom Stevens labels major man:

> Can we compose a castle-fortress-home,
> Even with the help of Viollet-le-Duc,
> And set the MacCullough there as major man?   [CP, 386]

Canto viii of "It Must Be Abstract" gives us the transformation of MacCullough, ordinary man, into the MacCullough, major man, by depicting the contemplative moment in which MacCullough "lounging by the sea, / Drowned in its washes, reading in the sound, / About the thinker of the first idea" begins to "take habit" (CP, 387) from the emotion generated by an attitude that Mauron characterizes as immersion in the present. "Through our very immobility," he notes, "the excitement is multiplied. From nerve-centre to nerve-centre it rolls, re-echoing. Thus we learn ourselves to be more profoundly and subtly sensitive than we had imagined" (AP, 37). For Stevens's major man, who is his embodiment of Mauron's contemplative man, in the depths of such immersion it is

> As if the waves at last were never broken,
> As if the language suddenly, with ease,
> Said things it had laboriously spoken.   [CP, 387]

The achievement or failure of achievement of such moments in *Notes* takes many forms and is figured in a number of fables and fabulous personages including the Arabian, Adam and Eve, MacCullough, the planter, Nanzia Nunzio and Ozymandias, the blue woman, the great captain and Bawda, and the Canon Aspirin. These fables, figures, marriage tales, and narratives provide a great variety of perspectives on the consummating experience the poem depicts. They tend to share the requisites for the aesthetic attitude as suggested by Mauron, the chief of which is the absolute separation of the active and contemplative emotions in the creator who "contemplates the universe without any idea of making use of it" (AP, 39). This, in its turn, leads to a secondary quality that Stevens also emphasizes. "Only the artist enjoys to the full the world's diversity," Mauron concludes; the artist "alone can love the individual, for nothing obliges him to go beyond his own enjoyment" (AP, 48). And Stevens's marginal commentary characterizes the artist as one "who dwells in detachment and in contemplation and thus conceives a tenderness for the thing contemplated."[11] The artist is the world's lover, *un amoureux perpétuel*.

It is perhaps this secondary effect of contemplation that leads Stevens to his marriage fables in *Notes*. The "mystic marriage in Catawba" (CP, 401) between the great captain and Bawda is Stevens's figure for the tenderness the contemplative attitude engenders. Their union is a marriage of mind and place, an illustration that "we make of what we see, what we see clearly / And have seen, a place dependent on ourselves":

> The great captain loved the ever-hill Catawba
> And therefore married Bawda, whom he found there,
> And Bawda loved the captain as she loved the sun.
>
> They married well because the marriage-place
> Was what they loved.   [CP, 401]

The confrontation between Nanzia Nunzio and Ozymandias, however, warns us against the illusion that the contemplative moment can be stripped to bare reality. The point of view is that of the "contemplated spouse" (CP, 396) who, like Mrs. Alfred Uruguay of a poem written at about the same time, misreads the moment, fails to understand that what we see clearly in the union of self and world is not the thing itself but "a place dependent on ourselves":

> Then Ozymandias said the spouse, the bride
> Is never naked. A fictive covering
> Weaves always glistening from the heart and mind.   [CP, 396]

This is another way of saying that it must be abstract. The moment of aesthetic contemplation has the power to marry mind and place, but Stevens is careful to rule out the sort of radical realism that has been so frequently urged in readings of the poem's early cantos.

In canto vii of "It Must Change" qualities of the artist as lover and as the contemplative who makes no use of the world he contemplates are combined in one of many passages given to depiction of the mood that was, for Stevens, the ground of poetry:

Charles Mauron and *Notes toward a Supreme Fiction*

> Tonight the lilacs magnify
> The easy passion, the ever-ready love
> Of the lover that lies within us and we breathe
>
> An odor evoking nothing, absolute.
> We encounter in the dead middle of the night
> The purple odor, the abundant bloom.
>
> The lover sighs as for accessible bliss,
> Which he can take within him on his breath,
> Possess in his heart, conceal, and nothing known. [CP, 394–95]

Here the "lover that lies within us" is the pure aesthetic emotion, roughly equivalent to major man—always potentially present, but released only by experience that is absolute, "evoking nothing," separated from the active world of consequence and reason. The moment is "accessible," possessed in the lover's heart, but not "known." Describing a similar experience later in the poem, Stevens labels it an "Irrational moment" (CP, 398), for the very fact that the intrusion of the reason, a quality of the utilitarian world, would destroy it. The reason must follow the contemplative experience:

> These are not things transformed.
> Yet we are shaken by them as if they were.
> We reason about them with a later reason.   [CP, 399]

The aesthetic emotion, Mauron argues, "is attributable neither to the intelligence . . . nor to instinct" (AP, 23–24).

In Chapter 8 of *Aesthetics and Psychology* Mauron examines the mental impulses that "upset the balance" achieved in contemplation and "thus lead us to abandon the aesthetic attitude" (AP, 62). As could be anticipated, they turn out to be impulses associated with the instinct or the conscious will that would lead us back into the active world. The sexual instinct, once excited, "never ceases to ponder on the actions to come" (AP, 62); consequently, "many artists, far from cultivating day-dreams, shun them, and shut their ears to the thunder of instinctive voices" (AP, 63). But the more conscious mental impulses involving the will, conviction, the sense of reason, and obligation are equally destructive:

> Most of the movements of our mind, whether feelings or convictions, are, like instinct, turned toward future action, and for that reason, as soon as they become at all evident they threaten the aesthetic attitude with the same dangers. That is

why so many artists dislike making their work a profession of faith or an act of propaganda. That is why Théophile Gautier, Flaubert, Baudelaire protested so strongly against the intrusion of morality into art. Others to-day are protesting against the intrusion of politics, and theoretically they are right, for here too we have an imperative, and nothing could be more contrary to a pause from living. [AP, 66]

Stevens makes essentially the same argument in "The Noble Rider" when he dismisses the moral, political, and social obligations of the poet: "The truth is that the social obligation so closely urged is a phase of the pressure of reality which a poet . . . is bound to resist or evade today" (NA, 28).

Of the mental impulses that Mauron finds most conducive to the aesthetic attitude, on the other hand, the strongest is memory. Only the greatest artists, he finds, can see a useful object as if it were of no use—that is, as an aesthetic object. The memory, however, gives us experience that cannot be transformed to utility or action: "the more we lose ourselves in memory, the more completely we forget, for its sake, all practical considerations—in short, the more completely we adopt the aesthetic attitude—the more chance there is that the latent beauty of the moment we are evoking will appear to us" (AP, 73). Because memory is disassociated from our present life, it is "the one inner reality which does not attempt to hurry us into action," and the poet "works upon his memories as the painter works on landscapes or groups of objects which have no practical interest for him" (AP, 72).

These considerations involving the mental impulses that hinder or promote the contemplative state would seem to have some bearing on one of the most opaque passages in *Notes*, the "blue woman" canto of "It Must Give Pleasure." The passage describes the blue woman's refusal to transform, through her imagination, the objects of a spring morning. At first it is difficult to understand her motive in resisting the desire to exercise her imagination on the scene and, further, what this denial has to do with the repeated line, "It was enough for her that she remembered" (CP, 399). In response to Hi Simons's request for help with the passage, Stevens recalled that the blue woman "was probably the weather of a Sunday morning early last April." He said of the curious references to memory: "In the memory, (the past, the routine, the mechanism) there had always been a place for everything, free from change, and in its place everything had been right. This validated the memory (the

past, the routine etc.) and in any event it gave an intensity express-
ible in terms of coldness and clearness" (L, 444). Although this is
not altogether intelligible as a reading, it suggests that the memory,
even though a mere "mechanism," has the capacity to impart two
qualities to the scene—the two qualities, interestingly enough,
that Mauron had attributed to the memory. First, it creates the illu-
sion of a suspension of time ("free from change") characteristic of
the aesthetic emotion; second, it gives the moment an intensity
that evokes its latent qualities. The conceit of the passage is that
the April weather is the meditation of the blue woman. Both the
weather itself and the meditation on the weather, she does not wish
to transform the world her contemplation creates: "It was enough
for her that she remembered." It is as if her memory of an April
morning fixes it for a moment beyond change and with an intensity
that obviates the necessity of metamorphosis (poetic figures that
turn clouds into foamy waves) or "abortive dreams" inspired by the
"sexual blossoms" (CP, 399). The clouds "Are nothing but frothy
clouds; the frothy blooms / Waste without puberty" (CP, 399). De-
sire for change and the sexual instinct are lost in the memory, and
the moment is experienced as "cold and clear" and, "except for the
eye, without intrusion" (CP, 400). The poem clearly has interests
beyond Mauron's delineation of the function of memory in the aes-
thetic attitude, but it is faithful to Mauron's psychology in assum-
ing that the memory is the one mental mechanism that intensifies
appreciation of "the latent beauty of the moment we are evoking"
(AP, 73).

In this and the other examples of such moments from Stevens
quoted above, the relationship to Mauron's psychology is oblique—
at times perhaps simply fortuitous. These passages best illustrate
an assumption about the artist's peculiar sense of the world for
which Mauron had provided a detailed and lucid description. Mau-
ron's contribution to Stevens's poetry in the late thirties and forties
was not in providing a new theory of art, but in justifying a concep-
tion of poetry already potentially present in Stevens, a conception
that lacked only the specificity and the order provided by *Aesthet-
ics and Psychology*.

The bulk of *Aesthetics and Psychology* is occupied not with
the description of the aesthetic attitude, which is rather quickly
disposed of, but with the *consequences* of that attitude, and it is
Mauron's analysis of these consequences that is most evident in
the development of *Notes*. The analysis constitutes a kind of "psy-

chology of pleasure" (AP, 33), since the general effect of the aesthetic focus is to give pleasure. This psychology is grounded in Mauron's assumption that pleasure is "a promise of satisfaction much more than a result of it" (AP, 35). That is, pleasure accompanies the stimulus, not the reflex, "and that is why all epicurean refinements consist simply in prolonging and enriching the approach to a denouement which remains unchangeable" (AP, 35). Such a pleasure principle is easily applied to Mauron's conception of art, since the contemplative state depends on prolonging the stimulus and suspending the reflex: "The artist puts before us something we can make no use of. He asks us to look, but not react. The obvious result is that he gives possible pleasures every possible opportunity, since our mind is suspended just at the point where pleasure becomes manifest, between the stimulus and the response. . . . The artist transforms us, willy-nilly, into epicures" (AP, 37–38). Since the attitude generated in the auditor by the work is the same one that the artist "must himself have cast, in the first place, on the world around" (AP, 39), the psychology of pleasure operates equally at both ends of the creative process.

If the ultimate aim of the work of art is to give pleasure, in what specific ways are these pleasures realized? There are, Mauron concludes, three specific effects of the aesthetic attitude. "To each effect of the aesthetic focus there corresponds a distinct pleasure, or rather class of pleasures" (AP, 45), and these he labels the pleasures of sensibility (Chapter 7), the pleasures of expression (Chapter 8), and the pleasures of organization (Chapter 9). A summary of these three consequences will quickly reveal their relevance to the structure of Stevens's poem, for (in a much revised and rearranged form) they become his three "notes" toward the supreme fiction.[12] More specifically, the first section of *Notes* incorporates elements of Mauron's second and third consequences; the second section includes Mauron's first; and the third section is devoted to the overall effect—that is, pleasure—of the aesthetic focus. This is, to be sure, something of an oversimplification, since *Notes* does not itself hold strictly to its three-part division. "Even in a text expounding *it must change*, it is permissible to illustrate *it must give pleasure* without any law whatever" (L, 445), Stevens said, and each of his three "notes" is illustrated as well by the other two sections of the poem. Perhaps it is more accurate, then, to say that the consequences of the aesthetic attitude analyzed in *Aesthetics and Psychology* parallel in a fairly consistent way the chief elements of Stevens's supreme fiction.

The first third of the poem, "It Must Be Abstract," has generated as much controversy as anything else by Stevens, and I have earlier entered the controversy in suggesting that Stevens's reading of Richards's *Coleridge on Imagination* was largely responsible for the somewhat peculiar use of the term *abstract* in this first note. Much of the substance of the section, especially the first two cantos, can also be traced to Mauron, whose contribution is perhaps more obvious than Richards's. The third consequence of the aesthetic attitude is summarized as *"Dissolution of the practical organization of reality, giving place to other possible organizations"* (AP, 42). Mauron's argument is that the aesthetic attitude cannot be maintained in "practical life in a world organized by our intelligence." The artist is required to penetrate the film of the familiar world so that it is stripped of its commonplace trappings and becomes alien to his impulse toward the active and utilitarian:

> By altering his focus, and treating as negligible the future and the conduct required in it, the artist of course loses all the advantages of this practical organization; it becomes perfectly foreign to him. At this moment I see through my window a landscape with a house, trees and hills. Certainly I know, as a result of long experience, how to behave towards these different objects. But if I consider them from an aesthetic, that is a static point of view, my knowledge becomes useless lumber. . . . Henceforth there is nothing in front of me but forms and colours between which strange affinities assert themselves. . . . What was distinct draws nearer, and what was mingled separates. The landscape I could find my way about so easily returns to chaos. [AP, 42–43]

This altered focus by which the familiar world becomes foreign is, of course, essential to the speaker's advice to the ephebe in the opening canto of *Notes*, which reflects Mauron's conclusion that "In the arts, as in poetry, the zero from which the artist starts . . . is a certain pre-existent organization of the world, which he will have to destroy in order to create new combinations" (AP, 79). If the artist remains at zero, the accustomed world, the audience will greet his work with indifference. Yet, paradoxically, the audience will protest any deviation from custom. Stevens wrestles with this paradox in *The Man with the Blue Guitar*, where the audience demands "A tune beyond us, yet ourselves" (CP, 165). The writer, Mauron concludes, is obliged to "deal cunningly with our mental habits," pretending to copy nature while superimposing the aesthetic effects that interest him (AP, 79). Stevens's marginal comment (on pp. 79–80 of *Aesthetics and Psychology*) is appropriate to the first canto of *Notes*: "There exists an organization of the world, which cannot be destroyed without protest and yet to which we are indifferent."

Notes begins, then, with the training by which the imagination achieves the aesthetic attitude. The first step consists of destroying the preexistent world, "this invented world" (CP, 380), to grasp the "first idea" (CP, 381). "If you take the varnish and dirt of generations off a picture, you see it in its first idea," Stevens explained. "If you think about the world without its varnish and dirt, you are a thinker of the first idea" (L, 426–27). The varnish and dirt, one assumes, are the meanings and associations built up through generations in the preexistent world. But it is in the perceiver's mind, in the attitude that the artist brings to the world, not in the world itself, that cleansing is required. To become a thinker of the first idea it is necessary to empty one's mind of the preexistent order, the utilitarian world:

> You must become an ignorant man again
> And see the sun again with an ignorant eye
> And see it clearly in the idea of it. [CP, 380]

It is the "ennui of apartments," the indifference with which we view the world of the multitudes, "That sends us back to the first idea" (CP, 381), to which, in turn, we grow indifferent.

The mental state sought in Stevens's program for achieving the first idea he calls *ignorance*, using the Vichian term to suggest a deliberate cleansing or emptying of the mind to reach a state approximating that of Vico's first poets. Here is Mauron's parallel instruction for achieving the proper aesthetic attitude: "The only training for the imagination—in Mallarmé's words—consists in looking at the picture a long time, with a mind at once curious and empty; little by little, under the 'natural' meaning of the work —portrait, landscape, or what not—certain plastic *insistences* appear. Their outstanding characteristic is often a certain oddity. . . . those details which are *foreign to the practical point of view* reveal most clearly the exigencies of aesthetics" (AP, 94–95). One notes here an emphasis on the strangeness, oddity, irrationality of the sight available to the aesthetic attitude, an emphasis apparent throughout *Aesthetics and Psychology*. The aesthetic universe "becomes at once richer and stranger." The spectator has the impression of having been "transported into another world, full of monsters and fascinating subtleties" (AP, 40). The "most absurd voyages are allowed," and "the whole field of abstract logic which is the native land of the active intellectual is forbidden the artist" (AP, 105). Aesthetic seeing, far from granting a more intense view of common reality, pierces the veil of what is "real" only by being familiar: "Everything like a firm grasp of reality is eliminated from the aesthetic field" (AP, 106).

This line of thought in Mauron, from which Stevens had quoted approvingly in "The Noble Rider," is without question related to his tendency in *Notes* to equate the most intense moments of contemplation with nonsense, the irrational, or the absurd.[13] The first instance in the poem occurs in canto iii of "It Must Be Abstract," when the speaker attempts to illustrate the "candor" (CP, 382) that aesthetic vision allows us to share:

We say: At night an Arabian in my room,
With his damned hoobla-hoobla-hoobla-how,
Inscribes a primitive astronomy

Across the unscrawled fores the future casts
And throws his stars around the floor. By day
The wood-dove used to chant his hoobla-hoo

And still the grossest iridescence of ocean
Howls hoo and rises and howls hoo and falls.
Life's nonsense pierces us with strange relation.   [CP, 383]

The verse is itself a kind of nonsense meant to illustrate the manner in which the aesthetic attitude transports us into a world where the preexistent order has been eliminated. Stevens said the Arabian was the moon (L, 434), but the Arabian is also, for Stevens, an emblem for the artist's transformation of the accustomed to the exotic. Mauron illustrates his concept of an "aesthetic combination" —that is, a formal relation of aesthetic elements—with the analogy of a journey "from one reality to another" (AP, 83), and he offers this example of its presence in a poetic image: " 'Tiger, tiger, burning bright.' Here the mental journey takes us from the idea tiger to the idea flame. Something changes—the object considered—something remains constant—the brightness streaked with black, the bound, the suppleness. The immobility of these elements has made possible the course of the metaphor. The poetic arabesque is formed by the mental leap thus accomplished" (AP, 84–85). Stevens's "poetic arabesque," the linguistic leap from the literal to the intricately contrived and irrational, manages to include the Arab himself, whose effect is to pierce us with life's "nonsense," as everything like a firm grasp of reality is eliminated from the object considered. The nonsense element of the passage is heightened by Stevens's intention of leaving the reader in the dark as to the exact nature of the figure: "the fact that the Arabian is the moon is something that the reader could not possibly know. However, I did not think that it was necessary for him to know" (L, 434). Obviously his intention has been to some extent compromised with the publication of the letter glossing the passage, yet even that information cannot domesticate an Arabian with "his damned hoobla-hoobla-hoobla-how" who "throws his stars around the floor," any more than, in Mauron's exemplary poem, Blake's stars, which "threw down their spears, / And watered heaven with their tears," are susceptible to rational analysis.

As I will suggest in the next chapter, which considers in greater detail Stevens's conception of obscurity and nonsense in poetry, his notion of irrationality is considerably more complex and more far-reaching than Mauron's, although they start from similar assumptions about poetry.[14] Here I want simply to suggest the links between the "Irrational moment" (CP, 398) in *Notes* and Mauron's theory of poetry as inactive contemplation. One such link is implied in Mauron's statement on training the imagination, quoted above. Once the mind is emptied of its preconceptions, he argues, "little by little, under the 'natural' meaning of the work," certain *insistences* appear, prompted by the object of contemplation. These *insistences* will appear odd to the perceiver since they are foreign to the familiar point of view (AP, 94–95). The nonsensical quality of the aesthetic emotion is thus the inevitable result of escaping for a moment from the commonsensical world, and the most difficult task of the artist is stripping the object of contemplation of its utilitarian function: "Only very great artists can see a useful object exactly as if it were good for nothing" (AP, 71). In *Notes* poetry is possible only after the familiar world has become alien: "From this the poem springs: that we live in a place / That is not our own and, much more, not ourselves. . ." (CP, 383). The value of this difficult task for the artist, however, is a fresh seeing or first idea that takes its qualities from the *insistences* of the object, rather than from the accustomed point of view of the active world.

In Stevens's most explicit treatment of the irrational moment in *Notes* (in the first canto of "It Must Give Pleasure") his emphasis is on both the difficulty of achieving such a moment and the value of capturing that moment's own irrational qualities. "To sing jubilas at exact, accustomed times," to be part of "a multitude" and "to exult with its great throat" is "a facile exercise":

But the difficultest rigor is forthwith,
On the image of what we see, to catch from that

Irrational moment its unreasoning,
As when the sun comes rising, when the sea
Clears deeply, when the moon hangs on the wall

Of heaven-haven. These are not things transformed.
Yet we are shaken by them as if they were.
We reason about them with a later reason.   [CP, 398–99]

These are not things transformed by the mind, which has been emptied of its customary point of view, the view of the multitude. Immersed in the experience, one has the sense of having captured "*from* that / Irrational moment *its* unreasoning." In a poem also written under the spell of Mauron's aesthetics—"Phosphor Reading by His Own Light"—Stevens makes the same point about aesthetic viewing:

Look, realist, not knowing what you expect.
The green falls on you as you look,
Falls on and makes and gives, even a speech.
And you think that that is what you expect. . . .   [CP, 267][15]

In both instances the assumption is that the qualities of the object of contemplation itself—Mauron's *insistences*—form the basis for the first idea, or fresh sight, which is the artist's triumph over the multitude's "exact, accustomed" seeing; this can occur, Stevens warns the artist, only if one approaches the object "not knowing what you expect."

Although Stevens extends the motif of irrationality beyond Mauron's rather clear limits, a number of the most obscure passages in *Notes* are approachable once we recognize that they result from the poet's attempt both to capture and to impart a quality of the aesthetic attitude the poem describes and simultaneously seeks to inculcate in the reader. That is, the poem resorts to nonsense in attempting to be faithful to its rendering of the aesthetic emotion, and it provides detailed instructions or notes for the reader's training in aesthetic seeing. The poet's obligation to his readers here, as Stevens suggested in "The Noble Rider," is "to make his imagination theirs and . . . he fulfills himself only as he sees his imagination become the light in the minds of others" (NA, 29). The "poet's gibberish" can become "The gibberish of the vulgate" (CP, 396), Mauron and Stevens suggest, if we adopt the same attitude that the artist "must himself have cast, in the first place, on the world around" (AP, 39). The poem describes a world which is "familiar yet an aberration" (CP, 406), and it settles for this aesthetic view at the end: "That's it: the more than rational distortion, / The fiction that results from feeling. Yes, that" (CP, 406).

A difficulty in Mauron's and Stevens's poetic, which proposes an absolute separation between the aesthetic emotions and other human emotions, is that the poet's audience cannot appreciate his achievement as long as it remains in its active state:

There's a meditation there, in which there seems

To be an evasion, a thing not apprehended or
Not apprehended well. Does the poet
Evade us, as in a senseless element? [CP, 396]

What appears to be the poet's evasion, however, the senseless element of the poem, is, to adopt Mauron's terminology, the product of the active mind attempting to share the aesthetic attitude. The poet's aim is not to evade "our bluntest barriers" (CP, 397)—our limitations as readers, as Stevens glossed the passage (L, 435)—but to transform us, willy-nilly, into epicures:

It is the gibberish of the vulgate that he seeks.
He tries by a peculiar speech to speak

The peculiar potency of the general,
To compound the imagination's Latin with
The lingua franca et jocundissima. [CP, 397]

To suggest that the poet seeks "the gibberish of the vulgate" is, on the surface, to suggest his attempt to employ the common language, but to "compound the imagination's Latin" with the vulgate is also to transform the common language to the gibberish of the poet. In the end, one of the poet's obligations in Notes is to cultivate readers whose gibberish matches his own, whose contemplative "ignorance" before the work of art allows them to accept the irrationality of the aesthetic emotion.

The artist's or auditor's initial ignorance at the moment of contemplation is not the final state. The second consequence of the aesthetic attitude that Mauron considers helps us to understand how the experience terminates in a fiction or why, in Stevens's and

I. A. Richards's terminology, it must be abstract. Mauron himself uses the term *abstract* in a conventionally negative sense, but his examination of the dynamics of the second of the contemplative pleasures, that of artistic expression, is in perfect accord with the notion of abstraction that Stevens apparently took from Richards.

To summarize Mauron's detailed examination of the pleasures of expression in *Aesthetics and Psychology*, we may say that the contemplative emotion is double-edged. While its focus is on the external object, it also awakens in us "distant repercussions . . . a hubbub of past impressions, feelings and desires" (AP, 40). In our active life we pay little attention to these mental echoes, since they have almost no practical importance. "But the artist listens. Indeed . . . he is obliged to listen, since he will not allow himself to act." Here we enter "the obscure domain of allusions, interpretations and symbols. Here a colour is not only a colour, but, for example, a haze of memories. A window is not merely a window, but the aspiration to some vague deliverance. A note is not merely a note, but a cry of hope or a convulsion of anguish" (AP, 41). In short, the "man who pauses" finds himself observing "this inner landscape with the same contemplative detachment as if it were part of the outer world" (AP, 60–61). He must be double-minded; one part of him "seethes with echoes, impulses, desires, emotions; the other, unmoved, savours and appreciates" (AP, 61).[16]

The effect of the awakening of these internal echoes by the contemplative state can be seen in the artist's need for expression. In Mauron's psychology, the aesthetic emotion is all stimulus and no reflex, since the reflex carries us away from contemplation and back to the world of action. Artistic expression, then, becomes the aesthetic equivalent of reflex: "It is as though, possessing a certain amount of accumulated energy, we were obliged to expend it, either through the channel of the reflexes, or through that of expression" (AP, 58). Expressive art is the culmination of the aesthetic emotion for the artist, and it differs from the simple transmission of sense impressions—colors, shapes, sounds: "The difficulties—and the expressive side of art—begin from the moment when the creator aims at transmitting *something other* than the sensations which compose the work of art" (AP, 54). By *something other*, Mauron means "states of mind," and the transmission of a state of mind, "impossible directly, requires the medium of symbols" (AP, 57). How is this transmission accomplished? "Clearly, by means of the internal echoes. . . . A sensation in our nervous system cannot remain isolated; it links up with past impressions; it awakens feelings; it excites desires. If the links thus formed are strong enough, a moment comes when it may symbolize, signify, and thus transmit these acquired secondary elements" (AP, 55).

The significance of this step for a psychology of art is that it bridges the gap between the "ignorant man," passive before the contemplative object, and the artist conceiving a formal work of art. For Mauron, the dynamics of contemplation "necessarily end in the creation of a language. And a language was what expressive art required" (AP, 57). Readers of the early cantos of "It Must Be Abstract" who have interpreted Stevens's epistemology as an act of perception that seizes a reality that "cannot be transcribed into mental conceptions"[17] have some difficulty reconciling this view with the resulting fiction or poem. This is clearly not a problem for Mauron, who incorporates both Stevens's initial ignorance before the object of contemplation and his "fiction that results from feeling" (CP, 406). Mauron's psychology of aesthetic response suggests a path by which "the first idea becomes / The hermit in a poet's metaphors" (CP, 381). It suggests why it is the "ennui of apartments," the utilitarian world of the "multitude," that "sends us back to the first idea" (CP, 381), why the "monastic man," the contemplative removed from the active world, "is the artist" (CP, 382), and how the "poem refreshes life so that we share / For a moment, the first idea" (CP, 382).

Realist misreadings, which have dominated discussion of the aesthetics of *Notes*,[18] have not taken sufficient account of the fact that Stevens pursues in the poem a "fictive abstract" that is "immanent in the mind of the poet" (L, 434). This characterization appears in his comments on canto vi of "It Must Be Abstract." Both the passage and the commentary take on a fresh coloring when read in the light of Mauron's doctrine of "internal echoes" awakened by the contemplative mood.

Not to be realized because not to
Be seen, not to be loved nor hated because
Not to be realized. Weather by Franz Hals,

Brushed up by brushy winds in brushy clouds,
Wetted by blue, colder for white. Not to
Be spoken to, without a roof, without

First fruits, without the virginal of birds,
The dark-blown ceinture loosened, not relinquished.
Gay is, gay was, the gay forsythia

And yellow, yellow thins the Northern blue.
Without a name and nothing to be desired,
If only imagined but imagined well.

My house has changed a little in the sun.
The fragrance of the magnolias comes close,
False flick, false form, but falseness close to kin.   [CP, 385]

The canto, in Stevens's reading, is "a constant reference from the
abstract to the real, to and fro." It is "a struggle with the inaccessi-
bility of the abstract," which "does not exist" but which, as "fictive
abstract," is "as immanent in the mind of the poet, as the idea of
God is immanent in the mind of the theologian." The weather, on
the other hand, "is not inaccessible and is not abstract" (L, 434). In
both the poem and the paraphrase Stevens has described the double
nature of the aesthetic experience, as suggested by Mauron. On the
one hand, the accessible weather ("The weather as described is the
weather that was about me when I wrote this" [L, 434]) is reduced
to aesthetic contemplation. It is perceived in terms of the forms,
colors, and brushwork of a painting ("by Franz Hals")—"Yellow, yel-
low thins the Northern blue." It is "without a name" in the sense
that the customary point of view has been successfully dissolved
so that the perceiver stands empty before it, accessible to its own
insistences. But this in itself is not enough to achieve the fictive
abstract. It must be "imagined but imagined well." The aesthetic
focus must awaken the abstraction, the symbols, feelings, and im-
pressions "immanent in the mind of the poet." These, because they
are fictive, not the thing itself, will be "False flick, false form, but
falseness close to kin." The resulting union of mind and world, of
latent symbols and objects stripped of familiarity, seems a paradox,
and the final two stanzas can speak of it only in contradictory
terms:

It must be visible or invisible,
Invisible or visible or both:
A seeing and unseeing in the eye.

The weather and the giant of the weather,
Say the weather, the mere weather, the mere air:
An abstraction blooded, as a man by thought.   [CP, 385]

The fictive abstract is the marriage of visible and invisible, world
and mind, and the "giant of the weather" is major man or man
stripped to pure aesthetic contemplation. The merger of the

weather and the giant of the weather is an "abstraction blooded" in the way that man, an abstract concept, is made real by conscious thought, which is itself a transaction between an accessible world and a personal and eccentric sensibility.

In "The Irrational Element in Poetry," the first of Stevens's exercises in poetic theory to be influenced by Mauron, he locates the irrational element in "the transaction between reality and the sensibility of the poet from which poetry springs," and he labels this act a "transposition of an objective reality to a subjective reality" (OP, 217). I believe Stevens describes such a transaction in the canto above, and it seems clear that the resulting fiction depends not on a perception of bare reality, the *Ding an Sich*, as we have been so often told, but on the ability of the poet to *abstract* reality, in Stevens's sense of the word, which he does by clothing it in the feelings and impressions that are, necessarily, prompted by the experience of the first idea. For the poet, the aesthetic emotion ends in a language, as it does in MacCullough's reading of the first idea, when "the language suddenly, with ease, / Said things it had laboriously spoken" (CP, 387). The candor of the first idea results in a speech that may be, as Mauron suggests, "more original than the clichés of ordinary speech" and "too personal even to be expressed in public; no one but the author would know what was meant" (AP, 41):

> We say: At night an Arabian in my room,
> With his damned hoobla-hoobla-hoobla-how,
> Inscribes a primitive astronomy. . . .   [CP, 383]

The link between our experience of the first idea and what "we say" may thus be so original that "only a psycho-analyst could hope, by long and painful effort, to unravel the skein" (AP, 41). "We move," Stevens said, "between these points: / From that ever-early candor to its late plural" (CP, 382), from first idea to fiction. The two are so closely related in the aesthetic emotion that it is difficult to separate them, as the Canon Aspirin discovers in canto vi of "It Must Give Pleasure."

"The Irrational Element in Poetry" contains an instructive example of such a transaction between reality and the poetic sensibility from which the poem springs:

> A day or two before Thanksgiving we had a light fall of snow in Hartford. It melted a little by day and then froze again at night, forming a thin, bright crust over the grass. At the same time, the moon was almost full. I awoke once several hours

before daylight and as I lay in bed I heard the steps of a cat
running over the snow under my window almost inaudibly.
The faintness and strangeness of the sound made on me one of
those impressions which one so often seizes as pretexts for
poetry. I suppose that in such a case one is merely expressing
one's sensibility and that the reason why this expression takes
the form of poetry is that it takes whatever form one is able to
give it. The poet is able to give it the form of poetry because
poetry is the medium of his personal sensibility.   [OP, 217]

In Mauron's terms, Stevens's description is that of the aesthetic
emotion, separated from the active world, characterized by a neces-
sary "strangeness," and followed by the artist's need for expression,
which in the poet must take the form of a poetry expressed in a
personal and original sensibility. The resulting poem, if it comes to
that, will represent the "attitude of the writer," a "manner" of ap-
prehending the world (OP, 220). It might well contain no notice of a
cat running across the snow:

Manner is something that has not yet been disengaged ade-
quately. It does not mean style; it means the attitude of the
writer, his bearing rather than his point of view. His bearing
toward what? Not anything in particular, simply his pose. He
hears the cat on the snow. The running feet set the rhythm.
There is no subject beyond the cat running on the snow in the
moonlight. He grows completely tired of the thing, wants a
subject, thought, feeling, his whole manner changes. . . . All
this is irrational. If the choice of subject was predictable it
would be rational. . . . One is always writing about two things
in poetry and it is this that produces the tension characteristic
of poetry. One is the true subject and the other is the poetry of
the subject.   [OP, 220–21]

If poetry springs from a transaction between a real event—a cat
running across the snow, for example—and the chance thoughts,
feelings, and rhythms awakened in the sensibility by the poet's sa-
voring of this moment, then the resulting poem must be granted an
irrational element. Stevens distinguishes here between the exter-
nal, "the true subject," and the internal, "the poetry of the subject,"
in suggesting the double-mindedness that Mauron grants the artist.

The transaction between reality and the sensibility of the poet is,
of course, the focus of *Notes*, and "It Must Change," the second
section of the poem, is devoted to the motivation that Stevens sug-

gests in "The Irrational Element in Poetry." "Why does one write poetry?" he asks. One reason is "because one is impelled to do so by a personal sensibility and also because one grows tired of the monotony of one's imagination, say, and sets out to find variety" (OP, 221). This is, for Mauron, the first and perhaps most important consequence of the aesthetic attitude, what he calls "the pleasures of sensibility." The term *sensibility* he uses in its strictest sense as "the perception of differences" (AP, 45). The artist "is sensitive when he distinguishes between two words which we should be apt to use indiscriminately" and equally sensitive in separating "two states of mind hidden in a common name" (AP, 46). The artist's motive is originality, which is the product of an individual sensibility: "Only the artist enjoys to the full the world's diversity. He alone can love the individual. . . . His sensibility takes a particular form which is worth considering separately: *the love of original beings*" (AP, 48). Artists are "the great explorers of new worlds, the great hunters of originality"; to them we owe "almost all our delicate perceptions in this field" (AP, 49).

While "It Must Be Abstract" is primarily concerned with the mental act by which the indifferent world is stripped of its indifference—the difficult realization of the aesthetic attitude and its expression—"It Must Change" details the pleasures of sensibility that overcome "the distaste we feel for this withered scene," the world "that has not changed enough" (CP, 390). After the opacity of the poem's struggle with the almost impossible articulation of the fictive abstract, "It Must Change" is surprisingly accessible, mirroring in its verse our refreshment in "a universe of inconstancy" (CP, 389) as revealed by the artist's sensibility. Such figures as the booming bees of canto i, the President of canto ii, who "ordains the bee to be / Immortal" (CP, 390), the statue of General Du Puy of canto iii, and the "idiot minstrelsy" (CP, 394) of wren and sparrow in canto vi reflect the "granite monotony" (CP, 394) of the familiar world. Stevens suggests, in "The Irrational Element in Poetry," that this world drives one to a personal sensibility for relief from "the monotony of one's imagination." Mauron is quite specific on this point, and his motive for the artist is in perfect accord: "A universe too monotonous or customary means a state of boredom which rapidly becomes unbearable. The only known antidote is surprise; and for the man sensitive to slighter impacts the number of surprises will be multiplied. Thus the artist and the scientist are hardly ever bored; some little difference, imperceptible to others, always turns up in time for their amusement" (AP, 47–48). Unfortunately for the scientist, the business of science is "the reduction of difference" to "austere and useful general laws," so the scientist's pleasure is soon ended (AP, 48). The artist's business, however, "is to enjoy"; the "great contemplatives . . . contrive to maintain their equilibrium and to love in every manner possible the universe before their eyes." They have attained this "point of detachment" through "pure sensibility—their perception of differences" (AP, 50–51).

To continue Mauron's terminology, one might then read almost the whole of "It Must Change" as an account of the universe of surprise granted the contemplative through the pure sensibility, the perception of differences awakened by the aesthetic emotion. In the concluding canto of the section Stevens incorporates the chief elements of Mauron's psychology in depicting what is, for both theorists, the moment from which the poem springs:

A bench was his catalepsy, Theatre
Of Trope. He sat in the park. The water of
The lake was full of artificial things,

Like a page of music, like an upper air,
Like a momentary color, in which swans
Were seraphs, were saints, were changing essences.   [CP, 397]

Stevens's gloss of the first line is this: "A bench as catalepsy is a place of trance" (L, 434). That is, the poet on his park bench has attained the contemplative attitude; a firm grasp of reality has been eliminated from the aesthetic field, which in this case is a lake full of swans. Properly double-minded, the poet is equally attuned to the internal echoes awakened in a sensibility that changes swans to seraphs and saints. The "true subject" (swans on a lake) has been transformed to "the poetry of the subject" (swans as aesthetic objects, "artificial things"). The motive for this transformation is the poet's need to satisfy a sensibility that contains the same "will to change" characteristic of the inconstant world he observes:

The west wind was the music, the force
To which the swans curveted, a will to change,
A will to make iris frettings on the blank.

There was a will to change, a necessitous
And present way, a presentation, a kind
Of volatile world, too constant to be denied. . . .   [CP, 397]

The paradox contained in this artificial act of seeing—present as well in Mauron's theory—is that the inconstant world of change that furnishes the model for the imagination's desire for novelty is unavailable to what might be called a "realistic" point of view, one "faithful" to the object of perception. For Stevens and Mauron, only when we attain an aesthetic attitude, one in which swans are transformed to objects of artifice, is the perception of differences realized. At this point the world becomes "The eye of a vagabond in metaphor / That catches our own" (CP, 397). Although we may acknowledge that change is a property of the external world, it is a change that awaits our own transformation:

> The casual is not
> Enough. The freshness of transformation is
>
> The freshness of a world. It is our own,
> It is ourselves, the freshness of ourselves,
> And the necessity and that presentation
>
> Are rubbings of a glass in which we peer.
> Of these beginnings, gay and green, propose
> The suitable amours. Time will write them down. [CP, 397–98]

These "beginnings, gay and green," which originate outside of time through "catalepsy," a condition of suspended animation, enter time in the poem, where they will, ironically in Stevens's poetic, experience the same fate as the birds' song of canto vi—"A single text, granite monotony" (CP, 394).

The desire for the "freshness of transformation," which is the "freshness of ourselves," is relentless in Stevens and is chiefly responsible for his obsession with originality. "As a man becomes familiar with his own poetry, it becomes as obsolete for himself as for anyone else," Stevens notes. "From this it follows that one of the motives in writing is renewal" (OP, 220). He offers a similar explanation for a poetic drought: "Poetry is like the imagination. It is not likely to be satisfied with the same thing twice" (L, 680). His insistence on change as a vital element in the conception of the supreme fiction, in fact, answers Mauron's objection that novelty, as such, has not been accorded "the importance it should have in aesthetic theory." The true artist "has a horror of repeating himself." The motive for the artist "consists in obeying solely his aesthetic pleasure"; consequently, "a combination twice repeated pleases him no longer" (AP, 100). Although Stevens was celebrating change in his poetry long before he read *Aesthetics and Psychology*, he discovered in Mauron an aesthetic that not only granted the concept of change an important place in the theory of poetry but also integrated it with other qualities he valued. His marginal notes in Chapter 8 suggest his impression of Mauron's account of the pleasures of sensibility: "The perception of differences is agreeable in itself, in one way to the scientist, in another to the artist[.] For the artist, it leads to an original being who dwells in detachment and in contemplation and thus conceives a tenderness for the thing contemplated. L'artiste est un amoureux perpétuel." The perception of differences that engenders change is thus merged with the original being whom Stevens insisted the poet become, with detachment and contemplation and, finally, with the awakening of desire, the love for the world with which *Notes* concludes.

As many of its readers have observed, *Notes* enlarges its perspective with each phase of its triadic structure. From the rather professorial and technical instruction to the ephebe in the early cantos it builds toward the celebration of pleasure. Except for the unfortunate anticlimax of the epilogue addressed to the soldier, it achieves its most ecstatic moments in the final cantos, attempting to answer the question that opens canto viii: "What am I to believe?" (CP, 404). The structure of the poem reverses the organization of *Aesthetics and Psychology*, which begins with a psychology of pleasure and proceeds to the dynamics of the three pleasures of sensibility, expression, and the decreation of the utilitarian world, concluding where *Notes* begins. Mauron's assertion that art must give pleasure is not confined to any one section of his study; it is his given, implicit in his psychological approach. It is the assumption upon which his theory of art rests, as is suggested in his conclusion: "If I had to sum up in a sentence the results of my enquiry, I should say that art appears to me to seek everywhere the psychological conditions *best suited* to the growth of pleasures which *may remain contemplative*" (AP, 106). His restrictions here are important to note. Life obviously affords other pleasures, but in art "the pleasure accompanies the stimulus rather than the satisfaction" (AP, 109), and it therefore must remain contemplative, savoring the moment rather than anticipating future action.

In answering the question "What am I to believe?" in the final three cantos of *Notes*, Stevens reverts again to this concept of contemplative pleasure. Imagining an "angel in his cloud" (CP, 404), a figure for our traditional need, as in "Sunday Morning," for "some imperishable bliss" (CP, 68), the speaker recognizes that his pleasure derives not from the "golden destiny" (CP, 404) represented by the angel, but from the very experience of imagining an angel:

Am I that imagine this angel less satisfied?
Are the wings his, the lapis-haunted air?

Is it he or is it I that experience this?
Is it I then that keep saying there is an hour
Filled with expressible bliss, in which I have

No need, am happy, forget need's golden hand,
Am satisfied without solacing majesty. . . .   [CP, 404–5]

Is not the earthly and attainable experience of imagining an angel
the equivalent of the state we imagine that angels enjoy—a state
in which we forget worldly need and are satisfied for the moment
without the consolation of some external power? If this can be at-
tained in the moment of contemplating angels, then "there is a
day / There is a month, a year, there is a time / In which majesty is
a mirror of the self" (CP, 405). Stevens is here proposing the cultiva-
tion of a habit of mind—what Mauron calls the aesthetic attitude
—that is the secular parallel to the mind that created the earliest
fictions by which the "external regions" (CP, 405) were peopled
with gods and angels. The poem has thus returned us to the point
where it began, "a heaven / That has expelled us and our images"
(CP, 381). In its conclusion, it proposes the aesthetic emotion, the
pleasure of experiencing the moment for itself without thought of
future need or action or fate, as the fiction that will replace the
fiction of angels.

Canto ix describes this moment of contemplative pleasure, a
"thing final in itself and, therefore, good," having no more conse-
quence than the "Mere repetitions" of the songs of birds:

These things at least comprise
An occupation, an exercise, a work,

A thing final in itself and, therefore, good:
One of the vast repetitions final in
Themselves and, therefore, good, the going round

And round and round, the merely going round,
Until merely going round is a final good,
The way wine comes at a table in a wood.   [CP, 405]

Mauron, as I noted earlier, uses a similar figure to describe this
moment: "In ordinary life we sometimes pause in this way before a
tree, a landscape. . . . or at table even, with a mouthful of wine, our
attention concentrated wholly on the delicate black savour which

we are rolling between the palate and the tongue" (AP, 32). In the same discussion he employs another example of the inactive and inconsequential nature of the aesthetic experience. "What reflex is there," he asks, "to respond to a spiral painted on the bottom of a dish?" (AP, 36–37). Stevens's figure for the pleasure of aesthetic contemplation at the conclusion of the canto parallels this inconsequential spiral, shifting it from art to life:

And we enjoy like men, the way a leaf
Above the table spins its constant spin,
So that we look at it with pleasure, look

At it spinning its eccentric measure.   [CP, 406]

These may be no more than fortuitous parallels, but they help to show an affinity of minds that is difficult to discount in following the argument of *Notes*.

It is also difficult to ignore the possibility that Mauron was partly responsible for the theme of the canto that serves as an epilogue to *Notes*. It is, in essence, an explanation for the poet's necessary resistance to the pressure of reality, and it may have been inspired by a passage in Mauron that Stevens noted in his flyleaf index. Among several notations on the back flyleaf of *Aesthetics and Psychology* is this entry: "70 nothing is more foreign to the artist's nature than combat." Here is a portion of the discussion to which Stevens alludes:

... the essence of [man's] life is struggle, against nature or against his fellows. But nothing is more foreign to the artist's nature than combat. We may deplore it, but we cannot alter it. When the whole world is crying Forward, he stands still. If the artist, then, claims to express the essence of the human soul, he is wrong; and if the combatant, on his side, tries to make the artist join in the fray, then *he* is wrong. Biologically, human pleasure is a luxury. . . . Art is part of this luxury. We add aesthetic joys to our life as we add condiments to our soup, to give it a little more flavour. I should agree with the reader if he were to say that the condiment is not the essence of the soup; I should agree even more if he declared a soup without flavour uneatable.   [AP, 70–71]

The poet wishes to impart something like this to the soldier in the epilogue to *Notes*. He argues that there is another war, one "between the mind and the sky" in which the poet engages: "It is a war that never ends" (CP, 407). The soldier may return from his war to a celebration of "six meats and twelve wines," or he may die. In either case, he "is poor without the poet's lines" (CP, 407), for the poet provides the words by which life and death are celebrated. Stevens implies that the poet contributes with his words the flavor of life, like the condiments added to food:

> How simply the fictive hero becomes the real;
> How gladly with proper words the soldier dies,
> If he must, or lives on the bread of faithful speech.   [CP, 408]

After the sustained eloquence of the last three cantos of *Notes*, the epilogue is something of a disappointment. Its function, it seems to me, is not what Harold Bloom has suggested—a personal address to "anyone that fights for the mind in the 'war between the mind / And sky.' "[19] Rather, it is the apologia of the contemplative man justifying his inaction to the man of action. Writing a poem like *Notes* during a time of war would no doubt seem, from the point of view of the utilitarian world, an indulgence. Although the epilogue is not successful in dispelling that impression, Stevens's motive was, I believe, to explain the poet's function to the combatant; his explanation, like so much else in the poem, assumes a view in which the poet seeks the conditions best suited to pleasures that may remain contemplative.

If, as I have suggested, Mauron's psychology of pleasure plays a large part in the poem as a whole, we may approach passages such as the epilogue with a more substantial context. If we recognize that, in the concept of poetry Stevens accepted from Mauron, "nothing is more foreign to the artist's nature than combat," we see why Stevens felt the epilogue necessary and how it is connected with the larger interests of the poem. This is not to suggest that *Notes*, as a poem, is altered appreciably; rather, *Notes* as an argument about poetry is clarified to some extent once we grasp certain assumptions about the psychology of creativity that Stevens seems to have taken from *Aesthetics and Psychology*. I have attempted in this discussion to examine the passages in *Notes* that appear to be most faithful to Mauron's aesthetic. If I have exaggerated Mauron's importance in particular passages, that is no doubt because the conceptions of poetry held by the two theorists were so close as to be expressed in similar language and images. On the other hand, the importance of Mauron in the formulation of Stevens's conception of poetry in the late thirties and early forties is difficult to exaggerate, and to read the poem as if it incorporated details from *Aesthetics and Psychology* yields results valuable enough to justify it as a strategy. Such a reading renders the overall argument of the poem accessible. It provides an approach to passages that have troubled commentators, and it helps us to recognize that *Notes* is less concerned with a definition of poetry or a supreme fiction than with a depiction of the inner dynamics of the poet in the process of conceiving the world as poetic material. In "The Irrational Element in Poetry" Stevens struggles unsuccessfully to define what he calls variously the "manner," "attitude," "bearing," or "pose" of the writer, which he says has "not yet been disengaged adequately" (OP, 220). *Notes* is clearly his most successful attempt to articulate it. What he may have gained, finally, from Mauron was a theory and a systematic framework for describing the artist's attitude toward the world and the consequences of that attitude. That is not, however, the full extent of Mauron's contribution. In the next chapter I shall examine a link between Mauron's aesthetics and one of the distinctive traits of Stevens's later style.

5

RESISTING THE
INTELLIGENCE
Stevens, Mauron,
and a Theory of Obscurity

Assumptions about poetry's necessary inaccessibility to the intellect begin to emerge conspicuously as theme or figure in Stevens's verse at about the point when his own style becomes most disruptive—with *Parts of a World* and *Notes toward a Supreme Fiction* in 1942. Although he had already gained a reputation for obscurity with his earlier volumes, the sixty-three poems in *Parts of a World* introduce into the Stevens canon the first sustained indecipherability, which continues through *Transport to Summer* (1947) and *The Auroras of Autumn* (1950) before disappearing into the clear and barren style of his last poems in *The Rock*. In the manner in which Eliot noted the adjustment of the canon necessitated by the appearance of the really new work, the opacity of the poems published between 1942 and 1950 makes Stevens's earlier volumes appear suddenly lucid. It is usually with *Parts of a World* that the casual reader of Stevens's poetry surrenders in dismay, returning with some degree of confidence only with the verse of *The Rock*. I am concerned here with two aspects of Stevens's obscurity—the theoretical basis for the disjunctive nature of his verse, especially as this relates to his reading of Mauron's *Aesthetics and Psychology*, and the manner in which the theory informs the theme, figuration, and style of the later poems.

"The poem must resist the intelligence / Almost successfully": so Stevens begins one of his characteristic poems about poems, an exercise in theorizing with the unlikely title "Man Carrying Thing" (CP, 350). The aim of the poem is ostensibly to illustrate its opening pronouncement through a two-part analogy: first, a concept of the poetic work figured as the unidentifiable man of the title, who on a winter evening carries something that also escapes identity; then the uncertain details of a poem seen as the first scattered flakes of snow that trouble our thoughts through a winter night. The apparent argument of "Man Carrying Thing" is that we must accept our lack of immediate comprehension until these doubtful elements have time to accumulate, until the "bright obvious stands motionless in cold" (CP, 351).

It is possible to read the poem as a dispute against interpretation, or at least against the "necessitous sense" that is not content with the "obvious whole" and endeavors to reduce poetry to paraphrase (CP, 350–51). But it is not simply that, since the conclusion suggests that a poetic work grasped as a whole will eventually surrender its ambiguous parts. It is perhaps more accurate to say that the poem is an attempt to articulate the state of mind most favorable to the reading of texts, one in which the reader is content to remain in an indeterminate condition, prolonging the moment of contemplation, resisting the intellectual urge to exhaust each figure or connection. The poem also hints at the assumption behind this argument, the notion that the too obvious, the too easily comprehended, is antithetical to the reader's pleasure.

"Man Carrying Thing" expresses an attitude toward the reading of poetry that came to Stevens through at least two sources. The first is related to the custom he maintained throughout his career of explicating, sometimes at great length, passages of his verse for readers. The second may be discovered in his careful study of Charles Mauron's *Aesthetics and Psychology*.

In 1940, a few months before Stevens began his reading for "The Noble Rider and the Sound of Words," he completed a series of detailed letters to Hi Simons, one of his earliest advocates, in which he offered paraphrases or explanations for passages of his verse.[1] This exercise prompted Stevens to consider again the questions of poetic meaning, intention, and interpretation. As early as 1928 he had declared himself opposed to close scrutiny and paraphrase. "Your analysis of this poem is much too close," he wrote to L. W. Payne, Jr., in regard to Payne's reading of "Le Monocle de Mon Oncle." In the same letter he commented on "Domination of Black": "I am sorry that a poem of this sort has to contain any ideas at all, because its sole purpose is to fill the mind with the images & sounds that it contains. A mind that examines such a poem for its prose contents gets absolutely nothing from it" (L, 251). Several years later he amplified this objection in a letter to Ronald Lane

Latimer: "I have the greatest dislike for explanations. As soon as people are perfectly sure of a poem they are just as likely as not to have no further interest in it; it loses whatever potency it had" (L, 294).

His initial response to the long questionnaire he received from Simons early in 1940 was the same as his previous comment to Latimer. As was often the case, however, Stevens's kindness toward an admirer won out over his principles, and, after offering sound reasons for refusing to explain his poems (including an interesting anticipation of the formalists' intentional fallacy), he readily complied:

> A long time ago I made up my mind not to explain things, because most people have so little appreciation of poetry that once a poem has been explained it has been destroyed: that is to say, they are no longer able to seize the poem. Moreover, even in a case like your own, or in the case of any critic, I think that the critic is under obligation to base his remarks on what he has before him. It is not a question of what an author meant to say but of what he has said. In the case of a competent critic the author may well have a great deal to find out about himself and his work. This goes to the extent of saying that it would be legitimate for a critic to make statements respecting the purpose of an author's work that were altogether contrary to the intentions of the author. Notwithstanding this, you are so interested in what I have done that I shall be glad to answer your questions. . . .   [L, 346–47]

In the course of answering queries about passages from a great number of poems from *Harmonium, Ideas of Order, The Man with the Blue Guitar,* and *Owl's Clover* in letters that ran from January through August 1940, Stevens continued to protest even as he compiled pages of paraphrase.[2] After offering readings for more than a dozen poems, he noted that his explanations seemed "a good deal more fixed" than he would have liked, and his mild disclaimer to Simons reveals that he had been pondering the whole question of interpretation:

> Obviously, it is not possible to tell what one's own poems mean, or were intended to mean. On the other hand, it is not the simplest thing in the world to explain a poem. I thought of it this way this morning: a poem is like a man walking on the bank of a river, whose shadow is reflected in the water. If you

explain a poem, you are quite likely to do it either in terms of
the man or in terms of the shadow, but you have to explain it
in terms of the whole. When I said recently that a poem was
what was on the page, it seems to me now that I was wrong
because that is explaining in terms of the man. But the thing
and its double always go together.   [L, 354]

Characteristically, Stevens has here converted the abstruse issue
into a metaphor that manages simultaneously to heighten and to
obscure it. To think of a poem as a man and his reflection, the one
clear, the other shadowy, is to suggest the sense of doubleness that
Stevens recognized in his own attempts at commentary, a distinc-
tion between what is on the page and what is more elusive and
obscure. As is the case with many of Stevens's illustrative figures,
this one itself escapes exact paraphrase and leaves us at the level of
the unparaphrasable poem, the concept that the figure was invented
to clarify. The man seems to represent the printed poem, what is on
the page, but it is unclear whether the reflection represents the
poem's meaning or content, the poet's intention, the reader's re-
sponse, or something even more elusive. It is equally difficult to
determine from the metaphor the relationship between the two, the
"whole" that ideally is the object for explication. Stevens returned
to this basic figure—man and shadow, "the thing and its double"—
in "Man Carrying Thing" with somewhat the same ambiguous re-
sult. Stevens there renders the figure even more complex by incor-
porating Mauron's discussion of this issue.[3]

One conclusion resulting from Mauron's equation of the aes-
thetic attitude with the contemplative state of mind—and one that
held great interest for Stevens—has to do with the degree to which
a work of art is accessible to the audience. As we have seen, this
question had been occupying Stevens for some time prior to his
encounter with Mauron. Aesthetics and Psychology, however, of-
fered a theoretical justification for a position that Stevens had held
more or less instinctively.

Mauron's view of poetic meaning in the relationship between the
artist and the audience is based on his assumption that the creation
of art is a product of a contemplative state that is attempting only
to prolong the present, to enjoy the moments of existence instead
of allowing them to pass unnoticed. This premise yields an inter-
esting conclusion: "The 'expressive' artist uses a language without
really aiming at being understood" (AP, 59). The artist is interested

not in communicating something, but in expressing himself for the pleasure of expression. Or, as Stevens paraphrases Mauron's argument in the margins of pages 58–59 of *Aesthetics and Psychology*, "the artist does not use this language to say something to others but to express himself. . . . We listen and understand, in part or not at all."

For Mauron it is the "expressive" or symbolic artist who is most susceptible to misreading, since his art involves "the transmission of states of mind through a language" (AP, 59). In fact, Mauron is willing to grant that misreading is the rule rather than the exception, and he finds it curious (in his pre-deconstructive innocence) that so few aestheticians have seen the "incredible complications" and great ironies of a symbolic art in which transmission is involuntary and misreading inevitable: "Having each a different psychological make-up and different experiences, by what mystery should we make the same reality correspond to any given symbol? And if we remember that every artist creates his own idiom according to the inward echoes peculiar to himself, it will be admitted that his chance of being understood (even if he wished to be) is comparatively slight. . . . Certainly *something* passes from artist to auditor; but that the transmission must needs be bad who can deny? Happily a veil of illusion softens what would be too shocking in the admission of misunderstanding . . ." (AP, 60).

Mauron would thus agree with contemporary theorists like Bloom and Miller that attempts to arrive at a definitive or unequivocal reading of a text are doomed to failure. Where he diverges from most contemporary theory on interpretation is in finding "the lack of comprehension a trifling difficulty" (AP, 60). On the contrary, since the proper mental state for the enjoyment of art is one of passive detachment comparable to that of the artist (the auditor's version of prolonging the present), the absence of immediate understanding is a desirable condition. Paradoxically, the reader who "really shares the passion expressed in the work . . . is soon carried out of the aesthetic attitude . . ." (AP, 68). Feelings and convictions "are like instinct, turned toward future action, and for that reason, as soon as they become at all evident they threaten the aesthetic attitude" (AP, 66); any thought of future action returns us to the utilitarian world, breaking the contemplative mood.

One consequence of this line of argument for Mauron is to devalue content and to elevate technique. He notes that, after a time, the content of a work of art becomes alien to the spectator: "The model which the artist has been at such pains to reproduce in every detail is of little interest to him, or it 'dates,' becomes hackneyed, ridiculous, incomprehensible. But the technical discovery remains, and remains admirable" (AP, 75). Mauron uses a geological metaphor for the process that sees texts leaving mere vestiges of the history of their creation: "their trace remains, like an imprint left in the rock long ago by a creature to-day unknowable. The slightest vital shade has been transmitted to us, but in the form of a graphic or sonorous inflection. We do indeed attempt to attribute to these curves certain meanings, suggested by our own inner echoes; but the diversity of our interpretations proves them so fanciful that it would be better, perhaps, to admit the brutal fact; the hieroglyph has become in great part indecipherable" (AP, 76).

Fortunately for Mauron—and for Stevens, who follows him—in missing one mark the work hits another, and its compensation is suggested by Mauron's metaphor. Like a fossil, the work has been emptied of its content and can now be known only through its form, its general outline, which can be preserved. "In so far as the spectator differs from the artist," Mauron notes, "language-art, not understood, necessarily becomes object-art" (AP, 76). Furthermore, to be agreeably lost in the work's form (as opposed to its content) is to prolong the contemplative mood essential to the aesthetic experience. The following passage, which follows from such assumptions, may sound vaguely familiar to the reader of "Man Carrying Thing":

> . . . two elements in a work of art may very well be connected by a relation deliberately introduced by the artist, but unperceived by the spectator, especially at first sight. Aesthetic order is meant to be felt rather than analyzed; the existence of a combination produces a vague and delightful impression of continuity and order; we feel ourselves in a harmonious atmosphere. But the more intimate analysis of this delight of the shades and causes, requires technical knowledge which the spectator does not necessarily possess. Moreover . . . aesthetic order, if it is to become a source of pleasure, must remain hidden in a sort of twilight where we may have the joy of discovering it. So if the reader does not perceive at a glance the system of combinations in a work which yet he feels has "form," I advise him to be patient; to-morrow, or perhaps ten years hence, he will see it revealed to his astonished eyes. [AP, 87–88]

Here is the essential conception of Stevens's poem. In his January 1940 letter to Hi Simons, Stevens figured the poem as "a man walking on the bank of a river, whose shadow is reflected in the water."

In "Man Carrying Thing" he retains the figure of the man but alters the reflection to a shadowy thing he carries. In the original analogy the man was clear, the reflection elusive. Now, however, both man and thing are cast into the "sort of twilight" that Mauron recommends for the proper reception of art:

> A brune figure in winter evening resists
> Identity. The thing he carries resists
>
> The most necessitous sense. Accept them, then
> As secondary (parts not quite perceived
> Of the obvious whole, uncertain particles
> Of the certain solid, the primary free from doubt. . . .
>
> [CP, 350–51]

The "obvious whole" here, Mauron's form, is stated by the title—it is a man carrying a thing. Only the secondary elements are, in Mauron's words, "unperceived by the spectator, especially at first sight." Since "aesthetic order is meant to be felt rather than analyzed," Mauron's spectator, from whose point of view the poem is given, is presented with an image resistant to the analysis that would produce identity and thereby destroy the contemplative moment.

In the final six lines of the poem Stevens shifts the image from the vague figure to the atmosphere of the winter evening itself. The floating "parts not quite perceived" become the first snowflakes of a winter storm. Here Stevens's image again seems to owe something to two passages in Mauron. The first is the conclusion to the passage already quoted, where the reader who "does not perceive at a glance the system of combinations in a work" is advised to be patient so that "to-morrow . . . he will see it revealed to his astonished eyes." The second passage, a few pages later, states the issue in slightly different terms: "I am theoretically certain that all the *unexplained* harmony which remains in a work of art after the most scrupulous analysis, hangs on correspondences felt in their entirety but almost undistinguishable one by one, lost in minute inflections where we should be almost ashamed to look for them" (AP, 96).

In "Man Carrying Thing" the details, barely distinguishable one by one but felt in their entirety, are the "Things floating like the first hundred flakes of snow / Out of a storm we must endure all night." The revelation of that entirety which comes tomorrow to our astonished eyes is contained in the poem's brilliant conclusion: "We must endure our thoughts all night, until / The bright obvious stands motionless in cold" (CP, 351). Stevens's metaphor manages to convey the essential elements of Mauron's more abstract formulation without surrendering its own unparaphrasable quality. It suggests the wonder of what is passively experienced after a prolonged period of troublesome thought, as the night's analysis of the portent of scattered snowflakes gives way to the morning's easy realization of their accumulated significance. There is even something here of the chagrin implied in Mauron's statement that correspondences felt in their entirety may have been lost "in minute inflections where we should be almost ashamed to look for them." The thoughts endured all night indeed seem foolish in light of the "bright obvious" so effortlessly gained.

It is, however, misleading to imply that Stevens's poem yields its meaning as quickly or finally as this analysis may suggest, and herein lies an interesting complication of the theory of reading it expounds. Behind the poem lies the assumption held by Mauron and Stevens that the too easily apprehended, like the clichéd and hackneyed, works to undermine the pleasure of art. When Stevens noted to Simons and Latimer that a poem loses its potency through explanation, he anticipated a similar discussion by Mauron. His distinction between the active and the contemplative attitudes leads Mauron to a concept of originality as an essential element of the aesthetic emotion. The motive of the artist, he notes, "consists in obeying solely his aesthetic pleasure," and he finds pleasure only in an original discovery (AP, 100). He will avoid analogies already known; "he will delight, on the contrary, in resemblances buried in the complexity of the real, those that are felt and divined rather than perceived distinctly." Moreover, he will avoid a systematic or logical linking of resemblances: "the interest, for him lies in tasting a spiritual atmosphere rather than in reaching definite conclusions. It is enough that the work should convey an impression, even though vague, of a reality richer in unforeseen correspondences than the ordinary world" (AP, 104).[4] For this reason the "sincere artist has a horror of repeating himself" (AP, 100).[5]

The horror that Mauron's artist feels in the unoriginal, the too familiar and definite, finds its way into the poem in a curious line that at first seems barely connected to the adjacent passages: "A horror of thoughts that suddenly are real" (CP, 351). Although Stevens presumably shifts this reaction from poet to audience, the distinction hardly matters, since Mauron's assumption is that the spectator's experience is a lesser version of the artist's in the act of creation. However, the tangled syntax of the sentence in which Stevens's line appears leaves open the question of whether it is the poet or the reader who is horrified at the immediately obvious. This is but one instance of his tendency to blur the links and connections of the poem. It slips almost imperceptibly from the opening analogy of man and thing to the metaphor of the snowstorm. The *them* of line five starts as a reference to the obscure figure and the object he carries; it ends by referring to the "first hundred flakes of snow." The reader may well wonder what logic has led from the external world of vague objects to the internal world of the mind. In fact, the secondary elements of the poem are left unresolved, and the "necessitous sense" that seeks a logic in the connection between the two primary images will remain frustrated. The poet here illustrates his own "horror of thoughts that suddenly are real," casting the entire poem in a syntax so hazy as to make exact paraphrase impossible.

There is, then, a subtle irony in the opening two lines, which read in full, "The poem must resist the intelligence / Almost successfully. Illustration. . . ." To illustrate is, in one sense, to make clear by giving examples, and the poem begins as if it were attempting to clarify its generalized opening statement. But of course it is itself an example of the thing it is to clarify, and this forces an apparent dilemma. If a poem must resist the intelligence, how may a poem be used to set forth this aspect of poetry? If it is clear and definite, it violates its nature as poetry; if it retains its necessary obscurity, it fails as illustration. Stevens finds one escape from this paradox in the qualification *almost*, but he does not rest with that. The triumph of "Man Carrying Thing" is that it is, as a poem, a perfect exemplification of its own theory. We apprehend it as a whole but lose our way in its structure, which keeps the mind suspended until the last line produces the impression of a resolution. It is only an impression, however, since the "bright obvious" of the conclusion has only the most tenuous relation to the initial puzzle of man and thing.

The word *illustration* in the second line is thus an instance of the poem's necessary ambiguity. The apparent function is to point to the remainder of the poem as a set of examples, but, because the examples themselves resist analysis and the form of the poem evades the intelligence, we discover that a second sense of the term also applies. That is, the poem does not simply offer a set of illustrations of a proposition but is itself, in its form, an illustration of the proposition that the poem (both *a* poem and *this* poem) must resist the intelligence almost successfully.

"Man Carrying Thing" is not one of Stevens's more widely discussed theoretical poems, yet it reveals an attitude toward poetry that clearly influenced the nature of his verse. The assumptions about poetry that prompted it seem directly related to the evasive and difficult style of the later poems which have so successfully resisted the efforts of commentators. Stevens has easily acquired the reputation of the most obscure of our major poets—in Harold Bloom's words, "the most advanced rhetorician in modern poetry and in his major phase the most disjunctive."[6] Stevens's conception of reading poetry, modified and buttressed by his study of Mauron, provided a strong theoretical justification for his disjunctive form. To resist the intelligence is, in Stevens's view, to preserve the potency of poetry, to maintain an interest in it as art against the destructive tendency of the intellect to reduce it to statement. His attitude toward explanation is, in effect, an early version of Susan Sontag's well-known argument in "Against Interpretation" that interpretation violates art: "To interpret is to impoverish, to deplete the world—in order to set up a shadow world of 'meanings.' "[7]

If this attitude has merit, it may help to account for the fact that a writer who is acknowledged as the least accessible of all modern poets has maintained the interest of a growing body of commentators and has risen, as a recent assessment puts it, "to a commanding position as *the* modern American poet."[8] It may also help to account for the fact that attempts to trace the ideas of "Man Carrying Thing" to their sources in Stevens's letters and Mauron's aesthetics are unable to exhaust the poem. Stevens's and Mauron's ideas on the psychology of reading are accessible to analysis outside the poem, but what is essential to the poem itself remains *almost* impervious to the intellect.

The attitude toward the reading of poems suggested by "Man Carrying Thing" is pervasive in the verse published between 1942 and 1947. In both *Parts of a World* and *Transport to Summer* the reading of difficult or obscure texts and the elevation of nonsense or the irrational over the sensible and familiar become, for Stevens, habitual patterns of thought or feeling; paradoxically, they render accessible a condition of his coexistence with his world with which he is chiefly concerned. Frequently the poems establish antitheses in which clarity and simplicity are dismissed in favor of obscurity or nonsense. That which has become intellectualized, mastered, explicated is relegated to the junk heap, and the speaker's desire is directed toward that which is beyond the intellect, beyond direct articulation or paraphrase. It is as if the desired world were an obscure poem or song not yet understood, and the familiar world were the stale poem reduced to cliché by the very fact of its accessibility.

Parts of a World is to some degree given over to the obscure articulation of a conception of obscurity. The best gloss on many of the poems in the volume is, not surprisingly, *Notes toward a Supreme Fiction.* (Although *Notes* gives the appearance, in the *Collected Poems*, of coming much later than *Parts of a World*, it was written at about the same time and first published the same year.) Frequently a motif or movement that barely achieves form in the cryptic verse of *Parts of a World* is treated more explicitly in *Notes*, or perhaps it is only that the numerous readings of *Notes* over the last forty years have made what is still ultimately untranslatable appear more accessible. At any rate, in what follows I have found it helpful to move back and forth from the poems of *Parts of a World* to the notes for the supreme poetry provided in Stevens's most explicitly theoretical poem.

"Montrachet-le-Jardin" (CP, 260), which reads like a warm-up for *Notes*, contains in ample form what is sometimes only hinted at in the surrounding verse of *Parts of a World*. It begins as if it were to be an extended variation on the first line of *Notes*: "And for what, except for you, do I feel love?" (CP, 380). It is, in fact, an almost inaccessible commentary on the mysterious "you" of the first line of *Notes* in that it is devoted to the conditions under which continuing love of the world is possible. (In this regard it is another version of canto ii of "It Must Be Abstract.") It begins by establishing what, in *Notes*, is called the "ancient cycle" of ennui and desire in which to have nothing more to love is "the beginning of desire":

> What more is there to love than I have loved?
> And if there be nothing more, O bright, O bright,
> The chick, the chidder-barn and grassy chives
>
> And great moon, cricket-impresario,
> And hoy, the impopulous purple-plated past,
> Hoy, Hoy, the blue bulls kneeling down to rest.
>
> Chome! clicks the clock, if there be nothing more. [CP, 260]

The bulk of the poem is given to the recovery of desire; here Stevens's buried analogy of the world as obscure text or aphonic song provides access to the "something" that must be without a name, remaining impervious to the intellect. "There is a point at which intelligence destroys poetry" (L, 305), Stevens had noted some time before beginning the poems of *Parts of a World*, and

in "Montrachet-le-Jardin" this principle is applied one step earlier
—to the imaginative seeing of the world which is preliminary to
the poem. The "something more to love" is present in the poem
only in figures that preserve its inaccessibility to the intellect. In
the mind of the lover it is a "shadow," "a senseless syllable," "a
flourisher / Of sounds resembling sounds" (CP, 260). Neither as
name nor as sound does it acquire intelligibility. The sources of
these shadowy nonsense syllables and sounds are equally obscured.
They are "other shadows, not in the mind"; they are "futura's fud-
dle-fiddling lumps," shapeless clods producing confused sounds on
instruments that are paradoxically called "aphonies," from *apho-
nia*, loss of voice (CP, 260). These silent instruments suggest both
an echo and a reversal of Keats's sweeter unheard melodies, a rever-
sal that seeks to awaken desire in change, to produce the transient
"breathing human passion" that Keats attempts to transcend in
stasis.

This teasing absence-presence, what Stevens in a much later
poem calls the "pre-history" of an emotional season, given before
"The life of the poem in the mind has . . . yet begun" (CP, 522), has
the effect of reawakening desire by allowing an obscure glimpse of
new objects of desire (actually the old objects freshly seen) and of
freeing the imagination from its imprisonment in habit and cus-
tom. As his players of aphonic melodies recall Keats, Stevens's fig-
ure for the familiar world that is newly ratified or sanctified with
an "amen" echoes another traditional symbol for the weight of cus-
tom, the enemy of imaginative seeing—Wordsworth's prison house
from the "Intimations" ode. Starved by thought and imprisoned in
a place that has become "our accustomed cell," the world emptied
and shrunk by routine, the would-be lover is reduced to the "words
on the wall," the stale words of the accustomed past (of which
Wordsworth's prison house figure, revivified, serves as an instance):

> But if there be something more to love, amen,
> Amen to the feelings about familiar things,
> The blessed regal dropped in daggers' dew,
>
> Amen to thought, our singular skeleton,
> Salt-flicker, amen to our accustomed cell,
> The moonlight in the cell, words on the wall.   [CP, 260]

The process by which the prisoner of custom becomes the poet-
hero is as obscurely recorded in the poem as the shadowy sources
that inspire the transformation, but it appears to be roughly analo-
gous to the passage in *Notes* in which MacCullough, any man,

becomes *the* MacCullough, major man or hero. In *Notes* I, viii, MacCullough, "drowned" in the undecipherable washes of the inexplicable sea, begins "reading in the sound, / About the thinker of the first idea"; that is, he reads the obscure text of nature and searches for a new imagining of his world ("The first idea is an imagined thing") that will reawaken his desire for it (CP, 387). At the point where MacCullough becomes the MacCullough in *Notes*, he becomes a "hypothesis," a "form to speak the word / And every latent double in the word." If this transformation were to take place—that is, if the world were to lose its familiarity and become again properly unnamable and inexpressible—then Mac-Cullough, the ordinary, customary man, might become for a moment the "thinker of the first idea," the "leaner" poet-hero who renames the world in words never before spoken:

> He might take habit, whether from wave or phrase,
>
> Or power of the wave, or deepened speech,
> Or a leaner being, moving in on him,
> Of greater aptitude and apprehension,
>
> As if the waves at last were never broken,
> As if the language suddenly, with ease,
> Said things it had laboriously spoken.   [CP, 387]

This process, which begins with the reduction of the familiar world to obscure text and ends with the poet's newest poem, appears in an almost identical form in "Montrachet-le-Jardin." The "feelings about familiar things" give way to "night's undeciphered murmuring," which in turn becomes the sound in "the hero's throat in which the words are spoken" (CP, 261). Just as MacCullough begins to "take habit" from the "deepened speech" occasioned by the transposition of life to a "senseless syllable," so the prisoner of "Montrachet-le-Jardin" is delivered by the poet-hero inside himself, the "leaner being" who, in singing "of an heroic world beyond the cell," is "echoing rhetorics more than our own" (CP, 261). The result of all this is a sense of newness, originality that "satisfies / Belief in an immaculate beginning" (*Notes*, CP, 382). Stevens's various treatments of this cycle all emphasize the priority of firstness, and the first idea of *Notes* is his best-known and least understood designation of this crucial point in the imaginative cycle. In "Montrachet-le-Jardin" the analogous terms are *earliest* and *youngest*:

He hears the earliest poems of the world
In which man is the hero. He hears the words,
Before the speaker's youngest breath is taken!   [CP, 261]

To be first, earliest, or youngest, it is of course necessary to start again at zero. This is accomplished in poems like "Montrachet-le-Jardin" by a process that produces, variously, the ignorant man, an immaculate beginning, or a world reduced to aphonia, "tuned in from zero and / Beyond" (CP, 260).

What is crucial in Stevens's assumption about the creation of poetry is that it can begin only at the point where the world becomes, in terms of customary usage, unintelligible; only then, reduced to zero, is it amenable to the distinct and unique language of the poet. In *Aesthetics and Psychology* Mauron states the point: "In the plastic arts, as in poetry, the zero from which the artist starts is not, as in music, pure chance, but a certain pre-existent organization of the world, which he will have to destroy in order to create new combinations" (AP, 79). The relationship between the poet and the world as obscure text is then necessarily repeated in the relationship between the resulting poem and its readers. "Montrachet-le-Jardin," for example, is continually poised at the brink of senseless syllables from its title (the name of a rare French wine) through such terms and figures as *hoy, chome, efflorisant, blessed regal dropped in daggers' dew, futura's fuddle-fiddling, salt-flicker, x-malisons, plus gaudiest vir,* and *root-man.* It is thus an enactment of the process it depicts, an obscure poem that attempts to transform the too well known to its own status of unintelligibility. When a young poet complained of being baffled by parts of his poetry, Stevens responded that "every poet's language is his own distinct tongue. He cannot speak the common language and continue to write poetry any more than he can think the common thought and continue to be a poet" (L, 873). "Montrachet-le-Jardin," like the first third of *Notes,* is governed by a conception of poetry in which the reduction to nonsense destroys the preexistent world and precedes the poet's distinct language.

In *Parts of a World* Stevens plays a number of interesting variations on this movement from familiarity to obscurity, which is for him synonymous with creation. The most accessible poems in the volume (predictably, those that are best known and most amenable to paraphrase) are those like "The Poems of Our Climate" (CP, 193) and "The Man on the Dump" (CP, 201) that deal with the stale images and poses of the overly familiar world and the mind's consequent revolt against it. In "The Poems of Our Climate" we are given what amounts to an image of perfection, reduced to "complete simplicity": "Clear water in a brilliant bowl, / Pink and white carnations." This image of perfect clarity is not only accessible in itself but renders the day equally accessible:

> The day itself
> Is simplified: a bowl of white,
> Cold, a cold porcelain, low and round,
> With nothing more than the carnations there.   [CP, 193]

In a much later poem, "The Ultimate Poem Is Abstract" (CP, 429), the speaker is "Hopelessly at the edge" of a day that refuses to come clear, a day of "dodges to and fro," "writhings in wrong obliques and distances" (CP, 429–30). He concludes that it "would be enough / If we were ever, just once, at the middle, fixed"; it would be "enough to be / Complete, because at the middle, if only in sense" (CP, 430). "The Poems of Our Climate" achieves this desire with an image that is fixed, complete, at the middle of a day that itself is fixed and complete. Yet the clarity, the accessibility and fixity of the image render it inadequate and reveal at the same time the illusion of the desire to be at the middle, the desire to provide a wholly adequate description or paraphrase for a day seen, in "The Ultimate Poem Is Abstract," as the text of a lecturer who "hems the planet rose and haws it ripe" (CP, 429) without ever once coming to the point.

In Stevens's cycles of ennui and desire, one is always seeking the opposite state, just as "Two things of opposite natures seem to depend / On one another. . . . / This is the origin of change" (Notes, CP, 392). In "The Ultimate Poem Is Abstract," the day is a badly delivered text that never achieves clarity, and one consequently desires more. "The Poems of Our Climate," at the opposite end of the cycle, gives us perfect access to a day clarified in a "brilliant" image. We recognize that its clarity, its very accessibility to the mind, its completeness, is the problem; it leaves nothing to be desired:

> There would still remain the never-resting mind,
> So that one would want to escape, come back
> To what had been so long composed.   [CP, 194]

The mind, which thrives on change, cannot rest in one image, however perfect and clear, since its perfection guarantees its monotony—"so long composed"—like the satirical description of a static paradise of "Sunday Morning." "The imperfect is our paradise" (CP, 194) for the very reason that it provides relief from the too long composed.

The concluding lines of the poem offer the surprising argument—surprising in its sudden appearance—that the "imperfect" art of poetry therefore provides a pleasure denied the more "perfect" visual arts, a "delight" that "Lies in flawed words and stubborn sounds" (CP, 194). The flaw of language that prohibits the clarity and simplicity of the pictorial (the picture's ability to reproduce the look of the real object) and the stubbornness of sounds that refuse to yield their complete meanings produce an art that can never be fully mastered by the never-resting mind. As an obscuring rather than a clarifying medium, poetry is the art most in accord with our imperfect world, our climate. The poems of our climate would presumably be flawed and stubborn poems that retain a measure of inaccessibility.

"Prelude to Objects" (CP, 194), which follows "The Poems of Our Climate" in *Parts of a World*, also argues that the imperfect and fortuitous are better suited to our peculiar human climate than are the static perfections of painting. If one is attentive to "what he hears and sees," without "sentiment" or "pathos," then "he has not / To go to the Louvre to behold himself" (CP, 194). Granted, painting mirrors reality, but not in the changeful and haphazard way that the world mirrors it, that is, "not by chance": "It comes to this: / That the guerilla I should be booked and bound" (CP, 195). The passage continues with references to mystics who exchange foolscap for wigs and academies that rise "as of a tragic science" (CP, 195). The implication of Stevens's imagery is that the "guerilla I," the violent, rebellious self, is captured and enfeebled by static depiction or academic explication or analysis. Consequently, it is the poet, not the painter or the pedant, who is asked to "conceive" the "diviner health / Disclosed in common forms." The distinction is that the poet's "conceits" by which "We are conceived" are composed of "nonsense foamed / From the sea" (CP, 195), the unparaphrasable modeled on the "inscrutable world" that the sea represented for Stevens as early as "The Comedian as the Letter C" (CP, 27). Like "The Poems of Our Climate," "Prelude to Objects" elevates poetry on the premise that it successfully resists the intelligence.

A number of the poems of *Parts of a World* record the moments in which conventional seeing is destroyed through reduction of the commonsensical to a kind of obscurity. Although "Study of Two Pears" (CP, 196) is not usually read in this manner, it is in part an exercise in freeing the world of conventional meaning, reducing the pears to "blobs." The exercise begins by resisting the impulse to see the pears through analogy with familiar objects, which would domesticate them, rob them of their uniqueness: "The pears are not viols, / Nudes or bottles. / They resemble nothing else" (CP, 196). The temptation to think of them in terms of *paintings* of pears is also resisted ("They are not flat surfaces / Having curved outlines" [CP, 196]), and the result is to convert them to form and color—"yellow forms / Composed of curves" . . . "touched red" . . ."round / Tapering toward the top" (CP, 196). The farther from the conventional descriptions of pears the poem retreats, the more unpearlike the objects become. They reveal uncharacteristic "bits of blue," and the pear-yellow now "glistens with various yellows, / Citrons, oranges and greens" (CP, 196–97). The final stage in this reduction is that of a formlessness in which the object loses its familiar look and resists the mind's attempt to dictate its appearance or meaning:

The shadows of the pears
Are blobs on the green cloth.
The pears are not seen
As the observer wills. [CP, 197]

Properly obscure, the pears are now presumably ripe for the "early" or "first" seeing, a result not of the will or intelligence but of what Stevens in *Notes* calls "candid" seeing, an "ever-early candor" by which "Life's nonsense pierces us with strange relation" (CP, 382–83).

To term the moment of fresh sight *candid* is to suggest not only freedom from the bias that marks customary seeing but, as in photography, the capturing of subjects naturally or spontaneously without their being posed. In the words of *Notes*, it is "to catch from that / Irrational moment its unreasoning" (CP, 398), to accept life as beyond the reason, beyond the intelligence. Opposed to the candid moment are such concepts as the pose and the "evading metaphor" (CP, 199), both of which appear in "Add This to Rhetoric":

In the way you speak
You arrange, the thing is posed,
What in nature merely grows. [CP, 198]

The conventions of all art—"The poses of speech, of paint, / Of music" (CP, 199)—deny the possibility of the candid view by posing the subject, denying the natural by substituting the contrived. In

Stevens's relentless cycle this is the point of ennui, the recognition of the pose. By depicting this moment literally—the moment of weariness, of tired phrases and exhausted conventions—"Add This to Rhetoric" demonstrates that the pose leads to ennui; the earth (like a model) is worn-out from being constantly arranged to prohibit spontaneous seeing:

> The poses of speech, of paint,
> Of music—Her body lies
> Worn out, her arm falls down,
> Her fingers touch the ground.   [CP, 199]

But the ennui of the posed, stale world "sends us back to the first idea" (CP, 381), and the termination of one movement—the point at which the earth becomes exhausted in her poses—is the origin of another, which commences in obscurity:

> Above her [the exhausted earth], to the left,
> A brush of white, the obscure,
> The moon without a shape,
> A fringed eye in a crypt.
> The sense creates the pose,
> In this it moves and speaks.
> This is the figure and not
> An evading metaphor.   [CP, 199]

Paradoxically, this first obscure, shapeless seeing is the beginning of another pose created by the sense after rejecting the tired poses of the past. It is an early seeing or first idea in which, for the moment, "the figure moves and speaks." It "*is* the figure," not an "evading metaphor," but only until the point at which the figure is exhausted by what can be nothing other than a pose. Stevens's pun on *figure* here is interesting, in light of the fact that the poetic figure is most conspicuously posed. The figure contains within itself Stevens's paradox, since it is both the escape from ennui—the occasion of a new way of seeing (the obscure presence of the shapeless moon figured as "A fringed eye in a crypt")—and the return to ennui: the poetic figure's posed, arranged quality ("In the way you speak / You arrange") exhausts it the more rapidly. "May there be an ennui of the first idea?" the speaker of *Notes* is apparently asked by the ephebe. "What else, prodigious scholar, should there be?" (CP, 381).

This paradox of "ever-early candor" become "evasive metaphor" is contained in parallel passages in "Add This to Rhetoric" and the first canto of *Notes*. In both the poet uses an obscure figure to re-name the sun, which, to be seen candidly, "Must bear no name" (CP, 381); that is, once named in a figure or metaphor, however fresh, the sun begins its inevitable decline into cliché. It loses "the difficulty of what it is to be," a difficulty that Stevens equates with obscurity, nonsense, the irrational—all of which call forth the poet's desire to possess the object in a new naming. Here is Stevens's statement of the paradox in *Notes*:

> The sun
> Must bear no name, gold flourisher, but be
> In the difficulty of what it is to be.   [CP, 381]

The poem itself, which must name in figures, however resistant to the intellect (i.e., "gold flourisher"), exposes the impossibility of leaving the object in the "difficulty" of mere being, without a name. The corresponding passage in "Add This to Rhetoric" suggests that the only way out of this apparent contradiction is the one adopted by Stevens—his conception of cycles, fluctuations between poles in which the sun, in its own cycle, survives its images to rise in its original vitality each new dawn:

> To-morrow when the sun,
> For all your images,
> Comes up as the sun, bull fire,
> Your images will have left
> No shadow of themselves.   [CP, 198]

In the passages in both *Notes* and "Add This to Rhetoric" the imageless sun is suggested in an image, almost as if, for a moment, the unconventional or fresh naming were not the evading metaphor but the figure itself. Initially, a candid figure such as "bull fire" may appear sufficiently fresh and resistant to the intellect to challenge the potency of the object it names, but as it tires it is revealed as nothing more than an image that eventually, unlike the sun, leaves no shadow. The difficulty in Stevens's cyclical conception of creativity is that the vitality of any specific work of art is short-lived, doomed from the moment of its birth. The optimistic note is that the world of change transcends any attempt to fix it in particular works, so that the cycles need never end. There is no point at which readers have sufficient poetry or at which poets are content with the poems of the past.

In a poem celebrating the fortuitous nature of reality, "The Sense of the Sleight-of-Hand Man," Stevens toys again with his images for the sun:

It is a wheel, the rays
Around the sun. The wheel survives the myths.
The fire eye in the clouds survives the gods.   [CP, 222]

The sun as a vital force survives our attempts to name it, although the poet cannot resist the temptation (with "fire eye") at the moment when he admits its futility. Given, then, a world in which things "Occur as they occur" and a mind equally haphazard in assigning arbitrary and evasive figures—"To think of a dove with an eye of grenadine / And pines that are cornets, so it occurs"—it is no wonder that every conscious reading of the world is ultimately a misreading. Only the reader with no preconceptions or chance associations could "mate his life with life." This would of course be the "ignorant man" (CP, 222), who reappears in the first canto of *Notes* in search of the first idea. "Having each a different psychological make-up and different experiences, by what mystery should we make the same reality correspond to any given symbol?" Mauron asks in *Aesthetics and Psychology*, in a passage that reads like a gloss on "The Sense of the Sleight-of-Hand Man." He continues, "And if we remember that every artist creates his own idiom according to the inward echoes peculiar to himself, it will be admitted that his chance of being understood . . . is comparatively slight" (AP, 60). Both Mauron and Stevens concede the impossibility of fixing reality in language, and from this apparent defeat at the hands of a flawed and stubborn language Stevens conceives a provisional poetic based on the endless fluctuations between the two poles of inaccessibility and overfamiliarity.

There is a further paradox in Stevens's assumptions about the obscure and the explicit, in that the world that *seems* accessible in its familiarity—the world, for example, of "The Man on the Dump" (CP, 201)—actually denies us access by the very fact of being explicit. We no longer desire it; it has become the "trash" that is rejected in "The Man on the Dump": "One grows to hate these things except on the dump" (CP, 202). Conversely, and equally paradoxical, it is the undecipherable, the obscure or nonsensical that grants us access to itself precisely because its present inaccessibility *in language* awakens our desire for it. This is the "purifying change" of "The Man on the Dump" that occurs exactly when "One rejects / The trash" (CP, 202), discards the stale literary descriptions so that the object is stripped of all previous images:

That's the moment when the moon creeps up
To the bubbling of bassoons. That's the time
One looks at the elephant-colorings of tires.

> Everything is shed; and the moon comes up as the moon
> (All its images are in the dump). . . .   [CP, 202]

This is the paradox of an object that can be known only after all our
words for it have been discarded—or, to put it in Stevens's terms,
that can be known only by the completely ignorant man. Stevens
turns the conventional notion of obscurity and accessibility on its
head, since, in terms of language, it is at the point of its greatest
(or absolute) obscurity that the object is most accessible. The prob-
lem for the poet attempting to capture this moment is that it is a
nonlinguistic phenomenon; the closest the poet can come to it is in
an unconventional figure, one that refuses to name the moment in
a traditional way or to suggest an identifiable connection with the
object. Thus the moon devoid of its images in "The Man on the
Dump" is described with an outrageous image: "the moon creeps
up / To the bubbling of bassoons." This, then, is the paradox of the
moments of "accessible bliss" (CP, 395) described in inaccessible
language.

A variation on this paradox is that, when we recognize the truth
of something, we lose access to it; when we deny its truth, we
recover it. In "On the Road Home," the poem that follows "The
Man on the Dump," the speaker and his companion conclude that
" 'There is no such thing as the truth' ":

> It was at that time, that the silence was largest
> And longest, the night was roundest,
> The fragrance of the autumn warmest,
> Closest and strongest.   [CP, 204]

Implicit in the argument of the poem, as in "The Latest Freed
Man," which follows it, is that the "truth," any preconceived doc-
trine or description of the world, gives us a false view, since it pre-
vents us from seeing it in "the difficulty of what it is to be," with-
out a name. The freedom referred to in "The Latest Freed Man" is
the freedom from an explicit description or doctrine of the land-
scape, the landscape as treatise, explicable words and sentences.
Freed from this description at the moment when the sun is most
"vaguely seen," the world makes itself available in an absolute way:

> Tired of the old descriptions of the world,
> The latest freed man rose at six and sat
> On the edge of his bed. He said,
>   "I suppose there is
> A doctrine to this landscape. Yet, having just

Escaped from the truth, the morning is color and mist,
Which is enough: the moment's rain and sea,
The moment's sun (the strong man vaguely seen),
Overtaking the doctrine of this landscape."   [CP, 204]

Since the chief feature of the experience is the denial of its verbal qualities, in effect erasing the text of the landscape, the latest freed man is hard pressed to communicate it. He resorts finally to personifying the sun as a "man without a doctrine" (CP, 205) and to a construction using *how* that manages to imply that the act of seeing takes priority over its description in words: "The light he gives— / It is how he gives his light. It is how he shines" (CP, 205). The effect of all this is a kind of repetitive baby talk or prattle that abandons any pretense of adequately conveying the experience itself: "It was how the sun came shining into his room," and later:

It was how he was free. It was how his freedom came.
It was being without description, being an ox.
It was the importance of the trees outdoors,
The freshness of the oak-leaves, not so much
That they were oak-leaves, as the way they looked.   [CP, 205]

The last two lines are particularly revealing of the poet's dilemma in describing what is by nature "without description." It is utterly irrelevant to the quality of the experience that the tree happens to be named *oak* (a classification that takes us back to the doctrine of the landscape); yet, without the recourse to doctrine and description, obviously no poem could exist, because no reader could participate in it. The prattle that occurs at the moment when the old world is reduced to first idea must give only the *illusion* of nondescription; it must resist the intelligence *almost* successfully. Otherwise, only the experience itself counts; the poem of the experience ceases to matter. The ideal reading, whether of poem or world, Stevens suggests, would encounter something unexpected, something alien to the familiar world, yet something at the same time instantly accessible on some elemental level.

This conception of reading—in a figure in which the world is a difficult text approached by two different sorts of readers—comprises the substance of "Phosphor Reading by His Own Light." The poem treats the paradox of the two poles of reading that is implicit throughout *Parts of a World*. The first reader, who reads by his own light, "knows what it is that he expects." It is therefore ironic that the world which is his text is both "difficult" and "dark." It is not simply that he misreads it but that the "page is blank or a frame without a glass / Or a glass that is empty when he looks" (CP, 267). The text itself is a blank because readers who bring their own readings with them can never arrive at a text independent of their preconceptions. The second reader, whom the persona addresses directly, comes to the text unprepared, "not knowing what you expect" (CP, 267); ironically, he finds that the alien text is immediately available, although only on its own terms. The reading from familiarity becomes a misreading (or nonreading), and the reading from obscurity produces accessibility to the text itself. The distinction is that, in the first reading, the text is governed by the preconceptions of the reader—"Phosphor Reading by His Own Light"— and in the second the reader, emptied of language, is "given" a speech by the text so that his reading can only be in terms of the text itself:

Look, realist, not knowing what you expect.
The green falls on you as you look,

Falls on and makes and gives, even a speech,
And you think that that is what you expect,

That elemental parent, the green night,
Teaching a fusky alphabet.   [CP, 267]

At the moment of Stevens's ideal reading of the world as text, it both *makes* and *gives* a speech, making it difficult to distinguish between what is a property of the text itself and what is traceable to the act of reading it. Likewise, although the text is not "what you expect," the language it prompts is in such momentary accord with one's own reading that "you think that that is what you expect." Such a reading, in which the reader is content to accept the text on its own terms without paraphrase or translation, teaches a new language, prompts new words and figures, "a fusky alphabet." *Fusky* is the poem's one alien word that carries Stevens's paradox. If we are reading well, the word will seem unexpected yet perfectly at home, suggesting a dark, mysterious language. The word *fusky* is, in fact, foreign to our language—it does not exist in *Webster's Unabridged*—yet one feels that it *should* be there, that one has heard it before. It is offered as an instance of the text's ability to master the reader as it "Falls on and makes and gives, even a speech. / And you think that that is what you expect."

Stevens's designation of the successful reader as a "realist" might tempt us to take the view of so many of Stevens's own readers—

the view that the ultimate goal of all his poetry is the apprehension of naked reality freed from conventional seeing and naming. What such a reading fails to recognize, however, is that the moment of the first idea is a transient point along a continuum, rather than a stopping place. The realist in "Phosphor Reading by His Own Light" is immediately furnished with a speech and an alphabet, for the new naming follows immediately on the heels of the "ignorant" seeing. The *poet's* ultimate goal is not the apprehension of the thing itself but the production of poems. The naked seeing that results in the first idea is a private experience; the resulting poem is a *shared* one: "The poem refreshes life so that we share, / For a moment, the first idea" (CP, 382). We share only for a moment because the poem is forced to communicate the first idea in words and figures that, in their turn, become the stale invention "That sends us back to the first idea, the quick / Of this invention" (*Notes*, CP, 381). And so on, in a cycle that never finds a resting place because it is conceived by Stevens as obeying the second law of his supreme fiction: "It Must Change."

In *Parts of a World* and *Notes toward a Supreme Fiction* Stevens explores the dilemmas generated by the impossible task he sets himself in attempting to share the first idea—that is, to make public a private experience, to make accessible in language something that is available only if it remains unnamed, to preserve the linguistic obscurity of the first idea and yet communicate it—in short, to resist the intelligence almost successfully. This dilemma is treated in one of the last poems of *Parts of a World*, "The Search for Sound Free from Motion." In the poem the sounds of nature are unintelligible because they are constantly in motion, never fixed. Stevens's metaphor for this is a gramophone that produces nonsense sounds:

All afternoon the gramophone
Parl-parled the West-Indian weather.
The zebra leaves, the sea
And it all spoke together.
              . . .
All afternoon the gramaphoon,
All afternoon the gramaphoon. . . .   [CP, 268]

But the poet's search is for the sound free from motion—that is, the word, the abstraction that will momentarily fix the world in a formulation: "it spoke all together, / But you, you used the word." The poet's dilemma is the choice between the world as nonsense (*Parl–parled, gramaphoon*) and, as Stevens puts it in the poem,

"The world as word" (CP, 268). It is not, however, an actual choice because the fiction, the poem, *must* be abstract. The poet, as poet, has no alternative to the world as word. The compromise for the poet, then, is frequently the world as nonsense word or the world as extravagant figure or image.

In the poem that follows, "Jumbo," the world is an "imager" because our response to it is in images: "There are no rocks / And stones, only this imager" (CP, 269). In both poems Stevens recognizes the paradox of the poet's search for the sound that would fix a world in motion. The chief source of the obscurity that characterizes his poetry throughout the forties is his desire to employ a language that is least susceptible to being fixed, a language that approaches the nonsemantic quality of the candid moment when the world is freed from conventional naming. If he cannot duplicate this moment in words, he can at least produce a poetry that resists as long as possible its inevitable exhaustion by the intellect into cliché and pose.

The poem "Country Words" sums up the ideal condition of both the poem and the reading of the poem implied throughout *Parts of a World*. The poet sings a kind of nonsense song that does not easily yield its meaning:

I sang a canto in a canton,
Cunning-coo, O, cuckoo cock,
In a canton of Belshazzar
To Belshazzar, putrid rock. . . .   [CP, 207]

This is later described as "An edge of song that never clears." And what is the poet's motive for his obscurity—"What is it that my feeling seeks?"

It wants Belshazzar reading right
The luminous pages on his knee,
Of being, more than birth or death.
It wants words virile with his breath.   [CP, 207]

For Stevens, "reading right" means preserving the original potency of the poem, apprehending the poem on the model of the poet's perception of the first idea ("words virile with his breath"). The reader, that is, must confront the poem in the difficulty of its own being, rather than imposing a familiar meaning on it. That, in turn, means that the poem must avoid being intellectualized: "As soon as people are perfectly sure of a poem they are just as likely as not to have no further interest in it; it loses whatever potency it had" (L, 346–47). In "Country Words" the poet also thinks of the power of the poem in terms of sexual potency, virility, and to preserve the potency of the poem he sings a "rebellious" song that "never clears." *Country* words are, first of all, words *of* the country, native words natural to their region: the poet's "canto" almost matches the "canton" in which it is sung. But country words are also rude, unlettered, provincial words that are out of place in the capital and that might well be misunderstood. In light of the buried sexual metaphor of the poem, it is also difficult to avoid Hamlet's pun on "country matters"—that is, to suggest that the poem's appeal to Belshazzar "reading right" is analogous to an appeal to his virility. Stevens's creative cycle from ennui to desire is, after all, based on a sexual analogy that is never far from the surface. The awakening of desire occurs when the object for which desire has flagged through familiarity is made once again desirable by appearing as a new love, as if encountered for the first time.[9] The first idea is a form of first love, with all its innocence and naiveté. Moreover, the love object's initial inaccessibility in language awakens desire, so the poet's new naming, which gives him a momentary entry into the being of the object, is the consummation from which the cycle runs its downward course to ennui, to continue the analogy, a kind of post-coital depression. One need not read Stevens overingeniously to discover the sexual nuances of his themes and figures. At any rate, whatever reading of *country* one chooses to describe the poet's language, the result is a text to which one responds naturally, naively, or instinctively, rather than intellectually.

Although the verse of *Transport to Summer* (1947) continues these assumptions about language's resistance to the intellect, a few subtle shifts in emphasis in the later volume merit notice. One is suggested in the second poem, "Certain Phenomena of Sound": "There is no life except in the word of it" (CP, 287). The poems of *Transport to Summer* perhaps recognize more explicitly than those of *Parts of a World* that the abstracting quality of language is not simply an evasion of the real—the "evading metaphor"—but may be itself a source of refreshment and the awakening of desire.

This shift in emphasis is made clear in the third poem of the volume, "The Motive for Metaphor," which can be read against its corresponding poem in the preceding volume, "Add This to Rhetoric." In the earlier poem the posed, static quality of language is compared unfavorably to nature, which "merely grows." In the later poem, however, the poet recognizes that language itself can be a source for change. The motive for metaphor suggested in the title is the desire to create in language the obscure "half colors of quarter-things" that characterize the fortuitous moments of accord with the real world. Autumn is pleasurable because it is indefinite, in a state of flux where the wind among the leaves "repeats words without meaning." Spring is equally evasive:

> The obscure moon lighting an obscure world
> Of things that would never be quite expressed,
> Where you yourself were never quite yourself
> And did not want nor have to be. . . .   [CP, 288]

Metaphor, the poem implies, has the same capacity to leave the object in a state of uncertainty, not quite expressing it, or expressing it in an unfamiliar way. Whereas in *Parts of a World* language and metaphor were often seen as the enemy of candid seeing, here the situation is reversed. The motive for metaphor is associated with the "exhilarations of changes," the "shrinking from / The weight of primary noon / The A B C of being." The weight of stark reality here is a burden, this "arrogant, fatal, dominant X" (CP, 288). Although value has temporarily shifted from world to word, the same assumptions about obscurity prevail. One shrinks from the thing itself because it is too much itself—the primary, as basic as A B C or the nameless X. Metaphor, on the other hand, preserves a certain obscurity; its inability to "bring a world quite round" (CP, 165) elevates it for the moment over a reality that appears fixed and monotonous in its domination. Although "The Motive for Metaphor" may appear initially to contradict the view of metaphor suggested in the verse of *Parts of a World*, its argument is prepared for in the earlier poetry's motif of change in which things of opposite nature depend on each other to awaken desire, as "the imagined / On the real" (CP, 392), or language on the nameless and arrogant X that language seeks to name.

Another of the motifs carried over into *Transport to Summer*, with slight alterations, is the juxtaposition of antithetical readings of texts. In "The Lack of Repose" (CP, 303) a young man, "Andrew Jackson Something,"[10] reads a book in which the ghost of his grandfather mumbles. That is, like the first reader in "Phosphor Reading by His Own Light" (CP, 267), he reads in a traditional manner, "With an understanding compounded by death" (CP, 303). This act of reading in light of the past brings the illusion of understanding: "What a thing it is to believe that / One understands." Yet the praise in the poem is for the reader or writer who corresponds to the realist of "Phosphor Reading by His Own Light"—who comes to the text without knowing what to expect. It "is a good," the speaker notes, "not yet to have written a book in which / One is already a grandfather" (CP, 303). In the poem that follows, "Somnambulisma," the distinction between the two kinds of reading (and writing) is made more explicit. The world of Andrew Jackson Something is now the "geography of the dead," a static world in which our grandfathers lived and "lacked a pervasive being" (CP, 304). The poet of "The Lack of Repose" who refuses to become a grandfather is the "scholar" of "Somnambulisma," a "man feeling everything" who reads his world as if it "were his" and not the dead land of his grandfather (CP, 304). In both poems "an understanding compounded by death" is the enemy of candid reading because it cannot allow for change. *Pose, composed,* and *repose* are closely related in Stevens's negative poetic because they are characterized by stasis. To rest in the world of the past is merely to repeat the pose of one's grandfather.

Since *any* understanding, traditional or otherwise, acts as an obstruction to the candor that creates poetry (or reads it), one may wonder how, in Stevens's poetic, it is possible for a poem to come into being. How may poetry be produced in the absence of understanding, memory, intellect? Some of the most elusive passages in the verse of the forties are devoted to this difficulty—the MacCullough canto from *Notes*, for example—and in *Transport to Summer* Stevens attacks this problem directly with a poem called "The Creations of Sound," which describes the verse of a contemporary poet (called simply X[11]) who is "an obstruction, a man / Too exactly himself" (CP, 310). What X does not understand about the creation of poems is precisely Stevens's conception of candor or ignorance, in which the poet must be "without understanding" and in which the sounds of the poem are not consciously chosen by the poet, or chosen so freely that the poem appears to be "without a poet." Here is the crucial passage:

If the poetry of X was music,
So that it came to him of its own,
Without understanding, out of the wall

Or in the ceiling, in sounds not chosen,
Or chosen quickly, in a freedom
That was their element, we should not know

That X is an obstruction, a man
Too exactly himself, and that there are words
Better without an author, without a poet. . . .   [CP, 310]

The notion of a poem without a poet is, however, immediately qualified by the conception of "a separate author, a different poet, / An accretion from ourselves" (CP, 311). This postulation of a separate being who is purely a poetry-making self is necessitated by the quandary into which Stevens is led by his poetics of ignorance, the reduction of the poet to an "immaculate beginning." "The Creations of Sound" is thus a variation of the MacCullough passage in *Notes*, but here the poet X is unable to transcend MacCullough, his everyday self, to become the MacCullough, major man, "hypothesis," or "expedient" who represents the "leaner being" (CP, 387) stripped of the customary ways of seeing and knowing that make him "Too exactly himself" (CP, 310). In "The Creations of Sound" this being is said to be "intelligent / Beyond intelligence"; he is "an artificial man," a "secondary expositor, / A being of sound" (CP, 311). It is from this hypothetical poet who is in the end a fiction that the lesser poet receives his poems: "From him, we collect" (CP, 311).

This is also an earlier version of the "essential poem at the centre of things" of "A Primitive Like an Orb" (CP, 440). In both poems Stevens finds satisfaction in the fiction of an essence of poetry that cannot be known directly but is apprehended "in lesser poems" and "By means of a separate sense" (CP, 440). The fiction of major man or the poet-hero (the essential poet) is a variation of the essential poem. At the moment when the poet approaches the essence of poetry, what Stevens sometimes refers to as *pure* poetry, he becomes, in the fiction, a separate being reduced from the customary man to "a being of sound." Just as the ignorant man perceives the world stripped of its stale doctrines and descriptions, the pure poet, the "secondary expositor" of "The Creations of Sound," is able to speak a language stripped of its clichés and poses, so that his poems may be thought of as creations of pure sound. They are not, in Frost's terms, clarifications of experience but complications and obfuscations of ordinary experience:

Tell X that speech is not dirty silence
Clarified. It is silence made still dirtier.
It is more than an imitation for the ear.

He lacks this venerable complication.
His poems are not of the second part of life.
They do not make the visible a little hard

To see nor, reverberating, eke out the mind
On peculiar horns, themselves eked out
By the spontaneous particulars of sound.   [CP, 311]

To return, then, to the question of how poems may be created in the kind of ignorance or blankness that Stevens postulates as poetry's beginning, his answer is that restricting the intelligence, the understanding, reveals a hypothetical self more capable of producing poetry than the reason, a being of sound, of language "chosen out of . . . desire" (CP, 441). Like the Romantics, Stevens separates the poetry-producing faculties of the mind from the reason or intellect. In short, as he notes in "Pieces," "There are things in a man besides his reason," just as "There is a sense in sounds beyond their meaning" (CP, 351–52).

One practical result of this conception of poetry as outside reason and beyond meaning or intelligence is the discovery that a number of Stevens's poems of the forties—the verse of *Parts of a World* being perhaps the prime example—have been "frozen" in a disjunctive style so difficult to pierce that they have not been thawed by explication in almost a quarter century of reading. There is, of course, no single explanation for Stevens's rise to preeminence in the past few decades, but it may be argued that his emergence is related to the fresh appeal of his poems in comparison, say, to those of Eliot or Frost or Williams. Stevens, we may feel, holds promise for the critic and theorist because his *Collected Poems* have not yet been exhausted by explication. To put it another way, because any particular reading of Stevens can be challenged by another equally defensible reading, readers cannot be "perfectly sure of a poem" and consequently "have no further interest in it." Discussing the "authentic voice of Stevens as a poet," J. Hillis Miller has noted: "That voice is something unpredictable, savage, violent, without cause or explanation, irrational."[12] Quoting a passage of near-nonsense verse from "Montrachet-le-Jardin" as one example of the "disrupting element" in Stevens's poetry, Miller argues that the presence of this element forbids any understanding of the poetry by way of origins—including Stevens's reading in Western tradition—"or even in some intrinsic irrational property of language."[13]

In reference to an unequivocal or definitive explanation of this irrational element in Stevens, an explanation that is not itself the result of an earlier cause, Miller may be correct. However, he chooses to ignore an intriguing situation; namely, that a great part of the verse of *Parts of a World* and *Notes toward a Supreme Fiction* addresses the theoretical assumptions that result in the inexplicable voice he identifies as central to Stevens's greatness. Stevens's own explanation for the presence of this voice—in part a result of his reading in Western tradition—is frequently the subject of the poem in which the voice occurs. The voice is also directly related to Stevens's conception of the intrinsic properties of language—especially of language as the medium for art.

In the verse of *Parts of a World*, especially, Stevens explores two qualities of poetic language that argue for the presence of the inaccessible voice he so frequently employs in the volume. In comparison with other media, language is imperfect, flawed, stubborn; it produces an obscure art suited to minds that cannot rest in perfect clarity or static lucidity. Conversely, because language is static, fixed, it quickly assumes a pose, becoming exhausted or stale once it is mastered by the intellect. Stevens therefore assumes that it is to the poet's and the reader's benefit to delay mastery as long as possible by producing the kind of irrational style that Miller has identified as lying at the heart of his poetry. What Miller regards as one instance of the equivocal and disruptive nature of all texts may be seen, then, as a practical and quite deliberate result of a theory of art.

For Stevens, in opposition to deconstructive theory, the problem is not that texts are unreadable but that they are too readily available to explication and thus are depleted and enfeebled. However, the notion of misreading has a different implication for Stevens. He is not so much concerned with the validity of interpretation as with the psychology of reading. In his conception, a misreading may be more damaging to the poem's potency than a reading that is faithful to the spirit of the text. At the point where readers *believe* they have mastered the poem intellectually, whether or not they are in some unequivocal terms correct, the poem, Stevens believed, ceases to hold interest for them. A misreading (in Stevens's terms) —that is, an intellectual explication that attempts to clarify the details of the poem in terms of the *reader's* system or doctrine—is more destructive of the poem's power than a "right" reading of the sort Stevens recommends. This would be a reading that accepts the poem on its own terms and that is intent on the "obvious whole," rather than on details "not quite perceived" (CP, 350), allowing the poem to retain a candor that must elude the mind's propensity for explication and paraphrase.

One of his earliest commentators, R. P. Blackmur, pointed out in 1932 that the obscurity of Stevens's poetry was different in kind from that of Eliot and Pound, which had hitherto defined the difficulties of modernism. Blackmur also found that the peculiar merit of Stevens's obscure verse was "that it resists paraphrase and can be truly perceived only in the form of words in which it was given."[14] Anticipating Stevens's own argument of the forties, Blackmur notes: "The poems cannot be exhausted, because the words that make them, intentionally ambiguous at their crucial points, are themselves inexhaustible."[15] Ironically, Blackmur is referring here to what are now regarded as the "easy" poems, those of *Harmonium*, but, as he states, the obscurity of these early poems had already given Stevens a "bad reputation" among a certain class of readers,[16] and certainly the occasionally impenetrable quality of this early verse, which was to become more sustained in the forties, was widely regarded as one of Stevens's indulgences, one of his weaknesses as a poet, limiting the growth of any substantial audience. Perhaps the final irony is that the obscurity that retarded recognition of Stevens's achievement for decades has, in the end, contributed to his stature by preserving the bulk of his poems relatively unscathed through an entire generation of criticism. In Stevens we may have the example of a poet who outlasts his competition at least in part because his poems are more resistant to the intellect. Many of them have not yet been reduced to pose and cliché, and it may be that, with their built-in cycle of change, they are permanently resistant to the critics' systems and doctrines.

6

AFTER THE SUPREME FICTION

Stevens, Focillon,

and the Life of Forms

The second of the lectures collected in *The Necessary Angel*, "The Figure of the Youth as Virile Poet," reveals a shift in Stevens's conception of poetry that is increasingly evident in both the verse and the theoretical prose written after *Notes toward a Supreme Fiction*. Although the composition of the lecture was apparently underway less than two years after the completion of "The Noble Rider,"[1] its departures from the earlier lecture are significant, especially in light of the direction of the theory that follows in *The Necessary Angel*, which has its base in the position articulated in this pivotal lecture delivered in the summer of 1943. It is not that Stevens has changed his mind about poetry. One theme of "The Figure of the Youth as Virile Poet" advances the argument of "The Noble Rider" in identifying poetry with the personality of the poet and in locating the poem as the product of the "inescapable process of [the poet's] own individuality" (NA, 46). It is, rather, that an element has been added, one that is not easily reconciled with the conclusions reached in "The Noble Rider" concerning the poet's necessary resistance to or evasion of the pressure of reality.

In both "The Irrational Element in Poetry" (1936) and "The Noble Rider" Stevens's emphasis on the individualizing and internalizing nature of poetry-making—an emphasis encouraged by his reading of Charles Mauron—is accompanied by a need to neutralize the external world as an active force in the process. In "The Irrational Element in Poetry" this is accomplished by a conception of poetry as "the transposition of an objective reality to a subjective reality" or as the expression of the poet's "personal sensibility" (OP, 217). That is, in this early attempt to locate the source of poetry, its roots are traced to a "transaction between reality and the sensibility of the poet" (OP, 217) in which the sensibility, as absolute master, transposes something real—the sounds of a cat running over crusted snow, in Stevens's example—into something that has become an expression of a personal "manner" or "attitude." The irrational element enters the definition at the point where explanations are sought for the form the poem assumes. Stevens's argument takes this circular path: The poet transforms his experience of the external world into poetry because poetry is the medium of his personal sensibility. Because what gives a poet a particular sensibility cannot be known, we are left with a definition of poetry as one of the manifestations of "the individuality of the poet" (OP, 219). It is "irrational in the sense that it takes place unaccountably" (OP, 218). Stevens's early inability to account for a process that achieves a particular poetic form thus lies partly in the fact that consideration of any factor external to the poet's eccentric sensibility is absent. Why does the sound of a cat on snow prompt a poet to compose a poem? Stevens can only answer that "one is impelled to do so by a personal sensibility and also because one grows tired of the monotony of one's imagination, say, and sets out to find variety" (OP, 221). What relationship exists between the poem and the original experience? Stevens answers that "just as the choice of subject was unpredictable . . . so its development, after it has been chosen, is unpredictable." "All this is irrational," he concludes, and the retreat to irrationality testifies to the frailty of Stevens's earliest attempt to construct a viable aesthetic.

Some five years later, in "The Noble Rider," this exclusive focus on the internalizing nature of poetic composition is altered somewhat in Stevens's effort to find a place for a pressure from outside the poet. In the lecture's opening parade of noble riders, from Plato's figure of the soul to a contemporary painting called *Wooden Horses*, he appears to be attempting to introduce into a conception of art the external force—for Stevens, unfortunately, always the vaguely defined and undiscriminated "reality"—that had been missing earlier. We discover, in fact, that Plato's figure has lost its vitality because it "adheres to what is unreal" (NA, 7), and that Verrocchio's statue of Bartolommeo Colleoni in Venice and Clark Mills's statue of General Jackson in Washington are susceptible to the same objection. In Cervantes's Don Quixote and in the contemporary painting *Wooden Horses*, however, Stevens discovers an equilibrium between reality and imagination that supports his later assertion that the two forces are "equal and inseparable" (NA, 24). Following the argument of the first third of the lecture, one might feel that Stevens is consciously redressing an earlier imbalance too favorable to a personal sensibility or the individuality of the poet. This impression is illusory, however, for when Stevens introduces his concept of the "pressure of reality" as a vital force in the history of the imagination (NA, 13) the essay takes a curious turn, and by its conclusion this force is effectively neutralized.

In Stevens's definition of the pressure of reality as "a set of events, not only beyond our power to tranquillize them in the mind, beyond our power to reduce them and metamorphose them, but events that stir the emotions to violence, that engage us in what is direct and immediate and real" (NA, 22), we infer already a force not altogether favorable to the creation of art, since it is clearly a force outside the range of the poet's power to personalize or individualize experience, beyond the reach of a sensibility to reduce or metamorphose. Yet we discover that the pressure of reality is "the determining factor in the artistic character of an era" (NA, 22) as well as "the determining factor in the artistic character of an individual" (NA, 22–23). In what sense is this true? Does the artist reflect the particular reality, the events of the age, in such a way as to give the art of an era the peculiar and individual stamp of its own reality? By no means: "The resistance to this pressure or its evasion in the case of individuals of extraordinary imagination cancels the pressure so far as those individuals are concerned" (NA, 23). The pressure of reality is introduced as an element destructive to aesthetic contemplation, and its evasion is seen as a victory of the imagination over an alien force. If, in "The Noble Rider," Stevens has expanded the rather narrow field in which the poet of "The Irrational Element in Poetry" operated, he has done so only to negate the added force.

In "The Noble Rider" Stevens speaks fondly of poetry as "an interdependence of the imagination and reality as equals" (NA, 27), yet it is difficult to reconcile this view with his construction of the "possible poet," whose measure is "his power to abstract himself, and to withdraw with him into his abstraction the reality on which the lovers of truth insist"; the poet "abstracts" reality "by placing it in his imagination" (NA, 23). Following I. A. Richards's use of the term *abstract*, Stevens attempts in "The Noble Rider" to clear a place for the pressure of a reality beyond the individual imagination through the concept of abstraction—for him, the power by which the poet "creates the world to which we turn incessantly" and by which "he gives to life the supreme fictions without which we are unable to conceive of it" (NA, 31). However, at this point in his theory Stevens is unable to accommodate the pressure of reality as anything like an equal to the powerful abstracting imagination. Reality in one sense that he uses the term is a pressure that must be resisted or evaded. In a second sense it is "not that external scene but the life that is lived in it" (NA, 25); in yet another sense it is simply the world created by the poet, the world that we acknowledge "without knowing it" (NA, 31) and that we can conceive of only through the poet's fictions. "The Noble Rider" ends with the poet's role defined in terms of "whatever the imagination and the senses have made of the world" (NA, 30), with the mind ennobled as "the imagination pressing back against the pressure of reality" (NA, 36), and with Stevens defending "escapism" in art with the help of a series of quotations from Charles Mauron (NA, 30). "The Noble Rider" provides no place for a concept of reality that Stevens would later refer to in an essay on Marianne Moore: "reality as it impinges upon us from outside, the sense that we can touch and feel a solid reality which does not wholly dissolve itself into the conceptions of our own minds" (NA, 96).[2]

Against the background of these two early attempts to fix the relationship between the internal and external pressures on the poet, we may note the departure made in "The Figure of the Youth as Virile Poet" in 1943. Stevens's shift in perspective may be stated briefly as a tendency now to externalize what was previously located in the sensibility of the poet. The conception of poetry articulated in the lecture grants an importance to a world beyond the poet's mind and nerves never before attained in Stevens's critical prose. We learn, for example, that "poetic truth is an agreement with reality" (NA, 54) and no longer a resistance to the pressure of reality, and we are given a world that exists independent of the poet's intervention:

... standing in the radiant and productive atmosphere, and examining first one detail of that world, one particular, and then another, as we find them by chance, and observing many things that seem to be poetry without any intervention on our part, as, for example, the blue sky, and noting, in any case, that the imagination never brings anything into the world but that, on the contrary, like the personality of the poet in the act of creating, it is no more than a process, and desiring with all the power of our desire not to write falsely, do we not begin to think of the possibility that poetry is only reality, after all, and that poetic truth is a factual truth, seen, it may be, by those

whose range in perception of fact—that is, whose sensibility—
is greater than our own? From that point of view, the truth
that we experience when we are in agreement with reality is
the truth of fact.   [NA, 59]

The possibilities suggested here—that poetic truth is only factual
truth, that the personal sensibility is merely one's range in per-
ceiving fact, that creating is not invention but perception of a po-
etry that exists without any intervention on our part—are startling
partly because they follow so closely on the heels of "The Noble
Rider" and *Notes toward a Supreme Fiction*, both of which had
pointed us in the opposite direction, toward poetry as inwardly di-
rected contemplation and toward reality as a structure to be dis-
mantled through decreation by a poet seeking to become ignorant
again.

Because Stevens's key terms—imagination, poetic truth, fac-
tual truth, agreement with reality—are so evasive, one must always
hesitate to push the implications of pronouncements that seem
to come too easily to him. Yet the direction, the general drift of
Stevens's theoretical prose, is difficult to misjudge. There can be no
mistaking, for example, the consequences of his discovery in "The
Figure of the Youth as Virile Poet" that "imaginative objects" exist
"as they are, and without any intervention of the imagination"
(NA, 60). One such consequence is the rejection of a conception of
an all-powerful and incalculable imagination that pervades "The
Irrational Element in Poetry" and, to some degree, "The Noble
Rider"—the degree to which in that essay "everything like a firm
grasp of reality is eliminated from the aesthetic field" (NA, 30).
Here is Stevens's summation of his shift in perspective: "It is im-
portant to believe that the visible is the equivalent of the invisible;
and once we believe it, we have destroyed the imagination; that is
to say, we have destroyed the false imagination, the false concep-
tion of the imagination as some incalculable *vates* within us" (NA,
61). In "The Noble Rider" the pressure of reality—even if a false
conception of reality—was canceled or at least evaded by a "vio-
lence from within" (NA, 36). Now the necessary belief in an inde-
pendent visible world, a world of "absolute fact" that "includes
everything that the imagination includes" (NA, 60–61), works in
the opposite direction to destroy a conception of the imagination
that Stevens himself had so recently held.

There is without much question a personal, even confessional,
element in "The Figure of the Youth as Virile Poet," and it is con-

tained in a series of "poetic" passages interspersed with the more straightforward theorizing. Stevens characterizes the first of these as "an inscription above the portal of what lies ahead." It is an approach to a new belief that promises liberation: *"No longer do I believe that there is a mystic muse, sister of the Minotaur. This is another of the monsters I had for nurse, whom I have wasted. I am myself a part of what is real, and it is my own speech and the strength of it, this only, that I hear or ever shall"* (NA, 60). The virility of the poet in Stevens's title is, in fact, identified with the poet's discovery that he is a part of what is real, that poetic truth is the truth of fact, and that "the indefinite number of actual things . . . are indistinguishable from objects of the imagination" (NA, 62). That these discoveries were significant to Stevens beyond their usefulness in the argument of "The Figure of the Youth as Virile Poet" is made clear by the personal tone infused into the lecture by the four inscriptions above the portal with which it concludes; we may easily read them as a kind of ritual of purification on Stevens's part, a renunciation of old beliefs that has "washed the imagination clean" (NA, 62). They are "part of the purification that all of us undergo as we approach any central purity" (NA, 60). The importance of "The Figure of the Youth as Virile Poet" in the development of Stevens's fluid aesthetic is that, for the first time in his theoretical prose, he has been able to escape the rhetoric of the incalculable imagination and to find a place for a substantial reality that does not dissolve itself into the conceptions of the poet's mind.

The essays that follow "The Figure of the Youth as Virile Poet" in *The Necessary Angel* are proof that the "purification" reached there, and the place now granted a solid and independent reality, remained a part of Stevens's view of poetry-making for the remainder of the forties. The assumption of "Three Academic Pieces" (1947) is that "an accurate theory of poetry" necessitates an examination of "the structure of reality" (NA, 71), and it concludes with the principle that "the structure of poetry and the structure of reality are one" (NA, 81). "About One of Marianne Moore's Poems" (1948) is based almost entirely on a philosophical treatise, "On Poetic Truth" by H. D. Lewis, which argues that poetry "derives its significance from the reality to which it belongs" (NA, 93) and that the function of poetry is "contact with reality" (NA, 96). "Effects of Analogy" (1948) considers two theories of the imagination, both of which assume an external pressure that the poet must accommodate rather than evade. The first "relates to the imagination as a power within the poet not so much to destroy reality at will as to put it to his own use." Under the agency of this conception, the poet "comes to feel that his imagination is not wholly his own but that it may be part of a much larger, much more potent imagination, which it is his affair to try to get at" (NA, 115). The second of the two theories has to do with the imagination "as a power within him to have such insights into reality as will make it possible for him to be sufficient as a poet in the very center of consciousness" (NA, 115). Whether one chooses to regard the external field as a kind of cosmic imagination or as an independent reality, "in any art, the central problem is always the problem of reality" (NA, 116). In "Imagination as Value" (1949) the imagination has become "the only clue to reality" (NA, 137), and "The Relations between Poetry and Painting" (1951) returns us to an earlier conception of the cosmic imagination in which Stevens posits a "universal poetry that is reflected in everything" (NA, 160). Individual works of art then become not so much the products of the individuality of the artist as they are manifestations of "an unascertained and fundamental aesthetic, or order" (NA, 160). These essays are, of course, involved with many other matters; I am concerned with them here only as evidence that the externalizing tendency begun in "The Figure of the Youth as Virile Poet" became a permanent addition to Stevens's critical rhetoric. After 1943 he is constantly aware of an external order or structure, however defined, to which the personal sensibility, the individuality of the artist, must be accommodated.

In summary, tracing the drift of Stevens's reflections on poetry from 1936, when he first attempted, however unsuccessfully, to frame an adequate poetics in "The Irrational Element in Poetry," past the end of the forties, when his theorizing in prose slackened, one discovers the most decisive break in his aesthetic in a shift in perspective traceable to the period between the delivery of "The Noble Rider" (May 1941) and the start of "The Figure of the Youth as Virile Poet" (spring 1943). During this period Stevens published *Parts of a World*, which collected the poems written between 1937 and 1942. He composed *Notes toward a Supreme Fiction*, which properly belongs with *Parts of a World* rather than *Transport to Summer*, where it is collected. (*Notes*, that is, marks the end of one phase of the imagination for Stevens, not the beginning of another.) Stevens also discovered in 1942 a theoretical work by Henri Focillon called *The Life of Forms in Art*.[3] Focillon is the presiding spirit of "The Figure of the Youth as Virile Poet," and his presence is decisive in moving the essay away from the route charted in "The Noble Rider." I believe Focillon's conception of art, more than any other theoretical influence, was responsible for the shift in Stevens's aesthetic after *Notes toward a Supreme Fiction* and "The Noble Rider."

The Life of Forms in Art served Stevens in a number of ways, not the least of which was as a source for one of his greatest long poems, "The Auroras of Autumn." Its most immediate effect was to counter Charles Mauron's considerable influence, which had dominated "The Noble Rider" and had culminated in *Notes*. Whereas Mauron's psychology of aesthetic contemplation had strengthened the imagination side of Stevens's imagination-reality complex, Focillon's aesthetic offered an approach to the other side, to a world of forms whose life seemed to exist independent of the psychology of the artist or the techniques of art. In examining Focillon's aesthetic of form and Stevens's use of it, I am interested in Focillon's impact on the direction of Stevens's theory of poetry in *The Necessary Angel*, as well as in the presence of the doctrine of *The Life of Forms in Art* in the verse that followed *Notes toward a Supreme Fiction*.

Stevens spoke of *The Life of Forms in Art* as "one of the really remarkable books of the day" (NA, 46), and his copy of the work[4] exhibits the same habits of careful reading and note-taking already observed in his scrutiny of *Coleridge on Imagination*, *The Life and Writings of Giambattista Vico*, and *Aesthetics and Psychology*. More than three-quarters of its seventy-six pages contain marked passages or marginal notations, and the index Stevens prepared on the back flap of the dustjacket guides us to several significant uses he made of Focillon's theory of form:

Renewal as metamorphosis 6 67
Form is a mobile life in a changing world 5
Style 8
Transfiguration 25
The builder—according to . . his own spirit 25
Metamorphosis as transfiguration 25
The chief characteristic of the mind is to be constantly
    describing *itself* 52
Delacroix 60
Centuries as landscapes of time 64
Art is action 66

Almost all of the passages identified here eventually found a place in his prose or verse, and one of them furnishes a clue as to when

Stevens first encountered *The Life of Forms in Art*—apparently while he was still at work on *Notes toward a Supreme Fiction* in summer 1942.

Stevens's references to "The builder—according to .. his own spirit" and "Metamorphosis as transfiguration" lead us to the conclusion of Focillon's discussion of a figure familiar to readers of *Notes*—Viollet-le-Duc, the nineteenth-century architect and restorer of medieval structures. Focillon's discussion allows us to see how Viollet-le-Duc got into the poem, and it also clarifies Stevens's allusion to him in a difficult passage:

> Can we compose a castle-fortress-home,
> Even with the help of Viollet-le-Duc,
> And set the MacCullough there as major man?   [CP, 386]

The general intent of the passage is evident. The canto that it introduces proposes the notion of major man as the humanist extension of God, and the opening lines ask if it is possible to build a structure, a system of belief, in which man can find a home as the new hero of his world—MacCullough, the ordinary man, transfigured as *the* MacCullough, major man. But how would Viollet-le-Duc aid in this enterprise?

Frank Kermode has argued that the theme of the canto is that "our 'giant' cannot be like one of the old gods"; therefore we "cannot restore such a mythical concept for our own use" in the way that Viollet-le-Duc restored French medieval buildings.[5] Harold Bloom's reading is essentially the same: "Unlike Viollet-le-Duc, Stevens is not interested in that kind of restoration in which you put false fronts on edifices."[6] Both readings are open to the same objection—that they run counter to the speaker's willingness to allow even "the help of Viollet-le-Duc." The passage does not contrast Stevens's restoration of man with the restorations of Viollet-le-Duc, but instead offers an analogy with the help of the nineteenth-century architect.

The nature of this help is suggested in Focillon's discussion of Viollet-le-Duc's work on medieval cathedrals: "Relying upon the height of the bases and the dimensions of the portals, Viollet-le-Duc makes it clear that even the largest cathedrals are always at human scale. But the relation of that scale to such enormous dimensions impresses us immediately both with the sense of our own measure—the measure of nature itself—and with the sense of a dizzy immensity that exceeds nature at every point. Nothing could have determined the astonishing height of the naves of those cathedrals save the activity of the life of forms: the insistent theorem of an articulated structure, the need to create a new space" (LF, 24). Viollet-le-Duc's example, then, can aid Stevens in composing his supreme fiction "at human scale" so that major man might truly be at home. Just as the permutations of the compound "castle-fortress-home" suggest the stages of restoration of a single edifice from the medieval world to the present, the structure that the poet proposes may attain, in his architectural analogy, a scale that reminds us both of our own measure and of the immensity that exceeds us. When Stevens asks if we can compose an edifice for man that would be the modern equivalent of the medieval cathedral, he accepts the model of Viollet-le-Duc's restructuring of these cathedrals to human scale.

Focillon concludes that the architectural details of such edifices testify to the continuous metamorphosis of form. They "are like symbols of the eternal transfiguration that is forever at work upon the forms of life, and that is forever extracting from it different forms for another life." The builder, he notes, "does not set apart and enclose a void, but instead a certain dwelling-place of forms," and he assumes "different personalities in different degrees, according to the demands of his own spirit and to the state of the style in which he is working" (LF, 25). Stevens came upon *The Life of Forms in Art* too late for it to have played a significant role in *Notes*, but in Focillon's discussion of Viollet-le-Duc, the "eternal transfiguration" of forms, and the builder who creates a dwelling-place according to his own spirit and the state of his style he recognized a figuration for his construction of a dwelling for major man, "This foundling of the infected past" (CP, 388). Focillon contributed not merely the model of Viollet-le-Duc and the architectural figure, but also a conception of form in which vitality persists from age to age through metamorphosis.

Stevens's borrowing of Viollet-le-Duc from Focillon does not, however, suggest that Focillon's theory of form is present in *Notes*. On the contrary, Focillon's approach runs counter to the aesthetics of *Notes*, and a more extensive use of the doctrine of *The Life of Forms in Art* would have been enough to wreck the poem, or at least to confuse its point of view. The use Stevens makes of Focillon in *Notes* is, rather, the influence of a memorable but essentially self-contained passage. The same is true of a second passage from Focillon appropriated for the poem "Description without Place," begun in 1945.[7]

Stevens said that the subject of the poem was that "we live in the description of a place and not in the place itself" (L, 494). This is the difference between "seeming" and being, and Focillon furnished him with an example of such seeming in the discussion labeled in Stevens's index "Centuries as landscapes of time." Focillon offers the concept of the century as an example of our confusion "between chronology and life, between points of reference and fact, between measurement and action" (LF, 64). Although the century is no more than a way of computing time, we attribute to it a life and an identity of its own: "These measurements presently become frames, and the frames then become bodies. We personify them. Nothing, for instance, could be more curious in this respect than our concept of the century. We find it difficult not to think of a century as a living entity, or to refuse it a likeness to man himself. Each century reveals itself to us with a color and a physiognomy; each century's shadow has a clearly defined silhouette. It is, I think, an entirely defensible procedure to give configuration to these vast landscapes of time" (LF, 64).

This is precisely the point of the second canto of "Description without Place," where Stevens gives the century or the age as an example of something "seeming" whose identity is revealed to us as a living entity or a color:

An age is a manner collected from a queen.
An age is green or red. An age believes

Or it denies. An age is solitude
Or a barricade against the singular man

By the incalculably plural. Hence
Its identity is merely a thing that seems,

In the seeming of an original in the eye,
In the major manner of a queen, the green

The red, the blue, the argent queen.   [CP, 340]

Focillon excuses this " 'centurial' mysticism" as a necessary "collective fiction" (LF, 64). Without recourse to such fictions, space and time would become nondescript: "The historian of a world that was perpetually flooded with steady light, a world without day or night, month or season, would be able to describe only a more or less complete present" (LF, 64). Stevens ends the canto with the same justification for the fiction of the age. Without it, appearance would be flat, eternally present, and unexplained:

If not,
What subtlety would apparition have?

In flat appearance we should be and be,
Except for delicate clinkings not explained.   [CP, 340]

The third canto of "Description without Place" also relies on Focillon for an example of what Stevens calls "potential seemings" (CP, 340). Such seemings occur in the artist's ability to realize mentally "intentions of a mind as yet unknown" (CP, 341), as in the musician's power to conceive a composition not as a written score but as the sounds and rhythms of its performance:

There are potential seemings, arrogant
To be, as on the youngest poet's page,

Or in the dark musician, listening
To hear more brightly the contriving chords.   [CP, 340]

The seemings on the youngest poet's page are only potential because they have not yet become a part of the reader's sense of the world, and the "dark" musician, hidden in the mind, hears the chords before they are played for an audience. These are "seemings that are to be" (CP, 342), as yet disclosed to no one but the artist. Focillon furnishes this example in arguing that, for the artist, mental forms are always tactile or visual: "Even as the musician hears, in his own ears, the design of his music not in numerical relationships, but in timbres, instruments, and whole orchestras, so likewise the painter sees, in his own eyes, not the abstraction of his painting, but the tones, the modelling, and the touch" (LF, 55).

As in the case of Viollet-le-Duc's appropriation for *Notes*, the usefulness of *The Life of Forms in Art* for "Description without Place" is as a sourcebook for striking examples or figures that may be severed from the larger argument they are meant to illustrate. *Notes* and "Description without Place" represent a rather haphazard use of *The Life of Forms in Art*; in other poems and in his prose Stevens is more concerned with the substance of Focillon's theory. Before examining those instances, however, we need to have in mind some sense of the argument of *The Life of Forms in Art*.

It may seem surprising, given Stevens's view of poetry in 1942, that *The Life of Forms in Art* should have been attractive to him as theory. Its approach does not initially appear applicable to a conception of poetry, for it is concerned with the plastic arts and architecture, works or structures that exist in the realms of matter and space and that thereby illustrate the metamorphoses of form. Moreover, Focillon's approach clearly runs counter to the conception of art that Stevens was articulating at the time, the notion of poetry as a process of the sensibility, the individuality, or the personality of the poet. Focillon's aesthetic implicitly rejects this focus on the artist and substitutes for it a conception of a world of forms that exists seemingly independent of the ideas, feelings, instincts, images, recollections, and skills of the individual artist. While it is true that form is "realized" at the hands of the artist, Focillon prefers to think of form as a living entity that obeys "a secret principle, stronger and more rigorous than any possible creative conceit" (LF, 9). Reversing the notion that man creates art, Focillon proposes an aesthetic in which art "creates man, creates the world, and sets up within history an immutable order" (LF, 1).

He begins with the assumption that, in order to be understood, art must be isolated, separated from the intentions, commentaries, and memoirs of artists. "In order to exist at all, a work of art must be tangible. It must renounce thought, must become dimensional, must both measure and qualify space" (LF, 3). A work of art, then, is form (form is defined loosely as "the measure of space" [LF, 2]) that makes itself known to us. However, Focillon is less interested in form as manifested in individual works of art than in a conception of a "world" of form, or form as an "order of existence" that may be spoken of in biological terms: "It is my conviction that we are entirely justified in our assumption that such forms constitute an order of existence, and that this order has the motion and the breath of life. Plastic forms are subjected to the principle of metamorphoses, by which they are perpetually renewed, as well as to the principle of styles, by which their relationship is, although by no means with any regularity of recurrence, first tested, then made fast, and finally disrupted" (LF, 6). The key terms here are *metamorphoses* and *styles*. In the first principle Focillon avoids a static conception of form and provides a means for its survival; in the second, by redefining style, he offers a theory by which form maintains its priority over individual artists and schools of art.

To be considered a living entity, form must be capable of renewing itself, and the principle of its perpetuation is metamorphosis. A work of art may seem motionless, arrested, but "in reality it is born of change, and it leads on to other changes" (LF, 6). Focillon conceives of a work as containing the rough drafts, experiments, and false starts that preceded it, as well as variations that will follow:

"Rembrandt's sketches swarm across Rembrandt's paintings. The rough draft always gives vitality to the masterpiece" (LF, 6). In even the most formal and standardized of arts, say the geometric combinations of ornament, the life of change is evident: "deep within them, a sort of fever seems to goad on and to multiply the shapes; some mysterious genius of complication interlocks, enfolds, disorganizes, and reorganizes the entire labyrinth. Their very immobility sparkles with metamorphoses" (LF, 7). For Focillon, the mobility of art is evidence that "the life of forms has absolutely no aim other than itself and its own renewal" (LF, 8). That is, the principle of metamorphosis guarantees the life of forms, and the principle of style points to the presence in art of a formal logic impervious to "alien elements" and responsive only to its own needs: "ornamental style takes shape and exists as such only by virtue of the development of an internal logic, of a dialectic worth nothing except in relation to itself. Variations in ornament are not occasioned by the incrustation of alien elements or by a merely accidental choice, but by the play of hidden rules. This dialectic both accepts and demands new contributions, according to its own needs. Whatever has been contributed has already been demanded" (LF, 10).

By employing a language that attributes to art "needs" and "demands" (which are met by a style), Focillon confers on form the life he assumes. A style "is a development, a coherent grouping of forms united by a reciprocal fitness, whose essential harmony is nevertheless in many ways testing itself, building itself, and annihilating itself" (LF, 8). Just as the work of art "accepts and demands new contributions, according to its own needs," the concept of style, separated from the artist, is conceived of as the agent of form in its realization of new embodiments. The evolution of a style is a series of experiments in the process of "defining itself and then escaping from its own definition" (LF, 9). Furthermore, the successive states of a style testify to the independent life of forms: "Each style passes through several ages and several phases of being. This does not mean that the ages of style and the ages of mankind are the same thing. The life of forms is not the result of chance. Nor is it a great cyclorama neatly fitted into the theatre of history and called into being by historical necessities. No; forms obey their own rules" (LF, 12). The proof that forms obey their own rules is that their life cycle remains the same under different historical and cultural circumstances. Focillon's four ages of the life of forms (the experimental age, the classic age, the age of refinement, and the baroque age), dictated as one style comes to an end and another begins, "present the same formal characteristics at every epoch and in every environment." We may note affinities between Greek archaism and Gothic archaism, between the baroque state of Gothic and eighteenth-century rococo art (LF, 12). In mankind's tendency to "revaluate these styles over and over again" Focillon locates an "identity of the human spirit" (LF, 12) that may be attributed ultimately to the presence of a living world of forms.

The bulk of *The Life of Forms in Art* is devoted to explorations of this notion of form as an independent order of existence in relation to Focillon's conceptions of space, matter, the mind, and time. In the second chapter, "Forms in the Realm of Space," he pursues the argument that the work of art does not simply exist in or occupy space: it "treats space according to its own needs, defines space, and even creates such space as may be necessary to it" (LF, 19). Architecture, for example, by "lending definite form to that absolutely empty space . . . creates its own universe" (LF, 24).

"Form in the Realm of Matter" introduces the principle of "formal vocation," which Stevens borrowed for "The Figure of the Youth as Virile Poet." Because matter is always structure and activity (that is, form), different kinds of matter are subject to a "certain destiny" or to a "certain formal vocation." Different kinds of matter are chosen by artists "not only for the ease with which they may be handled, or for the usefulness they contribute to whatever service art renders to the needs of life, but also because they accommodate themselves to specific treatments and because they secure certain effects. Thus their form, in its raw state, evokes, suggests, and propagates other forms, and . . . this is because this form liberates other forms according to its *own* laws" (LF, 38). That is, the structure and activity of the external world of matter propagates and shapes forms according to formal properties, characteristically, for Focillon, limiting the area of "creativity" of the individual artist and enlarging the area in which art is created according to formal demands.

The same tendency may be seen in Focillon's conception of technique, which he defines not as an instrument of the artist in pursuit of a craft but as a process of form "for the achievement of metamorphoses" (LF, 42). Stevens, struck by this notion, wrote in the margin of page 42: "Definition of technique: *a process not an instrument.*" Focillon's implication is clear. His aim is to shift the emphasis from the idea of an artist practicing a craft—technique as "the aggregate of the trade-secrets of a craft" (LF, 43), as a " 'means

to an end,'" or as "virtuosity" (LF, 44)—to the idea of form achiev-
ing the states of its fluid life through the experimentations and
variations of technique, seen as something larger than the craft of
the individual artist. The study of the genealogy of a work of art
would thus give us not simply a historical or cultural perspective, a
psychological perspective, or a study of successive states of con-
sciousness, but "the very technique of the life of forms itself, its
own biological development" (LF, 44).

In "Forms in the Realm of the Mind," the chapter Stevens seems
to have scrutinized most carefully and from which most of his
citation from Focillon comes in "The Figure of the Youth as Virile
Poet," Focillon seeks to address a problem inherent in his approach
to form. Up to this point, as he admits, he has conceived of form
and of the work of art as facts separated from human causality. That
is, he has ignored the artist as a cause in the creation of art. Con-
scious of this omission, he asks, "Where, within this multifarious,
and yet highly organized world, are we to consider mankind as
standing? Have we left in it room for the mind?" (LF, 51). The es-
sential questions are these: Do the forms that inhabit space and
matter also inhabit the mind? Is their external life merely the pro-
jection of their life in the mind? Focillon is willing to grant the first
possibility but not the second. Forms do live in the mind, and the
mind is constantly seeking to describe itself in form. Focillon re-
jects, however, the notion of "a work of art as the practically pas-
sive copy of some inner 'work'" (LF, 53). Interestingly, his argument
for this position is also a rejection of the conception of art that
Stevens seems to have held at the time he read Focillon.

Even in the essay in which he employs Focillon's aesthetic Ste-
vens accounts for poetry as "a process of the personality of the
poet" (NA, 45), a process of the poet's "own individuality" (NA, 46).
While Focillon grants that "the world of forms in the mind is iden-
tical in principle with the world of forms in space and matter" (LF,
52), he is eager to separate the laws governing form from those of
the life of the mind in general. He argues that the life of forms in
the mind is not taken from the artist's images and recollections (LF,
54); that a "profound difference" separates forms from ideas (LF,
55); and that form and feeling, although mutually activating—emo-
tion turns to form and form awakens feeling—are by no means the
same (LF, 55). The distinction he wishes to draw is between a con-
ception of art in which the artist's images, ideas, and feelings lead
to a particular and individual view of the external world (this is

very close to Stevens's early position) and a conception in which the world of forms that inhabits the mind directs or "tutors" the artist's images, ideas, and feelings:

> Between nature and man form intervenes. The man in question, the artist, that is, forms this nature; before taking possession of it, he thinks it, feels it, and sees it as form. The etcher sees it as etching, and chooses from it what may already be of technical profit to him. . . . The painter of half-tones, again, turns to the rain and fog which serve to harmonize his values: before him is a curtain of water, and he sees everything through it; whereas the painter of bright colors, such as Turner, has before him the glass of water in which he dips his brush, and he sees the sun—tenfold, refracted, and mercurial—within it. [LF, 56][8]

Focillon postulates that, just as there is a formal vocation of the substances of art by which a "definite technical destiny is implicit," so a corresponding vocation of minds recognizes or anticipates both material and technique (LF, 57). Furthermore, "a certain order of forms corresponds to a certain order of minds" (LF, 57), which leads to the conclusion that "there exist whole families of the mind or, as it were, families of form" (LF, 61). Such a concept suggests that one may discover affinities between artists of different times and different schools: "Between masters who have never had the slightest personal acquaintance, and whom everything has kept apart—nature, distance, time—the life of forms establishes an intimate relationship" (LF, 62). It is a matter not of influence, but of a kinship that exists through the presence of identical forms. The existence of such families of the mind is itself evidence for Focillon that the "life of forms *within* the mind is . . . not a formal aspect of the life of the mind" (LF, 58). In the creation of art, the life of forms within the mind supersedes and directs the life of the mind as it is displayed in intellect, imagination, memory, sensibility, instinct, character: "forms, as they work upon these data, train and tutor them ceaselessly and uninterruptedly. They create a new man, manifold and yet unified, out of animal man. . . . At the crossroads of psychology and physiology, forms arise with all the authority of outline, mass, and intonation. If for a moment we cease to regard them as anything but concrete and active forces powerfully at work among the *things* of matter and space, we will find ourselves touching in the mind of the artist no more than the larvae of images and recollections, or at best the most rudimentary gestures of instinct" (LF, 58–59).

Although we are forever attempting to discover the key to art among the details of the lives of great artists, Focillon notes, this attempt is doomed to failure, since these commonplace facts can never reveal the operation of form by which art arises. Equally doomed to failure, he remarks in the final chapter, "Forms in the Realm of Time," is the attempt to discover the key to art in the analysis of historical developments, natural and social environments. "The most attentive study of the most homogeneous milieu, of the most closely woven concatenation of circumstances will not serve to give us the design of the towers of Laon" (LF, 71). The moment of the work of art "does not necessarily coincide with an historical urgency; it may indeed even contradict it" (LF, 74). The state of the life of forms should likewise not be confused with a phase of social life: "The time that gives support to a work of art does not give definition either to its principle or to its specific form." Neither is the moment of a work of art necessarily "the moment of taste"; that is, it does not coincide with the history of taste as that reflects sociological conditions (LF, 74). The birth of a work of art is instead, in Focillon's phrase, "a phenomenon of *rupture*" (LF, 75), and for that reason no theory of biographical, social, or historical determinism can explain its appearance. Focillon's conclusion characteristically relegates the artist to the role of mechanic in the maintenance of a creative entity seeking its own realization: "Even as the artist fulfills his function of geometrician and mechanic, of physicist and chemist, of psychologist and historian, so does form, guided by the play and interplay of metamorphoses, go forever forward, by its own necessity, toward its own liberty" (LF, 76).

A view of art in which the role of the individual artist is so greatly diminished hardly seems promising as a source for a poet who tended to magnify sensibility and individuality. Yet Stevens employed Focillon extensively in the preparation of the first lecture delivered after reading him, and the theory of *The Life of Forms in Art* achieved an important place in his poetry and prose throughout the middle and late forties. Did Stevens misread Focillon, or did Focillon's theory of the life of forms fill a void in Stevens's aesthetic? It is relatively easy to show that both explanations apply to some extent. Stevens's initial use of Focillon in "The Figure of the Youth as Virile Poet" is not altogether faithful to the larger argument of *The Life of Forms in Art*; however, even in misreading him, Stevens was drawn irresistibly to Focillon's position by acknowledging the possibility of an imaginative and creative order external to the artist's private sensibility. Stevens did not, on the other hand, surrender his earlier reliance on the individuality of the poet, so the two rival conceptions exist uneasily side by side in the same work.

The effect of Focillon's theory is, of course, to externalize the origin of art, to posit a structure and an activity at work both in the natural world and in the world of art. For Focillon, every activity, aesthetic or otherwise, may be comprehended and defined to the extent that it assumes form (LF, 2), so that nature may be (and has been) regarded "as the work of some God-artist, some unknown and guileful Hermes, the inventor and contriver" (LF, 3). Art, likewise, may be regarded as the work of an imaginative force larger than the creative conceits or techniques of the individual artist, obeying its own laws and responsive to its own needs. Individual artists may participate in the metamorphoses of the life of forms, but their separate contributions cannot be equated with the world of forms itself. Rather, individual works testify to the presence of the larger aesthetic and mark the stages of its metamorphosis. Both of these concepts—the natural world as the scene of play of a cosmic imagination, and the abstraction of a colossal imaginative order in which individual imaginations participate—appear increasingly in Stevens's poetry and prose after 1943, and they form the basis of several of his finest late poems.

Stevens's initial use of Focillon's theory is tentative and somewhat misleading in support of an argument that runs counter to the basic contention of *The Life of Forms in Art*. Although he refers to the work several times in "The Figure of the Youth as Virile Poet," one example will suffice to suggest the degree to which he misread Focillon. In the third section of the essay Stevens argues that there can be no definition of poetry because there "can be no poetry without the personality of the poet" (NA, 46). In the course of the argument he cites this passage from *The Life of Forms in Art*: "Human consciousness is in perpetual pursuit of a language and a style. To assume consciousness is at once to assume form. Even at levels far below the zone of definition and clarity, forms, measures and relationships exist. The chief characteristic of the mind is to be constantly describing *itself*" (NA, 46; LF, 52). Stevens takes the passage as support for his thesis that "the mind of the poet describes itself as constantly in his poems as the mind of the sculptor describes itself in his forms, or as the mind of Cézanne described itself in his 'psychological landscapes' " (NA, 46). All of these examples, including the conception of "psychological landscapes," are taken from Focillon, but their implications in Stevens are in direct opposition to their implications in Focillon's theory.

Stevens's conclusion is that these examples point to poetry as the result of the poet's "whole personality" and that "the poet who writes the heroic poem . . . will accomplish it by the power of his reason, the force of his imagination and, in addition, the effortless and inescapable process of his own individuality" (NA, 46). For Focillon, however, the life of forms in the artist's mind is not to be confused with the personality, especially the individuality, of the artist. Likewise for Focillon, the forms of the sculptor could hardly be attributed to the process of his own individuality; they are, rather, the result of the life of forms as they "train and tutor" the "intellect, imagination, memory, sensibility, instinct, character" (LF, 58). Finally, Focillon's conception of "psychological landscapes" is not a notion of the mind of the artist projecting itself onto nature, as Stevens implies, but a part of Focillon's contention that forms as living entities "give birth to their own various types of social structure: styles of life, vocabularies, states of awareness" (LF, 16). That is, the effect of forms precedes states of individual awareness: "The life of forms gives definition to what may be termed 'psychological landscapes,' without which the essential genius of the environments would be opaque and elusive for all those who share in them" (LF, 16). Given this rather egregious misreading, one may question how well Stevens comprehended the implications of Focillon's theory of art, especially as it applied to his own conception of poetry.

A misreading may, however, be as helpful to a theory of poetry as a reading that is faithful to its source. Stevens clearly used Focillon for his own purposes in "The Figure of the Youth as Virile Poet." He was reluctant to surrender his conception of the imagination, and he attempted to accommodate a somewhat alien conception of art to a view that centered on the creative force of the individual imagination. The result was a tension between two conflicting theories of art in an argument that begins with the notion that poetry, as a process of the individuality of the poet, cannot be defined and ends by offering a definition of poetry as an agreement with reality. In the course of this argument Stevens announces that he has "washed the imagination clean" (NA, 62) by destroying a "false conception of the imagination as some incalculable *vates*

within us" (NA, 61). Focillon helped Stevens to modify his concep-
tion of the imagination by granting a legitimate place to an order of
existence external to the individual sensibility, an order with which
the poet must be in agreement.

Stevens's external order is not Focillon's world of forms, but that
world is approached obliquely at times in the essay: "In spite of the
absence of a definition and in spite of the impressions and approxi-
mations we are never at a loss to recognize poetry. As a conse-
quence it is easy for us to propose a center of poetry, a *vis* or *noeud
vital*, to which, in the absence of a definition, all the variations of
definition are peripheral. . . . We say that poetry is metamorphosis
and we come to see in a few lines descriptive of an eye, a hand, a
stick, the essence of the matter" (NA, 44–45). The language here is
Focillon's—not simply the notion of art as metamorphosis, but the
"moment" of the work of art as "a node, a protuberance" (LF, 73).
Although Stevens is uncomfortable with the notion, he returns to
it again and again, most notably in "A Primitive Like an Orb" (CP,
440). He returns to it in "The Figure of the Youth as Virile Poet" in
attempting to account for the way a poet feels in the process of
composing a poem that completely satisfies his intention: "It must
be this experience that makes him think of poetry as possibly a
phase of metaphysics; and it must be this experience that teases
him with that sense of the possibility of a remote, a mystical *vis* or
noeud vital" (NA, 49). This feeling is later described as an agree-
ment with reality, the sense "of a perfection touched, of a vocation
so that all men may know the truth" (NA, 51), and again the lan-
guage is from Focillon. Focillon's "formal vocation" (LF, 38) and his
"vocation of minds" imply that "a definite technical destiny is im-
plicit" both in the materials of art and in the artist's mind (LF,
57). This is to suggest that the artist experiences a sense of elation
when agreement is reached with a form implicit in the mind but
heretofore unrealized. Stevens cites a portion of the discussion:
"M. Focillon speaks of a vocation of substances, or technical des-
tiny, to which there is a corresponding vocation of minds; that is
to say, a certain order of forms corresponds to a certain order of
minds" (NA, 48). Focillon's conception of a vocation of minds is
somewhat more complicated than Stevens makes it appear, but his
own reading of it leads him to the lecture's final position of poetry
as an agreement with reality—"the possibility that poetry is only
reality, after all, and that poetic truth is a factual truth, seen, it may
be, by those whose range in the perception of fact . . . is greater than
our own." If we grant this possibility, then "the truth that we expe-

rience when we are in agreement with reality is the truth of fact" (NA, 59). The language here is Stevens's, not Focillon's, but Stevens's conception of poetry as an agreement with reality and his concession that "imaginative objects" exist "without any intervention of the imagination" (NA, 60) suggest a discernible shift in the direction of Focillon's theory.

I have already indicated how the pieces that follow in *The Necessary Angel* reinforce this shift in direction. Also apparent is the persistence of Stevens's version of what he called in the 1943 lecture "a center of poetry, a *vis* or *noeud vital*" to which individual expressions are peripheral. In "Three Academic Pieces" this is, rather vaguely, an "activity" at work in the world "that makes one thing resemble another" and to which Stevens attributes a "desire for resemblance" (NA, 76) in the artist that results in what he now labels "metamorphosis," by which he means "the creation of resemblance by the imagination" (NA, 72). The departure of "Three Academic Pieces" is to attribute to reality a "structure" and to suggest that there are degrees between the metamorphoses of poetry and the structure of reality. The lecture ends with this argument: since one resemblance is "always a little more perfect than another ... it is not too extravagant to think of resemblances and of the repetitions of resemblances as a source of the ideal" (NA, 81). This ideal, which "remains alive with an enormous life" (NA, 82) and by which the appropriateness of metaphors is measured, satisfies the demands of Focillon's world of forms by postulating a center of poetry with which the poet must seek agreement. Stevens's poetic version of this conception in "Study of Images II" postulates a center of metaphor to which individual metaphors are peripheral. The conceit of the poem is that there exists an ideal storehouse of images for things—the moon, for example—so that "the frequency of images of the moon / Is more or less." It is "As if the centre of images had its / Congenial mannequins, alert to please":

As if, as if, as if the disparate halves
Of things were waiting in a betrothal known
To none, awaiting espousal to the sound

Of right joining, a music of ideas, the burning
And breeding and bearing birth of harmony,
The final relation, the marriage of the rest.   [CP, 464–65]

The notion of the poet's obedience to a kind of cosmic imagination is repeated in "Effects of Analogy" in Stevens's articulation of the poet's constant sense "that his imagination is not wholly his own" and "that it may be part of a much larger, much more potent imagination, which it is his affair to try to get at" (NA, 115). In "The Relations between Poetry and Painting," the final lecture of *The Necessary Angel*, Stevens posits "a universal poetry that is reflected in everything": "This remark approaches the idea of Baudelaire that there exists an unascertained and fundamental aesthetic, or order, of which poetry and painting are manifestations, but of which, for that matter, sculpture or music or any other aesthetic realization would equally be a manifestation" (NA, 160). By the time of "The Relations between Poetry and Painting" (1951) Stevens has abandoned his earlier reliance on the poet's sensibility as the center for the origin of poetry. He now finds that "the operative force within us does not, in fact, seem to be the sensibility, that is to say, the feelings"; rather, it is "a constructive faculty" (NA, 164): "The point is that the poet does his job by virtue of an effort of the mind. In doing so, he is in rapport with the painter, who does his job, with respect to the problems of form and color, which confront him incessantly" (NA, 165).

The whole of "The Relations between Poetry and Painting" is instructive as a measure of how far Stevens's aesthetic has drifted from its original course in "The Noble Rider" ten years earlier. He now grants that "the total of the theories of poetry" appears "to become in time a mystical aesthetic, a prodigious search of appearance, as if to find a way of saying and of establishing that all things, whether below or above appearance, are one and that it is only through reality, in which they are reflected, or, it may be joined together, that we can reach them" (NA, 173–74). He quotes Klee's equally mystical aesthetic in which the artist "comes near to the secret places where original law fosters all evolution" and where "the organic center of all movement in time and space . . . determines every function" (NA, 174). The presence of these analogues to Focillon's world of forms does not mean, however, that Stevens embraces such a concept in his later prose. He toys with the idea of a coherent aesthetic order in most of the lectures that followed his reading of Focillon, but the idea is always marginal to other concerns. In "The Relations between Poetry and Painting" he notes that assumptions of "a fundamental aesthetic of which poetry and painting are related but dissimilar manifestations, are speculative" (NA, 160), and Stevens was more at home with such speculation in his poetry than in his prose. In Stevens's later theoretical poems

Focillon's theory makes its greatest mark, and there his influence can be most clearly detected.

Focillon's world of forms is granted an independent existence by his method of conceiving art and nature not as collections of individual works or objects, but as living entities that are never seen in their entirety but are glimpsed through the formal properties of individual works or objects. That is, we can know this world of forms only in particular states or stages of its metamorphosis. From this point of view, a work of art or a natural object is less important as a thing in itself than as marking a state of the entity of which it forms a small part. It is perhaps easier for us to grant this notion in regard to nature than in regard to art, but Focillon refuses to concede that the aesthetic world of forms is a mere metaphor, and he feels justified in applying to art the methods of the biological sciences (LF, 51). For Focillon, this greater aesthetic order actually exists; its existence is proven by the presence of the lesser works that constitute it, reveal its constant metamorphosis, and freeze it momentarily in a style from which it must eventually escape.

That Stevens found this point of view useful as one way of conceiving poetry is attested to by a poem based largely on Focillon's conception, "A Primitive Like an Orb." This speculative exercise from *The Auroras of Autumn* postulates an "essential poem at the centre of things," the knowledge of which involves "a difficult apperception." Like Focillon's world of forms, it can be known only in the existence of "lesser poems":

> We do not prove the existence of the poem.
> It is something seen and known in lesser poems.
> It is the huge, high harmony that sounds
> A little and a little, suddenly,
> By means of a separate sense. It is and it
> Is not and, therefore, is.   [CP, 440]

"A Primitive Like an Orb" is somewhat more wary than *The Life of Forms in Art* in its approach to the existence of this order. Focillon finds proof for its existence in his analysis of works, styles, and techniques at different stages of development. For Stevens, "One poem proves another and the whole" only "For the clairvoyant men that need no proof." "The lover, the believer and the poet" discover the presence of the central poem in words "chosen out of their desire, / The joy of language, when it is themselves." Stevens shifts

Focillon's theory from a critic's external approach to the study of art to the poet's inner sense of elation in achieving the "fulfillment of fulfillments" (CP, 441).

"A Primitive Like an Orb" is, to this extent, a poetic version—and therefore more extravagant in its claims—of the conceit of a "center of poetry" borrowed from Focillon, a conceit that I have already traced through the theoretical prose. Stevens uses it in "The Figure of the Youth as Virile Poet" to account for the "way a poet feels when he is writing, or after he has written, a poem that completely accomplishes his purpose," and the way he feels leads him to the possibility of "a remote, a mystical *vis* or *noeud vital*" (NA, 49). In his speculation about the nature of the central poem in "A Primitive Like an Orb" (published in 1948), Stevens returns to the language of the 1943 lecture and to Focillon's conception of an inherent aesthetic order evolving according to its own principles. The essential poem is

> A vis, a principle or, it may be,
> The meditation of a principle,
> Or else an inherent order active to be
> Itself, a nature of its natives all
> Beneficence, a repose, utmost repose,
> The muscles of a magnet aptly felt,
> A giant, on the horizon. . . .   [CP, 442]

Stevens chooses this last figure, a giant on the horizon, to embody his abstraction in the remainder of the poem. As a giant on the horizon, Stevens's version of Focillon's formal order approaches the giant imagination the poet senses in "Effects of Analogy," the lecture written about the same time as "A Primitive Like an Orb." In "Effects of Analogy," it will be recalled, the poet at times "comes to feel that his imagination is not wholly his own" but "part of a much larger, much more potent imagination, which it is his affair to try to get at" (NA, 115). In "A Primitive Like an Orb" Stevens's personification of this more potent imagination both humanizes it and renders it properly mythical or fictional, in keeping with the poem's view of the conception as a belief chosen out of the desire to believe rather than as the premise of a theory of art. It is "an abstraction given head" (CP, 443) in Stevens's private use of *abstraction* in reference to the fiction-making powers of the poet:

> Here, then, is an abstraction given head,
> A giant on the horizon, given arms,

A massive body and long legs, stretched out,
A definition with an illustration, not
Too exactly labelled, a large among the smalls
Of it, a close, parental magnitude,
At the centre on the horizon, concentrum, grave
And prodigious person, patron of origins.   [CP, 443]

The giant is prodigious in several punning senses—in its size; as a prodigy, something extraordinary or inexplicable; and finally as something prodigal, extravagant in its giving. As "patron of origins" and "crested with every prodigal, familiar fire" (CP, 442), this "essential poem begets the others" (CP, 441). It is not merely the total of poems but the source of their origin.

Canto x, which deals with the relationship between this giant imagination and the individual imagination, is the most difficult of the poem:

It is a giant, always, that is evolved,
To be in scale, unless virtue cuts him, snips
Both size and solitude or thinks it does,
As in a signed photograph on a mantelpiece.
But the virtuoso never leaves his shape,
Still on the horizon, elongates his cuts,
And still angelic and still plenteous,
Imposes power by the power of his form.   [CP, 442–43]

The key to the canto is in Stevens's play on *virtue* and *virtuoso*. The canto argues that the abstract imaginative order evolves constantly to retain its giant scale in relation to the lesser works by which it is known—"unless virtue cuts him . . . or thinks it does" by confusing the individual work with the imaginative order itself. *Virtue* is here used in its root sense, recalling the earlier *vis* and suggesting human strength or power in contrast to the strength of the *virtuoso*, the master of the arts, the giant imagination who "never leaves his shape"[9] despite attempts to cut him down to size. Just as the static "signed photograph" cannot be equated with its changing subject, so the power of the individual poem should not be confused with the evolving strength of the giant of poetry, who "Imposes power by the power of his form." Stevens's use of Focillon's language here reminds us that several of the concepts of the passage, including notions of the evolution of form and distinctions between form itself and its embodiments in individual works, are found in *The Life of Forms in Art*. The discussion of formal scale as a measure of an "immensity that exceeds nature at every point" can, in fact, be located in the discussion of Viollet-le-Duc that Stevens borrowed for *Notes toward a Supreme Fiction* (LF, 24). The argument of the canto is that the power of this abstract order is not exhausted by the individual works it begets. Its virtue is protected by metamorphosis, the same principle that guides Focillon's world of forms so that it always "is evolved, / To be in scale."

The poem ends with this notion of metamorphosis, and the final canto begins with the familiar and triumphant "That's it" we last heard at the conclusion of *Notes*. There is, however, a playful irony in its repetition here, for "A Primitive Like an Orb" reaches a somewhat different conclusion, and the implication is that a "giant ever changing, living in change" (CP, 443) is apt to produce a succession of such exclamations of certainty. The "That's it" of *Notes* preceded a conception of poetry as "The fiction that results from feeling" (CP, 406). The corresponding cry of "A Primitive Like an Orb" leads to a view of poetry as a part of something larger than the poet's "more than rational distortion" (CP, 406):

That's it. The lover writes, the believer hears,
The poet mumbles and the painter sees,
Each one, his fated eccentricity,
As a part, but part, but tenacious particle,
Of the skeleton of the ether, the total
Of letters, prophecies, perceptions, clods
Of color, the giant of nothingness, each one
And the giant ever changing, living in change.   [CP, 443]

"Even as the musician hears, in his own ears, the design of his music . . . so likewise the painter sees, in his own eyes, not the abstraction of his painting, but the tones, the modelling, and the touch," Focillon states in a passage (LF, 55) already noted as a source for "Description without Place." Interestingly, at the poem's conclusion Stevens suddenly enlarges his abstraction to find a place for the other arts. His oxymoronic "fated eccentricity," or destined freedom, recalls as well Focillon's theories of the formal vocation and the vocation of minds. Those theories imply, first, a "definite technical destiny" in the seemingly free play of the artist and, second, the notion that "a certain order of forms corresponds to a certain order of minds" so that the painter, the musician, and the poet will obey their formal destinies in different ways (LF, 57). Stevens's final conceit of each artist and art as part of a totality of art "ever changing, living in change" is precisely the assumption on which *The Life of Forms in Art* is grounded. "A Primitive Like an Orb" is Stevens's closest approach to Focillon's life of forms as theory.

Five years earlier Stevens had tried out Focillon's conception of form, as well as the term itself,[10] in "Chocorua to Its Neighbor" (CP, 296), a poem Harold Bloom sees as an early version of "A Primitive Like an Orb."[11] "Chocorua to Its Neighbor" features a figure who seems to represent the abstract form of man in the way that the giant of "A Primitive Like an Orb" represents the abstract form of poetry. At the beginning of the poem the mountain Chocorua sees men at a distance "without reference to their form" (CP, 296). Armies and cities are described as "forms in numbers" and a war is "a gesticulation of forms" (CP, 296), but these do not bring a knowledge of the essence of the form of man, the spirit or self, which is then embodied in the "prodigious shadow" who stands atop the mountain to represent "the self of selves" (CP, 297). "To think of him destroyed the body's form" (CP, 297), since he represents "not the person" but the "power" of man (CP, 299). This figure is described variously as "a central mind" (CP, 298), "the collective being" (CP, 299), "the total man" (CP, 301). He arose "because men wanted him to be":

> They wanted him by day to be, image,
> But not the person, of their power, thought
> But not the thinker, large in their largeness, beyond
> Their form, beyond their life, yet of themselves,
> Excluding by his largeness their defaults.   [CP, 299]

Although Stevens seems to have in mind Focillon's notion of a vital though hidden world of form, he does not exploit the implications of Focillon's theory in "Chocorua." Rather, he employs the terminology of *The Life of Forms in Art* to develop an earlier conception of his own, the notion of the hero or major man. What Focillon contributes is a rhetoric for depicting the relationship between the actual and the ideal by which is glimpsed a transcendent human form larger than any actual embodiment.

A similar use of Focillon's terminology occurs in the short poem "A Pastor Caballero," from *Transport to Summer*. The poem demonstrates the power of outward forms to embody an "image of the mind" (CP, 379), and it seems to represent a second misreading—the first occurs in "The Figure of the Youth as Virile Poet"—of Focillon's notion that "a certain order of forms corresponds to a certain order of minds" (NA, 48). In the poem the caballero becomes transfigured, attaining a spiritual quality through the evocations of form:

> The importance of its hat to a form becomes
> More definite. The sweeping brim of the hat
> Makes of the form Most Merciful Capitan,
>
> If the observer says so: grandiloquent
> Locution of a hand in a rhapsody.
> Its line moves quickly with the genius
>
> Of its improvisation until, at length,
> It enfolds the head in a vital ambiance
> A vital, linear ambiance. The flare
>
> In the sweeping brim becomes the origin
> Of a human evocation, so disclosed
> That, nameless, it creates an affectionate name,
>
> Derived from adjectives of deepest mine.
> The actual form bears outwardly this grace,
> An image of the mind, an inward mate. . . .   [CP, 379]

Stevens's assumption here is that an identical form is embodied in the sweeping brim of the hat, the expression of a hand in a moment of rhapsody, and the halo of the saint. Although this form is nameless, it "creates an affectionate name" derived from the "deepest mine," as if there were an unconscious storehouse of images in the mind (as in "Study of Images II") by which the "actual form bears outwardly this grace." Ultimately, the poem depicts a marriage of form and image, but it implies, contrary to Focillon, that the form is an image of the mind, a projection. In assuming that form is prior to any particular embodiment—in a hat, a gesture, a halo—it mirrors Focillon's approach; however, its implication that the mind describes itself in form "as the mind of the sculptor describes itself in his forms" (NA, 46) is a misreading of Focillon, although it is the same misreading that Stevens demonstrated in "The Figure of the Youth as Virile Poet."

One final example of Stevens's use of Focillon's theoretical language occurs in what is almost certainly his most opaque poem, "The Owl in the Sarcophagus" (CP, 431), composed a year before "A Primitive Like an Orb." Bloom labels the poem "uninterpretable,"[12] and it may well be that Focillon contributed to its uninterpretability by providing the rhetoric with which Stevens approaches "the mythology of modern death" (CP, 435). The occasion of the poem is the death of Henry Church, and Stevens adapts Focillon's aesthetic conception of form to his own purpose of positing vital forms for a secular version of death:

> Two forms move among the dead, high sleep
> Who by his highness quiets them, high peace
> Upon whose shoulders even the heavens rest,
>
> Two brothers. And a third form, she that says
> Good-by in the darkness, speaking quietly there,
> To those that cannot say good-by themselves.   [CP, 431]

One may read the poem's opening lines to say that a secular mind views death in terms of sleep, peace, and the memory of the dead, but Stevens is attempting to say much more than that—possibly more than can be said. Just as Focillon refuses to concede that his living world of forms is a metaphor, so Stevens predicates for his forms for death an actual existence in a realm where the material world is "prodigy," something marvelous or inexplicable:

> These forms are not abortive figures, rocks,
> Impenetrable symbols, motionless. They move
>
> About the night. They live without our light,
> In an element not the heaviness of time,
> In which reality is prodigy.   [CP, 432]

Bloom misreads "prodigy" in this passage as suggesting that the world Stevens describes "is not so much death as it is but rather *death as it will be*,"[13] thus missing Stevens's paradox of an order of existence so firmly predicated and so completely severed from "reality" that, from its perspective, the world of time can be thought of only in the way we now regard the supernatural.

In this attempt to grant the realm of death an independent existence, in which its forms "live without our light," the poem is most indebted to *The Life of Forms in Art*. Its achievement parallels Focillon's in the realm of art; the two works attempt to reverse our traditional conceptions of art and death by employing language that authenticates the existence of forms otherwise relegated to the status of images or modes of expression. The difference between the two is that, while Focillon never wavers from his stance of the biologist examining objectively the life forms of a separate order of existence, Stevens, as in "A Primitive Like an Orb," firmly grounds his conception in the notion of a fiction, believed momentarily be-

cause of an instinctive "will to believe" (L, 430).[14] The parallel
with "A Primitive Like an Orb" can be extended, for in both poems
the proof of the separate existence of an abstract realm, whether
that of the central poem or of the forms of death, is available only
to "the clairvoyant men that need no proof," whose acceptance pro-
ceeds "out of their desire" (CP, 441). Stevens was thus able to em-
ploy Focillon's theory only to the point at which the question of its
ontological status arises. At that point he reverts to a notion of his
forms as the offspring of desire, creatures of the mind, as in the
conclusion of "The Owl in the Sarcophagus":

> These are death's own supremest images,
> The pure perfections of parental space,
>
> The children of a desire that is the will,
> Even of death, the beings of the mind
> In the light-bound space of the mind, the floreate flare . . .
>
> It is a child that sings itself to sleep,
> The mind, among the creatures that it makes,
> The people, those by which it lives and dies.   [CP, 436]

Several other poems in *Transport to Summer* and *The Auroras of
Autumn*—including "The Pure Good of Theory" (CP, 329), "A Pas-
toral Nun" (CP, 378), "The Ultimate Poem Is Abstract" (CP, 429),
"Imago" (CP, 439), and "Study of Images II" (CP, 464)—propose aes-
thetic conceptions roughly analogous to those contained in *The
Life of Forms in Art*, but in none of these is Focillon's presence
clearly visible or decisive. "The Auroras of Autumn," however, bor-
rows freely from the language and imagery of *The Life of Forms in
Art* in Stevens's most successful effort to transpose Focillon's theo-
ries of form and metamorphosis into poetry.

7

AFTER THE SUPREME FICTION

Focillon's Life of Forms

and "The Auroras of Autumn"

The movement of the first six cantos of "The Auroras of Autumn" leads Stevens's speaker to the crucial question that begins canto vii:

> Is there an imagination that sits enthroned
> As grim as it is benevolent, the just
> And the unjust, which in the midst of summer stops
>
> To imagine winter?   [CP, 417]

The question derives ultimately from *The Life of Forms in Art*, where Focillon asks, "Do these forms sit enthroned like great goddesses in some remote region from which they descend to us only when we petition them?" (LF, 51–52). That the cosmic imagination of "The Auroras of Autumn" owes a great deal to Focillon's world of forms cannot be questioned, but the route that arrives finally at this conceit can also be attributed to Focillon, whose influence in this case extends beyond the theoretical assumptions behind the poem to include its personae and some of its figurative language. Sources for the poem have been located in, among others, Wordsworth, Dickinson, Emerson, and Shelley.[1] Focillon is, I believe, a more decisive source than any of these, an impression that is strengthened in reading "The Auroras of Autumn" alongside *The Life of Forms in Art*. The theoretical study does not distract us from the essential movement of the poem; rather, it makes the poem more accessible by clarifying its assumption that "Form is a mobile life in a changing world," a definition from Focillon that Stevens entered in his index to the book.

The poem's great symbol for the mobile life of form is the aurora borealis, everywhere present in the poem but mirrored as well in lesser figures reflecting its "lavishing of itself in change" (CP, 416).

The first of these is the serpent of the first canto, which functions, strangely, both as a metaphor for the auroras and as an autonomous emblem of flux. He is "the bodiless" whose "head is air" and whose eyes "open and fix on us in every sky" (CP, 411), but he is also a creature of the earth:

> This is where the serpent lives. This is his nest,
> These fields, these hills, these tinted distances,
> And the pines above and along and beside the sea.
>
> This is form gulping after formlessness,
> Skin flashing to wished-for disappearance
> And the serpent body flashing without the skin.   [CP, 411]

Although the traditional nature of the figure precludes the necessity of locating specific sources, Stevens's identification of the serpent as "form gulping after formlessness" derives from Focillon, for whom this emblem, employed in the interlace of ornament, "appears as a transitory, but endlessly renewed meditation on a chaotic universe that deep within itself clasps and conceals the debris or the seeds of humankind. The interlace twines round and round the old iconography, and devours it" (LF, 5). Focillon's description of the mobility of ornament later returns to the serpent: "It duplicates, coils back upon, and devours its own shape" (LF, 7).

For Stevens, too, the serpent represents not merely flux but an "endlessly renewed meditation on a chaotic universe." The phrase would not be far from the mark in suggesting the focus of the poem, for it is concerned not simply with the fact of change, which is its given, but with meditations at various levels on the source and principle of change. In this connection, the serpent is both the fact of change and its law. As an embodiment of flux, the serpent makes his nest on the earth; as the principle of flux, he lives in the sky "In another nest,"

> the master of the maze
> Of body and air and forms and images,
> Relentlessly in possession of happiness.
>
> This is his poison: that we should disbelieve
> Even that. His meditations in the ferns,
> When he moved so slightly to make sure of sun
>
> Made us no less as sure.   [CP, 411–12]

Later developments in the poem are implicit in this opening canto. Stevens's transformation of the serpent from a manifestation of flux to a symbol for the "master of the maze" anticipates the conceit of flux as an enthroned imagination in canto vii. The serpent is the object of the speaker's meditation on change, but the serpent's own "meditations in the ferns" will later become the poem's fiction for the source of change, for a universal mind "which in the midst of summer stops / To imagine winter" (CP, 417). The serpent's poison is that we are unable to accept this traditional emblem of evil and death as an innocent "master of the maze." That is, we are unable to accept the principle of change as "Relentlessly in possession of happiness," to accept the flux represented by the northern lights and the serpent as "An innocence of the earth and no false sign / Or symbol of malice" (CP, 418). This variation on the theme, developed in the final three cantos, is anticipated in our reaction to the serpent at the end of the first canto. Meditating in the ferns, the serpent moves slightly "to make sure of sun," a movement we interpret as a sign of malice:

> We saw in his head,
> Black beaded on the rock, the flecked animal,
> The moving grass, the Indian in his glade.   [CP, 412]

Stevens's figure of the "master of the maze" is also apparently taken from Focillon, in an odd way. One illustration in the 1942 edition of *The Life of Forms in Art*[2] is a reproduction of the first page of St. Mark's Gospel from the Book of Kells, intended to serve as an example of the use of the serpent in interlace. It can best be described as a maze, the passages of which are filled with the coils of countless serpents so intertwined that it is impossible to see where one ends and another begins. But the master of this maze is another figure who found his way into "The Auroras of Autumn," the father of cantos iv and v. In the upper right-hand corner of the illumination rests a godly figure whose lower body resembles the coils of the serpents but whose head and position are aptly described in the poem. He sits with his lower legs extended into the negative space outside the border of the ornamentation. His strongest features, seen in profile, are a large eye heavily outlined, dark eyebrow, and grim mouth. Stevens describes him thus:

> The father sits
> In space, wherever he sits, of bleak regard,

> As one that is strong in the bushes of his eyes.   [CP, 414]

In one arm the figure holds an animal, or at least the upper half of an animal that emerges from the border of the illumination. In the other hand he holds what appears to be a musical instrument, equally stylized. The poem's description of the father in canto v again mirrors the illumination:

> The father fetches his unherded herds,
> Of barbarous tongue, slavered and panting halves
>
> Of breath, obedient to his trumpet's touch.   [CP, 415]

Earlier, in canto iv, the father is addressed directly:

> Master O master seated by the fire
> And yet in space and motionless and yet
> Of motion the ever-brightening origin. . . .   [CP, 414]

The phrasing of this address is also taken from Focillon, who notes, in a discussion referred to in Stevens's index, "Both the man who sits by his fireside and the man who roams abroad are exposed at all points to these changes" (LF, 66).

Stevens's index to *The Life of Forms in Art* also leads us to an understanding of the role of the father (in canto v) as the master of pageants and festivals, but an intelligible reading of canto v must await a discussion of the three intervening cantos. Stevens introduces the father in canto iv as a culmination of the movement of the poem's second, third, and fourth cantos, each beginning "Farewell to an idea. . . ." These cantos, also implicit in the opening figure of the serpent as "form gulping after formlessness," extend the mobility of form in three stages. The second canto deals with the metamorphosis of form in the material and temporal realms. The *idea* of "Farewell to an idea" takes us back to what now seems the naiveté of the "first idea" of *Notes*, or, even earlier, to the presumption of "The Idea of Order at Key West," where, in a setting similar to that of canto ii, the singer through the power of her imagination "Mastered the night and portioned out the sea" (CP, 130). In "The Auroras of Autumn" such a belief in the ordering power of the individual imagination is shrunken in the face of an external power that does not seem to regard the man walking on the beach, who "turns blankly on the sand" and "observes how the north is always enlarging the change" (CP, 412). Similarly, the "idea" of the cabin on the beach does not originate in the perceiver but is derived from a larger context. It is the result of "custom," an "ancestral theme," or "as a consequence / Of an infinite course." Whatever the origin of the idea in custom or history, its principle, we learn by the end of the canto, is change—another version of "form gulping after formlessness":

Focillon's Life of Forms and "The Auroras of Autumn"

Farewell to an idea. . . A cabin stands,
Deserted, on a beach. It is white,
As by a custom or according to

An ancestral theme or as a consequence
Of an infinite course. The flowers against the wall
Are white, a little dried, a kind of mark

Reminding, trying to remind, of a white
That was different, something else, last year
Or before, not the white of an aging afternoon. . . .

    . . .

The season changes. A cold wind chills the beach.
The long lines of it grow longer, emptier,
A darkness gathers though it does not fall. . . .   [CP, 412]

"Farewell to an idea" also provides a kind of mark to remind
us of the drastic shift in the persona's perspective accomplished be-
tween *Notes* and "The Auroras of Autumn." Helen Vendler has ob-
served that "The Auroras of Autumn" and its companion piece
"Credences of Summer" (1947) are the first of Stevens's poems to
place the speaker "firmly in a landscape of the present moment."[3]
She notes that "spectatorship has turned into an immersion in the
scene, a scene which is at once fully made by the poet, fully ap-
parent of itself, and fully found, as if left, like Whitman's grass,
designedly dropped."[4] While it is true that the scene is fully appar-
ent and fully found, the question haunting both "The Auroras of
Autumn" and "Credences of Summer" is whether or not the some-
what inhuman world of these poems is in fact "fully made by the
poet." Both poems depict a setting that appears to operate according
to its own imaginative laws, in which it is "difficult to sing in
face / Of the object" (CP, 376). And "Credences of Summer" ends
with its own version of the cosmic imagination:

The personae of summer play the characters
Of an inhuman author, who meditates
With the gold bugs, in blue meadows, late at night.
He does not hear his characters talk. He sees
Them mottled, in the moodiest costumes,

Of blue and yellow, sky and sun, belted
And knotted, sashed and seamed, half pales of red,
Half pales of green, appropriate habit for

The huge decorum, the manner of the time,
Part of the mottled mood of summer's whole,

In which the characters speak because they want
To speak, the fat, the roseate characters,
Free, for a moment, from malice and sudden cry,
Complete in a completed scene, speaking
Their parts in a youthful happiness.   [CP, 377–78]

Vendler, oddly, identifies the "inhuman author" with the poet and not with the analogous enthroned imagination of "The Auroras of Autumn," but surely the force of the passage is to remove the personae of summer from the poet's control, to grant a separate and complete existence to the forms of summer as "appropriate habit for / The huge decorum, the manner of the time." The characters are "Complete in a completed scene," and they represent a moment or "style" in the mobile life of a changing world, a moment of complete satisfaction prior to that depicted in "The Auroras of Autumn," when the inhuman author "in the midst of summer stops / To imagine winter" (CP, 417). Both poems, that is, assume Stevens's version of Focillon's mobile life of external forms operating according to imaginative laws not supplied by the poems' speakers. The poems thus represent an externalizing of the imagination already noted in Stevens's theoretical prose, and in both the prose and the poetry the vision of a "completed" world "which is not part of the listener's own sense" (CP, 377) is usually accompanied by the conceit of an inhuman imagination in pursuit of its own ends.

Although "Credences of Summer" captures a static moment of the meditation of this larger imagination—"right ignorance / Of change still possible" (CP, 372)—the assumption of both poems is that it operates by the principle of metamorphosis. "The Auroras of Autumn," to return to the argument of the poem, is devoted to the consequences of this principle on a persona who is forced to acknowledge its presence. While canto ii illustrates the mobility of external forms, the dissolution of the meanings imparted to an architectural form such as a cabin on a beach, canto iii deals with a parallel internal dissolution, the dissolving of the feelings and memories that were the "purpose of the poem" (CP, 413). Canto iii contains the strange dislocations of dreams and memory in its description of mental forms gulping after formlessness:

Farewell to an idea . . . The mother's face
The purpose of the poem, fills the room.
They are together, here, and it is warm,

With none of the prescience of oncoming dreams,
It is evening. The house is evening, half dissolved.
Only the half they can never possess remains,

Still-starred. It is the mother they possess,
Who gives transparence to their present peace.
She makes that gentler that can gentle be.

And yet she too is dissolved, she is destroyed.
She gives transparence. But she has grown old.
The necklace is a carving not a kiss.

The soft hands are a motion not a touch.
The house will crumble and the books will burn.
They are at ease in a shelter of the mind

And the house is of the mind and they and time,
Together, all together. Boreal night
Will look like frost as it approaches them

And to the mother as she falls asleep
And as they say good-night, good-night.   [CP, 413]

It is not the mother but the memory of the mother's face that fills
the room and is the "purpose of the poem." However, the shelter
provided by the recollected scene is dissolved even as the mother
grows old in the course of the canto: "the house is of the mind and
they and time." The imaginative principle Stevens associates with
the aurora borealis is stronger than the individual imagination's
power to sustain itself with its storehouse of forms and feelings.
The poem's imagery assumes this force as a movement external to
the house of the mind, whose windows are lighted from outside:

                    Upstairs
The windows will be lighted, not the rooms.

A wind will spread its windy grandeurs round
And knock like a rifle-butt against the door.
The wind will command them with invincible sound.
                              [CP, 413–14]

The mother, who in canto v "invites humanity to her house /
And table" (CP, 415), has a number of associations for Stevens here,
among them peace, sleep, and memory, the same associations con-
veyed in her appearance as one of the three forms of death in "The
Owl in the Sarcophagus." She imparts the maternal affections of
the earth itself, but in both poems she is pictured in the act of

bidding farewell to her earthly children—"she that says / Good-by in the darkness" (CP, 431). The memory of the mother is thus another means of saying farewell to an idea and an acknowledgment that the forms of the mind are equally subject to the principle of flux. This figure, simultaneously comforting and chilling as "she too is dissolved," may have been suggested by another illustration from the 1942 edition of *The Life of Forms in Art*. Picasso's drawing, "A Mother Holding a Child," is composed of several studies of a mother and infant. Both the face and hands of the finished drawing of the mother are outlined lightly in identical poses to the right of the central figure, which gives the effect of the figure fading into the background. The more detailed drawing of the upper torso also dissolves into faint lines overlapping other studies of the hands below. Although the drawing had little influence on the characterization of the mother in the poem, which must have derived from something more deeply felt, it may have contributed to the canto the notion of a strong maternal figure who dissolves ultimately into the tentative lines and sketches of the artist. Like her necklace, she is ultimately revealed as a mere artifact, not a real presence, "a carving not a kiss."

Stevens's characterization of the father, however, is more clearly indebted to *The Life of Forms in Art*. While the father's initial appearance in canto iv is, as I have suggested, modeled on the godly "master of the maze" of the illumination from the Book of Kells, the father's function in the poem as master of pageants and festivals in canto v is most crucial to the poem's initial movement, which reaches its climax at the end of the fifth canto. The role of the father in the poem has been variously interpreted; he has been seen, for example, as a symbol for the creative imagination,[5] as the creator-father who becomes an object of contempt,[6] as a combination of Jehovah and Stevens's own father—"a failed Prospero,"[7] as the "Father-principle," suggesting, among other things, God the Father.[8] Focillon furnishes some help here in regard to Stevens's association of the father with pageantry—the musicians, dancers, and actors he summons to the tumultuous festival that concludes canto v. Stevens's index to *The Life of Forms in Art* contains the entry "Delacroix 60." On that page Focillon discusses both Delacroix and Rubens; the passage on Rubens is pertinent to the father's meaning for Stevens in the poem:

> ... Rubens, the diplomat and the producer of public festivals, delighted in the creation of pageants—of paintings, that is, not fashioned with canvas and brush. For this particular family of

minds has always taken actual, outward life as a plastic mate-
rial upon which it loved to impose, through the medium of
feasts and parades and balls, its own form. The substance of
art is then human life itself. In a more general way, the artist
faces life exactly as Leonardo da Vinci faced the ruined wall
that had been ravaged by time and weather, shaken by earth-
quake, stained by the waters of earth and sky, defaced by a
thousand cracks. The rest of us see in this wall only the marks
of ordinary circumstances. The artist sees in it figures of men
separately or in groups, battles, landscapes, crumbling cities—
forms. They powerfully affect his trained eyes, and are unrav-
eled and rebuilt.   [LF, 60]

In canto iv the father is introduced with the assertion that "The
cancellings, / The negations are never final" (CP, 414). The father
"measures the velocities of change" in saying "no to no and yes to
yes. He says yes / To no; and in saying yes he says farewell." Unlike
the mother, whose comfort depends on the illusion of stasis, the
father both accepts change and is "Of motion the ever-brightening
origin." The father faces life as da Vinci does in Focillon's example.
While the rest of us see, in the ruined wall ravaged by time, "only
the marks of ordinary circumstances," the father's trained eye and
ear are powerfully affected:

He assumes the great speeds of space and flutters them
From cloud to cloudless, cloudless to keen clear

In flights of eye and ear, the highest eye
And the lowest ear, the deep ear that discerns,
At evening, things that attend it until it hears

The supernatural preludes of its own,
At the moment when the angelic eye defines
Its actors approaching, in company, in their masks.   [CP, 414]

With the approach of the actors in their masks, the father as-
sumes his role as master of festivals, Stevens's figure for the artist.
Like Focillon's artist, he delights in the creation of pageants, for he
is of a "family of minds [that] has always taken actual, outward life
as a plastic material upon which it loved to impose, through the
medium of feasts and parades and balls, its own form." The father
demonstrates, as does Focillon's example of Rubens, that the "sub-
stance of art is . . . human life itself" and that the metamorphoses
of art are manifestations of the essential principle of flux at the
heart of the poem:

The mother invites humanity to her house
And table. The father fetches tellers of tales
And musicians who mute much, muse much, on the tales.

The father fetches negresses to dance,
Among the children, like curious ripenesses
Of pattern in the dance's ripening.

For these the musicians make insidious tones,
Clawing the sing-song of their instruments.
The children laugh and jangle a tinny time.

The father fetches pageants out of air,
Scenes of the theatre, vistas and blocks of woods
And curtains like a naive pretence of sleep.   [CP, 415]

The first half of the poem ends with the festival degenerated into riot, a "loud disordered mooch" with "brute-like guests" (CP, 415) in a pattern similar to the passage in Focillon that begins with Rubens as master of festivals and ends with da Vinci facing the chaos and ravage of nature and time. Focillon's artist, like Stevens's, says yes to no, as well as yes to yes. Helen Vendler reads this chaotic climax as the poem's "denial of meaning to poetic gesture," the father as creator having become an "object of contempt."[9] Bloom likewise interprets the conclusion of canto v as evidence that the father is "a failed translator, of desire into fiction."[10] These readings, however, appear to me too strong in their condemnation of the father, and they ignore the inevitable direction of the poem's initial five cantos, in which the opening image of form gulping after formlessness is traced progressively through the realms of matter, mind or feeling, and, finally, art. The progression seems deliberate, and it ends with the dissolution of what had been Stevens's most cherished defense against chaos, the supreme fiction of the artist. In the first half of the poem, however, all ideas of order are bid farewell, and the poem must begin anew with canto vi.

Its new beginning is foreshadowed in the theatrical imagery that concludes canto v:

We stand in the tumult of a festival.

What festival? This loud, disordered mooch?
These hospitaliers? These brute-like guests?
These musicians dubbing at a tragedy,

A-dub, a-dub, which is made up of this:
That there are no lines to speak? There is no play.
Or, the persons act one merely by being here.   [CP, 415–16]

These lines suggest, first, the inability of art to order permanently
that which is inherently without order—the pervasive flux that
changes "to no end, / Except the lavishing of itself in change" (CP,
416). There are "no lines to speak" because the force at work in the
universe can be contained only momentarily in language. But more
significant than this—and it is the conceit that controls the second
half of the poem—is the implication that the actors are part of a
play not of their making "merely by being here." That is, without
their lines to speak, they become the personae of an inhuman au-
thor whose theater is figured at the beginning of canto vi as the
auroras of autumn:

It is a theatre floating through the clouds,
Itself a cloud, although of misted rock
And mountains running like water, wave on wave. . . .[CP, 416]

Having bid farewell one by one to the comforting ideas of order
in the first half of the poem, the speaker must face directly the
remaining chaos—if it is indeed chaos. In canto vi the theater of
change represented by the auroras is seen at first as idle change
operating to no end except that of change itself:

It is of cloud transformed
To cloud transformed again, idly, the way
A season changes color to no end,

Except the lavishing of itself in change,
As light changes yellow into gold and gold
To its opal elements and fire's delight,

Splashed wide-wise because it likes magnificence
And the solemn pleasures of magnificent space.
The cloud drifts idly through half-thought-of forms.   [CP, 416]

An undercurrent in this passage qualifies the notion of purposeless
change. What is the ambiguous "it" described here—as in "it likes
magnificence / And the solemn pleasures of magnificent space"?
And who thinks the "half-thought-of forms"? The recurrence of
Focillon's language leads to the suspicion that even here, in the
midst of seeming chaos, something like Focillon's life of forms is in
motion—Stevens's fictional version of an unseen essence mani-

festing itself through metamorphosis. In his chapter "Forms in the Realm of Space" Focillon attributes the same motive to change, noting that "space as an environment . . . delights in the scattering of volumes, in the interplay of voids, in sudden and unexpected perforation . . . tumbled planes which rend the light asunder" (LF, 27). In his description of "the system of the labyrinth" in the same chapter, he might almost be describing Stevens's auroras: "As the eye moves across the labyrinth in confusion, misled by a linear caprice that is perpetually sliding away to a secret objective of its own, a new dimension suddenly emerges, which is neither a dimension of motion nor of depth, but which still gives us the illusion of being so" (LF, 20). What is evident in canto vi is Stevens's use of Focillon's language of metamorphosis, attributing to the caprice of change "a secret objective of its own" as well as the ability to manifest "half-thought-of forms" in the changing drifts of clouds.

Stevens differs from Focillon, however, in seeing this presence initially as a fearful phenomenon. The motive of the second half of the poem is to discover a means of confronting it without the conventional defenses:

> This is nothing until in a single man contained,
> Nothing until this named thing nameless is
> And is destroyed. He opens the door of his house
>
> On flames. The scholar of one candle sees
> An arctic effulgence flaring on the frame
> Of everything he is. And he feels afraid. [CP, 416–17]

Focillon notes that "time, like space, is nothing unless it has been really lived" (LF, 66), and this seems to be Stevens's sense in the first stanza above. An intellectual understanding of the phenomenon as "flux" or "metamorphosis" is nothing compared to the "nameless" experience of it. But to render it nameless by experiencing it directly is also to destroy it as a "named thing" by recognizing that the traditional names or ideas for it are now inadequate. The "scholar of one candle" is afraid, because he now sees the frailty of the individual imagination in the presence of an external intelligence that is of the same order as his one candle but that overwhelms it in its magnitude.

Examining the ambiguous images of the second half of the poem, Donald Davie observes, "We cannot tell from them whether we ought to believe that there is no principle governing the world except the principle of continual change, or that, in some way as yet unexplored, the metamorphoses of the world prove the existence of some more constant principle underlying them."[11] Davie here points to an issue that most readers of the poem have ignored or have successfully skirted, although the issue could be posed somewhat differently. One could say, rather, that Stevens's assumption in the second half of the poem is that the metamorphoses of the world imply the existence of some principle underlying them; we have some difficulty in knowing exactly how to respond to this assumption, however, because the speaker himself shies away from the implications of what he says. One of Stevens's favorite devices for hedging is to frame assertions as questions. This is the strategy for the three key assertions that begin canto vii, where, as we have already seen, Focillon's conception of a living world of forms becomes the poem's principle underlying the metamorphoses detailed in the preceding six cantos:

Is there an imagination that sits enthroned
As grim as it is benevolent, the just
And the unjust, which in the midst of summer stops

To imagine winter? When the leaves are dead,
Does it take its place in the north and enfold itself,
Goat-leaper, crystalled and luminous, sitting

In highest night? And do these heavens adorn
And proclaim it, the white creator of black, jetted
By extinguishings, even of planets as may be,

Even of earth, even of sight, in snow,
Except as needed by way of majesty,
In the sky, as crown and diamond cabala?   [CP, 417]

This interrogation plants the conception so firmly in the poem that, later in the canto, Stevens shifts from question to statement, dropping the tentative tone for a more assertive voice.

By the end of the canto Stevens is describing the nature of his cosmic principle and suggesting how it is made and unmade:

It leaps through us, through all our heavens leaps,
Extinguishing our planets, one by one,
Leaving, of where we were and looked, of where

We knew each other and of each other thought,
A shivering residue, chilled and foregone,
Except for that crown and mystical cabala.

But it dare not leap by chance in its own dark.
It must change from destiny to slight caprice.
And thus its jetted tragedy, its stele

And shape and mournful making move to find
What must unmake it and, at last, what can,
Say, a flippant communication under the moon.   [CP, 417–18]

The first two tercets here recall the chill of cantos ii and iii, in which "where we were and looked" and "where / We knew each other and of each other thought" are left a "shivering residue." The last two tercets are among the most difficult of the poem and have generally resisted the best efforts of readers. They deserve, therefore, a somewhat more detailed analysis.

Davie reads the argument of the passage this way: "An iron law of continual change *does* govern nature, but the presiding genius, the Father, has to make exceptions to this—'must change from destiny to slight caprice'—just so as not to be ruled by his own law."[12] The problem with this reading is that the passage seems to say the opposite. The "jetted tragedy" of Stevens's cosmic principle is that "it dare not leap by chance" and so, obeying its own law of change, its "stele" or "shape" moves "to find / What must unmake it." Bloom, who calls this "the most surprising passage in *The Auroras of Autumn*, and perhaps in all of Stevens," misreads the passage in a particularly willful manner, one that reveals why he finds the passage so surprising. Like Davie, he fixes on the term *caprice* as evidence that Stevens's borealis "is not a necessity at all, moving by laws of its own, but an interplay, and endless decentering of itself." In this reading "the flaring auroras are therefore only a kind of commemorative tablet whose shape and mournful making alike are subject to change, to whim, to an unmaking by man as the only maker of meaning, and by way of any flippant communication under the moon."[13] Such a reading ignores the entire first half of the poem. If it were so easy to dismiss the implication of the auroras, to make the principle of flux subject to the whim of the poet, then the first five stanzas would have no place in the poem and the magnitude of Stevens's fiction of the enthroned imagination would be greatly diminished. More than that, however, the syntax of the passage clearly makes the cosmic principle itself, and not the poet, the cause of its own unmaking. Helen Vendler reads the passage more carefully than either Davie or Bloom, but she achieves no more than a paraphrase that appears to her inadequate: "The only force regulating the leaper is its necessary polarity: 'it dare not leap by chance,' but it moves to unmake itself in comic flippancy—or so Stevens says."[14] An overpowering presence that can be undone by its own comic flippancy seems utterly unconvincing, and Vendler dismisses Stevens's conclusion as "an imposed order, not a discovered one."[15]

These readings can stand as illustrations of a range of failures to make this section of the poem accessible, although in fairness it should be noted that the opacity of the passage lies to some extent in Stevens's overly generous borrowing from his source. All of the crucial conceptions of the passage are from Focillon, and Stevens seems to have assumed too readily implications that were not available to his readers. Bloom asks: "Why dare the aurora borealis not leap by chance in its own dark?"[16] One answer is that Stevens patterned the presence represented by the aurora borealis after Focillon's life of forms, and Focillon insists that the "life of forms is not the result of chance. Nor is it a great cyclorama neatly fitted into the theatre of history and called into being by historical necessities. No; forms obey their own rules" (LF, 12). Stevens's cosmic principle is likewise neither happenstance nor necessity, but an originator of transient forms manifest through metamorphosis. "It must change from destiny to slight caprice," and the misreadings of this line have led Davie, Bloom, and the other commentators astray. The line has been interpreted as if it argued that the force represented by the auroras was formerly ruled by some law but now has shifted in its principle to caprice, caprice seen (as Bloom defines it) as freedom from law. But *caprice* suggests, in its operative meaning here, not lawlessness but an inexplicable law—a change that is impossible to explain or to predict for those who observe it from outside. Focillon uses the term in exactly this sense in an earlier-cited passage devoted to the metamorphoses of form. In a description of the "labyrinth" of mobile forms that "stretches itself out in a realm of glittering movement and color," like Stevens's aurora borealis, he notes that "the eye moves across the labyrinth in confusion, misled by a linear caprice that is perpetually sliding away to a secret objective of its own" (LF, 20). It is not that forms obey no law, but that they obey their own secret law, the ignorance of which renders their action capricious to the observer. The crucial lines, then, may be understood in this manner: Stevens's cosmic force changes its form neither by chance on the one hand nor by necessity or destiny on the other. It represents neither lawlessness nor subservience to a law external to itself. It obeys its own seemingly capricious laws so that its present forms may be unmade by what appear to us the lightest, most flippant of circumstances.

The second general misreading of the passage is that the force of the auroras is undone or destroyed at the conclusion of canto vii, the assumption of both Vendler and Bloom. Who could have guessed, Bloom asks innocently, "that the sinister splendor of the auroras would be undone by 'Say, a flippant communication under the moon' "?[17] The question is misleading on two counts. First, the auroras are not undone in Bloom's sense; second, their unmaking, in quite a different sense, is attributed to the auroras and not, as Bloom states later, to the poet who observes them. Reading the passage attentively, we see that the "jetted tragedy" of the auroras (or, more correctly, of the secret law they represent) follows from the fact that this law operates not by chance: "It must change from destiny to slight caprice. / *And thus* its jetted tragedy." The apparent tragedy suggested by the auroras is that they must obey their own law, one of constant flux. This means that the "stele / And shape and mournful making" of the presence in the northern sky must move "to find / What must unmake it," the "it" referring to its shape or form (as if it were a stone pillar constantly being destroyed and reshaped), and not the essence of the presence itself. Its making seems mournful to the speaker because its principle of creation is to escape whatever form currently manifests it. Since this form "leaps through us" and all our universe, "Extinguishing our planets, one by one," we and our world are the forms that now manifest it and that it must escape in its relentless pursuit of its own renewal in new forms.

Stevens is here quite faithful to Focillon, who observes repeatedly that the life of forms is maintained only through "the principle of metamorphoses, by which they are perpetually renewed ... first tested, then made fast, and finally disrupted" (LF, 6): "form is a will-o'-the-wisp, an uncertain note in a universe forever in flight. An examination, therefore, no matter how cursory, of the various conceptions of space shows us that the life of forms is renewed over and over again, and that, far from evolving according to fixed postulates, constantly and universally intelligible, it creates various new geometries even at the heart of geometry itself. Indeed, the life of forms is never at a loss to create any matter, any substance whatsoever of which it stands in need" (LF, 35). What thus may seem to an observer "form gulping after formlessness," a "will-o'-the-wisp," or even, "Say, a flippant communication under the moon" rather than "fixed postulates, constantly and universally intelligible" is the law by which the life of forms is sustained. They are simultaneously made and unmade by a principle that, for the first seven cantos of the poem, appears fearful and tragic, but that is finally accepted in canto viii as "a time of innocence / As pure principle" (CP, 418). I have lingered over the conclusion of canto vii because it is a crux of the poem, and one that has consistently been misread. It anticipates the "turn" of the poem from a kind of fearful stoicism to innocent acceptance, and the "time of innocence" of the last three cantos follows from the speaker's acknowledgment that the principle of metamorphosis represented by the auroras is, as in Focillon's aesthetic, a principle necessary to the continuing life of all natural forms.

The turn of the poem in canto viii was implicit from the first in the description of the serpent as "the master of the maze / Of body and air and forms and images, / Relentlessly in possession of happiness." The serpent's poison is "that we should disbelieve / Even that," but only after his transformation of the serpent to Focillon's principle of metamorphosis as a renewer of forms in canto vii does the speaker himself come to believe that the flux of the auroras is an "innocence of the earth and no false sign / Or symbol of malice" (CP, 418). *The Life of Forms in Art* is thus central to "The Auroras of Autumn" not only in providing a great deal of its incidental imagery and figuration, but also in suggesting a conception of change by which the issue of the poem finds a resolution. Stevens, it is true, broadens Focillon's aesthetic principle to include all natural life, and he transforms Focillon's principle into a metaphor or fiction that extends it beyond the realm of art. Stevens conceives a universal life of natural forms as the manifestations of an enthroned god-imagination that animates them in pursuit of its own secret ends. Yet even this extension of his conception is anticipated by Focillon, who notes, "Nature as well as life creates forms. So beautifully does she impress shape and symmetry upon the very elements of which she herself is made and upon the forces with which she animates them that men have been pleased to regard her from time to time as the work of some God-artist, some unknown and guileful Hermes, the inventor and contriver" (LF, 3). Stevens's enthroned imagination is not Hermes, but it has retained some of the qualities of Hermes as inventor and contriver, and the "happy world" of the poem's conclusion is referred to as "This contrivance of the spectre of the spheres, / Contriving balance to contrive a whole" (CP, 420). Stevens's use of the term *stele*—inscribed stone pillar—to describe the evolving form of his god-imagination also recalls Hermes, who was commemorated by the stelae representing his phallic origin. It is also possible that the appellation "goatleaper" was suggested by the Hermes myth, especially by Hermes's role as the father of Pan.[18] These associations may, however, be purely fortuitous, or at most incidental, for Stevens appears to regard his fiction of the enthroned imagination not as a god but as a god might be. It is more than an expedient to resolve the questions the poem raises, and less than an assertion of a supernatural power.

He hedges in a similar manner in his conception of innocence in canto viii. Innocence is Stevens's label for a condition of acceptance of the force enunciated in the preceding canto as benevolent, obeying its own laws, "relentlessly in possession of happiness." Innocence is first conceived as a time, "never a place" (CP, 418). It is a time, we learn later, in the sense that when "we partake thereof," we "Lie down like children in this holiness" (CP, 418). Yet even that sense of innocence is qualified:

> Or if there is no time,
> If it is not a thing of time, nor of place,
>
> Existing in the idea of it, alone,
> In the sense against calamity, it is not
> Less real. For the oldest and coldest philosopher,
>
> There is or may be a time of innocence
> As pure principle. Its nature is its end,
> That it should be, and yet not be. . . .   [CP, 418]

The notion of innocence as an "idea," a "sense against calamity," or a "pure principle" is close to Stevens's conception of the cosmic imagination in the preceding canto; its nature is that it both is and is not. It exists, like Focillon's life of forms, in particular manifestations, but its own existence is as principle or predicate:

> It is like a thing of ether that exists
> Almost as predicate. But it exists,
> It exists, it is visible, it is, it is.
>
> So, then, these lights are not a spell of light,
> A saying out of a cloud, but innocence.
> An innocence of the earth and no false sign
>
> Or symbol of malice.   [CP, 418]

Curiously, the existence of innocence is proven by the visible northern lights, which at this point have become the embodiment

of a benevolent force that (in canto ix) brings change and ulti-
mately death "Almost as part of innocence, almost, / Almost as the
tenderest and the truest part" (CP, 420).

Canto ix, like the penultimate section of "Sunday Morning,"
shows us the consequences of accepting the fiction urged in the
poem—to be "as Danes in Denmark all day long" (CP, 419), to re-
turn to a time of innocence modeled on the childhood world. The
final canto, however, returns to Stevens's great conception of the
enthroned imagination. His characterization of it here, had it come
earlier, would have made clearer the bridge between cantos vii and
viii, between the positing of such a presence and the recovery of
innocence. We are an "unhappy people in a happy world" (CP, 420),
the final canto argues, because we are unable to accept the premise
of the "rabbi" of the poem, the "scholar of one candle," who con-
cludes by reading to his congregation the lesson for today, a sum-
mary of the poem's implications:

Turn back to where we were when we began:
An unhappy people in a happy world.
Now, solemnize the secretive syllables.

Read to the congregation, for today
And for tomorrow, this extremity,
This contrivance of the spectre of the spheres,

Contriving balance to contrive a whole,
The vital, the never-failing genius,
Fulfilling his meditations, great and small.   [CP, 420]

It is a happy world because its changes are governed by a force
"Relentlessly in possession of happiness." We are an unhappy peo-
ple because we cannot achieve a state of innocence in which we
accept, as "pure principle," a life-giving and unfailing genius "Con-
triving balance to contrive a whole."

To conceive such a whole, as the poem does in the final two
tercets, is to adopt a conception of individual lives as the manifes-
tations of an essential life of forms, a conception that bears a re-
lation to these lives analogous to the relation that the essential
poem of "A Primitive Like an Orb" bears to individual poems: "It is
something seen and known in lesser poems" (CP, 440). The "never-
failing genius" of "The Auroras of Autumn" is conceived as the
essential life at the center of things, "miraculous multiplex" (CP,
442) of all lives, which he lives so that he might know all forms of
experience—not the stasis of "hushful paradise," but the exhilara-
tion of change. When he is introduced in canto vii, he stops in the

midst of summer to imagine winter, and the implications are grim. In the last line of the poem the cycle is completed, and we recognize at last that the principle he represents is as benevolent as it is grim:

> In these unhappy he meditates a whole,
> The full of fortune and the full of fate,
> As if he lived all lives, that he might know,
>
> In hall harridan, not hushful paradise,
> To a haggling of wind and weather, by these lights
> Like a blaze of summer straw, in winter's nick.   [CP, 420–21]

Clearly the force of the auroras was not undone at the end of canto vii, as has been suggested by the most practiced readers of the poem. The failure to take seriously Stevens's figuration of the contriving genius has led to oddly contorted interpretations of the poem's conclusion.

To return to the three distinguished critics whose readings of the poem I have set against my own, we may observe how each struggles with the final tercets. Davie, who offered his early reading as pure elucidation, innocent of the knowledge of any larger biographical or theoretical context, reaches this conclusion: "The poet decided that man's destiny is as it is because God requires in His Creation, before it can satisfy Him, an element of conflict to be reconciled, and hence a margin of freedom for man that leaves him capable of heroism."[19] This religious interpretation, hardly justified by the language of the poem, has at least the virtue of acknowledging the presence of some godlike force external to the poet's own imagination, an implication skirted by both Vendler and Bloom. Vendler's careful and detailed analysis of earlier cantos gives way to a noncommittal summary of the poem's conclusion: "Exposed to the auroras, Stevens, like Melville's dying soldier, has been 'enlightened by the glare,' and the final flippancy of the last canto, juggling discrepant phases of man's feelings and the world's landscapes, still yields, at the end, to the total reign of the auroras, 'these lights / Like a blaze of summer straw, in winter's nick.' "[20] Earlier in her reading she appeared closer to granting Stevens's serpent-aurora-spectre a more significant meaning in the poem, but she concluded that the reconciliation for which it reaches, "described in 'St. John and the Backache,' is not attained in *The Auroras of Autumn*, which remains bound in its glittering motion, a brilliant reproduction of Stevens's apprehensive compulsion in change."[21] Bloom ignores the implications of the final tercets, misreading Stevens's "spectre of the spheres" as "the never-failing genius of poetry," and concluding that it is the poet's imagination that knows "the full of fortune and the full of fate," as if it were the poet who "lived all lives."[22]

Given the extravagance of what the poem says, there is admittedly a temptation to have it say something more conventional. To ignore the implications of Stevens's central figure of the enthroned imagination, however, is to deny the poem its own fiction and to make nonsense of several key passages, most notably the concluding tercets of cantos vii and x. Moreover, to interpret Stevens's figuration of the auroras as merely a metaphor for the poet's imagination—Bloom's reading—is to conclude with Bloom that "all that the flash reveals to Stevens is change and ourselves as the origin of the meaning of change."[23] Such a conclusion overlooks one notable departure from the earlier verse implied in "The Auroras of Autumn," and that is Stevens's attempt to move beyond the individual imagination as the origin and measure of all meaning. The first half of the poem explicitly denies this assumption in its breaking down of all forms of order celebrated in Stevens's earlier verse. The second half of the poem is built on the elaborate conceit of an external imagination whose meditation, and not our own, is the origin and measure of our experience, "The full of fortune and the full of fate." The paradox of the poem is not that we imagine this presence but that it imagines us, not that we live its life vicariously but that it lives ours fully and completely. It is true that the absence of the individual imagination in the poem had itself to be imagined—that Stevens's depiction of the subservience of the poet's imagination to a more powerful external presence represents one of his greatest feats of the imagination—but that is a trap Stevens is forced to consider in the poems following "The Auroras of Autumn"; it occupies him throughout his last poems, as Helen Regueiro has shown in her study of Stevens's attempts to transcend the limits of the romantic imagination.[24]

Focillon's contribution to this effort, as I have tried to demonstrate, was a conception of art that transferred the center of creativity from the mind and craft of the individual artist to an essential life of art that obeys its own laws and, to this extent, transcends the purely personal and idiosyncratic rule of the artist. To put it in Stevens's terms in "A Primitive Like an Orb," it is a conception of art in which "The essential poem begets the others" (CP, 441), not the reverse (which would be something like Eliot's notion, in "Tradition and the Individual Talent," of a static ideal order of existing works of art, an ideal that is modified by the introduction of the new work). It is understandable that Stevens would not have been content to rest with this conception as a mere aesthetic principle, and in "The Auroras of Autumn" it becomes the cosmic principle underlying the phenomenon of flux. As a natural law it appears to exist on the same ontological basis as the aesthetic law of "A Primitive Like an Orb." We do not prove its existence; it is something seen and known in its lesser embodiments. Its ultimate ontological status for Stevens, it appears, was as one of the sustaining fictions of his last poems, for after its first significant appearance in "Credences of Summer," versions of the fiction of the inhuman author or of the world as the meditation of a cosmic mind appear with some frequency in the verse of the final two volumes.

In *The Auroras of Autumn* traces of this figure appear in "Large Red Man Reading." Ghosts, disappointed with a heaven that has turned out to be less than expected, return to earth to hear a mythic personage read from the "poem of life" (CP, 423). The large red man is apparently the earth itself; his poem, composed of the commonplaces of life—"the pans above the stove, the pots on the table, the tulips among them" (CP, 423)—is the reality that the ghosts "would have wept" (CP, 424) to feel again. The cosmic poet reads "from out of the purple tabulae / The outlines of being and its expressings, the syllables of its law" (CP, 424). In "The Ultimate Poem Is Abstract" the figure appears again as "The lecturer / On This Beautiful World of Ours" who "composes himself / And hems the planet rose and haws it ripe, / And red, and right" (CP, 429). The ultimate poem of the title is the abstraction or fiction of the world as the composition of a cosmic intellect—"Not an intellect in which we are fleet: present / Everywhere in space at once, cloud-pale / Of communication" (CP, 430). In "Metaphor as Degeneration" the figure is "a man in black space" who "Sits in nothing that we know, / Brooding sounds of river noises" (CP, 444), and in "Puella Parvula" the coming of autumn is the triumph of a "mighty imagination" that devours Africa and dissolves Gibraltar "like spit in the wind." The heart and mind of the man who observes the workings of this imagination are subdued by the force of "The dauntless master, as he starts the human tale" (CP, 456).

The fiction of the world as the meditation of a pensive nature "free / From man's ghost" (CP, 517–18) is treated at somewhat greater length in two poems of *The Rock*, "Looking Across the Fields and Watching the Birds Fly" (CP, 517) and "The World as Meditation" (CP, 520). Vestiges of this conceit also appear in several other of Stevens's last poems. In "An Old Man Asleep" the title refers equally to "The self and the world" (CP, 501), the world conceived as if its objects were the thoughts of a sluggish mind. "The Plain Sense of Things" toys with a notion of the change of seasons as the failure of a "fantastic effort" of imagination (CP, 502). In "Two Illustrations That the World Is What You Make of It," the wind is a "thought," though one that "was not his thought, nor anyone's"; it is "The breath of another nature" (CP, 513). These poems and others—"Final Soliloquy of the Interior Paramour" (CP, 524) and "Note on Moonlight" (CP, 531), for example—suggest that conceptions of the world as a "central mind" (CP, 524) or as a "poet revolving in his mind / The sameness of his various universe" (CP, 531) had become habitual with Stevens by the time of *The Rock*. At this point the figure has also become wholly Stevens's own; little trace of its origin in Focillon remains.

Curiously, however, in "Looking Across the Fields and Watching the Birds Fly" Stevens refuses to take responsibility for the conception, attributing it to an earlier scholar who appears to be modeled on Emerson. It is introduced as one of "the more irritating minor ideas / Of Mr. Homburg during his visits home / To Concord" (CP, 517). Having distanced himself from the extravagance of the concept, Stevens then proceeds to delineate it in a manner that both belies his disclaimer and reveals its un-Emersonian nature:

To think away the grass, the trees, the clouds,
Not to transform them into other things,
Is only what the sun does every day,

Until we say to ourselves that there may be
A pensive nature, a mechanical
And slightly detestable *operandum*, free

From man's ghost, larger and yet a little like,
Without his literature and without his gods. . . .   [CP, 517–18]

This pensive nature does not have its origin in the human imagination; it is "A thing not planned for imagery or belief, / Not one of the masculine myths we used to make" (CP, 518). Like the capricious master of flux detected in the auroras or the central poem known in lesser poems, the world as meditation is glimpsed in its natural manifestations. It is

What we know in what we see, what we feel in what
We hear, what we are, beyond mystic disputation,
In the tumult of integrations out of the sky,

And what we think, a breathing like the wind,
A moving part of a motion, a discovery
Part of a discovery, a change part of a change. . . .   [CP, 518]

Like the god-imagination of "The Auroras of Autumn," it also leaps
through us, so that what we think is equally a discovery of another
order of thought.

It is, in fact, as thought or meditation that Stevens comes closest
to the nature of this external presence free from his own spirit "and
yet a little like." Like many of the late poems, "Looking Across the
Fields and Watching the Birds Fly" attempts to preserve the inde-
pendent existence of a world that does not originate in the poet's
mind—to imagine the absence of the imagination, one of the chief
tasks of the late poems—and one means of its preservation is to
grant it a mind of its own as source, not consequence, of the poet's
thought:

The afternoon is visibly a source,
Too wise, too irised, to be more than calm,

Too much like thinking to be less than thought,
Obscurest parent, obscurest patriarch,
A daily majesty of meditation,

That comes and goes in silences of its own.   [CP, 518]

It is not, then, that the world exists as we think, but that "We think
. . . as the sun shines or does not. / We think as wind skitters on a
pond in a field" (CP, 518). In the same reversal contained in "The
Auroras of Autumn," Stevens here grants priority to external re-
ality, so that "The spirit comes from the body of the world," a world
"Whose blunt laws make an affectation of mind" (CP, 519). The
poem is presented finally as the reflections of "A new scholar re-
placing an older one," a scholar who "seeks / For a human that can
be accounted for" (CP, 519). It suggests the distance Stevens has
moved from the inwardly directed scholar of *Notes toward a Su-
preme Fiction*.

"Looking Across the Fields and Watching the Birds Fly" could
have been as appropriately entitled "The World as Meditation,"
and the poem of that title echoes its central fiction. "The World as
Meditation" is a late "Sunday Morning," with the addition of Ste-
vens's now familiar "inhuman meditation" (CP, 521) as a replace-
ment for the more general notion of change in the earlier poem.
Like the woman in "Sunday Morning," Penelope in "The World as
Meditation" desires one kind of comfort but receives another. The

reveries of the women in both poems are redirected by the persona toward the world of change as the source of satisfaction of their desires. The difference, however, and a measure of Stevens's own redirection between *Harmonium* and *The Rock*, is that while "Sunday Morning" moves inward, "The World as Meditation" moves outward. In "Sunday Morning" the woman is reminded that "Divinity must live within herself" (CP, 67), in the passions, grievings, elations, and emotions of her response to a chaotic world. Like the singer of "The Idea of Order at Key West," she is the single artificer of the world she makes. For Penelope, however, another artificer is present, and its "savage presence awakens the world in which she dwells" (CP, 520).

Penelope's meditation on the return of Ulysses leads to the awareness of another meditation greater than her own but of a like nature, as the approach of Ulysses from the east becomes the approach of the sun:

Is it Ulysses that approaches from the east,
The interminable adventurer? The trees are mended.
That winter is washed away. Someone is moving

On the horizon and lifting himself up above it.
A form of fire approaches the cretonnes of Penelope,
Whose mere savage presence awakens the world in which she
    dwells.   [CP, 520]

It is not, finally, Ulysses who comes, "only the warmth of the sun / On her pillow" (CP, 521). But the two have become one—"It was Ulysses and it was not"—since her desires are equally satisfied by this presence, "Friend and dear friend and a planet's encouragement." The mending of the trees and washing away of winter—household duties like those Penelope knows—are "an essential exercise / In an inhuman meditation larger than her own." Her world is neither chaotic nor foreign to her; rather, it is a coherent though inhuman presence always approaching from outside. Since "She wanted nothing he could not bring her by coming alone," Ulysses and the inhuman meditation have merged by the end of the poem:

She would talk a little to herself as she combed her hair,
Repeating his name with its patient syllables,
Never forgetting him that kept coming constantly so near.
                                                   [CP, 521]

Identifying his inhuman meditation with Ulysses allows Stevens to humanize it and to confer on it an existence separate from Penelope's own meditation. Ulysses is the object of her reverie, but his "interminable" adventures do not originate in her mind in the way that the divine object of desire in "Sunday Morning" can come "Only in silent shadows and in dreams" (CP, 67). What is noteworthy in a comparison of early and late Stevens is the degree to which the world of the later verse has acquired a separate external existence. This tendency, which becomes more noticeable after "Credences of Summer" and "The Auroras of Autumn," so frequently incorporates the conceit of the world as meditation or imagination that one feels justified in equating Stevens's use of the figure with his search for the conception of reality he describes in his theoretical prose: "reality as it impinges upon us from outside, the sense that we can touch and feel a solid reality which does not wholly dissolve itself into the conceptions of our own minds" (NA, 96). This was, I suspect, one appeal of Focillon's theory for Stevens, its ability to grant existence to a life of forms apart from their human creators. Focillon's contribution to Stevens's last two volumes almost certainly extends beyond those poems that contain verbal echoes of *The Life of Forms in Art*. His more general influence on the poetry, as is the case with the prose, was to provide an aesthetic model that ran counter to Stevens's earlier tendency to ennoble the individual imagination at the expense of the external world. That tendency subsided after *Notes toward a Supreme Fiction*, and "The Auroras of Autumn" is to some extent a farewell to that phase of Stevens's work. The direction in Stevens's poetry initiated fully by "The Auroras of Autumn" lasted, however, through *The Rock*, and the barren verse of the last volume may come closest to realizing an order of existence that impinges upon us from outside.

To posit a reality outside the mind and independent of the mind as source was one of Stevens's most persistent motives after "The Auroras of Autumn," expressed accurately in the title of the final poem of *The Rock*, "Not Ideas about the Thing but the Thing Itself." This last of the collected poems also demonstrates one of Stevens's most successful means of engendering a sense of a world outside the mind. In "The Auroras of Autumn" the successive annihilation of all forms of order leads to the conception of an order of existence beyond the mind's reach, and the same effect may be observed again and again in Stevens's last poems. In the world of *The Rock* we are "Natives of a dwindled sphere" facing the "stale grandeur of annihilation" (CP, 504–5). Merely to cull lines from these poems is to observe a diminished world:

> It is as if
> We had come to an end of the imagination. . . .   [CP, 502]

> Little by little, the poverty
> Of autumnal space becomes
> A look, a few words spoken.   [CP, 505]

> The effete vocabulary of summer
> No longer says anything.   [CP, 506]

> It is a kind of total grandeur at the end,
> With every visible thing enlarged. . . .   [CP, 510]

> It makes so little difference, at so much more
> Than seventy, where one looks, one has been there before.
>   [CP, 522]

> Even our shadows, their shadows, no longer remain.
> The lives these lived in the mind are at an end.   [CP, 525]

In these poems, however, the sense of having come to an end of the imagination, of the life of the mind, brings with it a concurrent enlargement of "every visible thing." Helen Regueiro has observed, in a discussion of "The Plain Sense of Things," that "the falling of the leaves points to the imagination's recognition of the barrenness that underlies every attempt at creation, but it suggests at the same time the imagination's realization that in questioning its capacity to transform and reconstruct reality it is capable of perceiving reality in its 'plainness' and its 'thingness.' "[25]

The plain sense of things, as well as the poverty of language in "Not Ideas about the Thing but the Thing Itself," gives us the sense of a final triumph over the mind. After more than five hundred pages of negotiation between mind and world, Stevens ends his collected poems by touching a separate reality outside the mind:

> At the earliest ending of winter,
> In March, a scrawny cry from outside
> Seemed like a sound in his mind.

> He knew that he heard it,
> A bird's cry, at daylight or before,
> In the early March wind.

> The sun was rising at six,
> No longer a battered panache above snow . . .
> It would have been outside.   [CP, 534]

Although the cry is at first located in the mind, the effort of the poem is to push it outside. Much earlier Stevens would have reversed the process, as he did in "The Irrational Element in Poetry" (1936); there, hearing a similar animal sound outside before daylight, he seized it as a pretext for poetry, an illustration that poetry is "the transposition of an objective reality to a subjective reality" (OP, 217).

The poem is insistent, however, that the scrawny cry is not part of a subjective reality, and its insistence on placing it outside is its only argument, the plainness and honesty of which are more compelling than theory or ingenuity. It is as if the mind's sluggish reaction to the world it wakes to discover is itself proof of that world's priority:

It was not from the vast ventriloquism
Of sleep's faded papier-mâché . . .
The sun was coming from outside.

That scrawny cry—it was
A chorister whose c preceded the choir.
It was part of the colossal sun,

Surrounded by its choral rings,
Still far away. It was like
A new knowledge of reality.   [CP, 534]

Like Penelope in "The World as Meditation," the speaker here is made aware of something colossal and inhuman; although still far away, it is always approaching from outside. His sense of it as outside the mind gives him, in the last line of the *Collected Poems*, "A new knowledge of reality."

In the "invented world" of *Notes toward a Supreme Fiction* the goal of the poet is to see the sun "in the idea of it" (CP, 380). By the time of *The Auroras of Autumn*, Stevens has said farewell to this idea, to the notion that the poet's imagination is the sole measure of his world, and at the conclusion of *The Rock* the sun, as an emblem of a colossal reality, has been firmly positioned outside the "ventriloquism" of the mind. If we are still at the end confronted with the struggle between the poet of imagination and the poet of reality, that is because Stevens chose to conduct his search in these terms in all phases of his career. I have suggested here something of the role played by Stevens's reading in critical theory in both major phases of his later poetry. The first, which owed much of its theory to Charles Mauron, reached its zenith in *Notes* in 1942; the second, indebted to Focillon, persevered to the end. The poems of imagination produced Stevens's earliest successes, but in his *Collected Poems* reality has the last word.

NOTES

CHAPTER ONE

1. "The Realistic Oriole," p. 161.
2. Ibid.
3. See, e.g., Baird, *The Dome and the Rock*, p. xix.
4. Vendler, *Wallace Stevens*, p. 32.
5. Ibid., p. 10.
6. Ibid., pp. 12, 39–40.
7. Ibid., p. 4.
8. See, e.g., Riddel, "The Contours of Stevens Criticism," pp. 265–67.
9. The idealist position may be found in Quinn, *The Metamorphic Tradition in Modern Poetry*, p. 49; the naturalistic argument is made by Frank Lentricchia in Ch. 5 of *The Gaiety of Language*.
10. A discussion of this issue appears in Hines, *The Later Poetry of Wallace Stevens*, pp. 213–15.
11. Richard Macksey argues for the dialectical pattern ("The Climates of Wallace Stevens," p. 191); J. Hillis Miller argues the opposite ("Wallace Stevens' Poetry of Being," p. 146).
12. See Schneider, *Symbolism*, p. 161.
13. The first view is held by Robert Pack in *Wallace Stevens*, pp. 147–48, 162; the second is argued in Baird, *The Dome and the Rock*, p. 281.
14. Perlis, *Wallace Stevens*, pp. 15–16.
15. Ibid., p. 150.
16. Ibid., p. 35.
17. Ibid., p. 97.
18. Regueiro, *The Limits of Imagination*, pp. 40–41.
19. Ibid., p. 149.
20. Ibid., p. 218.
21. Bloom, *Wallace Stevens: The Poems of Our Climate*, p. 168.
22. Ibid.
23. Vendler treats this subject in "The Qualified Assertions of Wallace Stevens," pp. 163–78. *On Extended Wings*, her study of Stevens's longer poems, includes some material from the earlier essay and is devoted to the same issue, as is much of her more recent study, *Wallace Stevens: Words Chosen Out of Desire*.
24. Vendler, "The Qualified Assertions of Wallace Stevens," p. 172.

25. Ibid., p. 164.

26. Ibid., p. 175.

27. Ibid., p. 164.

28. Donoghue, "Nuances of a Theme by Stevens," p. 227.

29. Miller, "Wallace Stevens' Poetry of Being," p. 146.

30. Donoghue, "Nuances of a Theme by Stevens," p. 228.

31. Miller, "Wallace Stevens' Poetry of Being," p. 146.

32. Miller, "Theoretical and Atheoretical in Stevens," p. 275.

33. Kermode, *Wallace Stevens*, p. 111.

34. Tindall, *Wallace Stevens*, p. 32.

35. See, e.g., Riddel, *The Clairvoyant Eye*, p. 41: "Indeed, the only contribution Stevens' poetics makes to modern thought is the perspectives it offers of his poems. Unlike Eliot's or even James's essays, Stevens' provide but few valid reflections of the essential nature of the artist's practice, or on the cultural phenomenon of his art. Here and there appear a few tacit suggestions on poetic form or style, on language, or the temper of the modern. But the essays in conjunction with the poems form a part of Stevens' Grand Poem."

36. I have attempted to suggest the reason for this distinction in the first section of Chapter Four.

37. All of these volumes are now located in the Special Collections of the University Library, University of Massachusetts at Amherst, along with Adams's *The Life and Writings of Giambattista Vico* and Focillon's *The Life of Forms in Art*. Richards's *Coleridge on Imagination* and Mauron's *Aesthetics and Psychology* are in the Wallace Stevens Archive of the Huntington Library.

38. He had attempted only one formal lecture, "The Irrational Element in Poetry," prior to accepting Church's invitation to participate in a series of four lectures at Princeton on "The Language of Poetry." Stevens had been dissatisfied with "The Irrational Element in Poetry" and did not include it in *The Necessary Angel*.

CHAPTER TWO

1. In letters written within a short span Stevens says both that the supreme fiction is and is not to be identified with poetry. A typical example of his attempt to avoid being pinned down is this statement to Hi Simons in January 1943: "I ought to say that I have not defined a supreme fiction. A man as familiar with my things as you are will be justified in thinking that I mean poetry. I don't want to say that I don't mean poetry; I don't know what I mean" (L, 435). See also pp. 407, 430, 438.

2. Pound, "A Few Don'ts by an Imagiste," p. 203. It is interesting that Pound, like Stevens after him, issued his pronouncement on abstraction under the guise of the "master" instructing the fledgling poet—Pound's "neophyte," Stevens's "ephebe."

3. *Stevens' Poetry of Thought* is, of course, Doggett's influential study of the ideas and concepts in Stevens's poetry. An earlier essay, "Abstraction and Wallace Stevens," was incorporated into *Stevens' Poetry of Thought*. Donoghue's remark appears in "Nuances of a Theme by Stevens," p. 235; he has examined the issue in more detail in "Wallace Stevens and the Abstract." Jarrell's famous attack on Stevens (later moderated) as "G. E. Moore at the spinet" may be found in his "Reflections on Wallace Stevens."

4. Jarrell, "Reflections on Wallace Stevens," p. 140.

5. Doggett, *Stevens' Poetry of Thought*, p. 213. Doggett defines Stevens's abstract fiction as "a mental construction based on perception and elaborated by thought" (p. 102).

6. See Doggett, *Wallace Stevens: The Making of the Poem*, pp. 107–8. Doggett notes that, by 1942, Stevens "recognized the shift that had occurred in notions of what was appropriate for poetry." By 1943, he "was committed to a recognition of the place of ideas in his poetry."

7. Donoghue, "Wallace Stevens and the Abstract," p. 391.

8. Ibid.

9. Ibid., pp. 398–99.

10. Ibid., p. 406.

11. Tompkins, " 'To Abstract Reality,' " p. 98. Like Donoghue, Tompkins assumes an identity between Stevens's prose statements on abstraction and his practice. Unlike Donoghue, however, Tompkins sees this practice as resulting not in an escape from reality to the structures of imagination but, paradoxically, as a tendency in the opposite direction: "The mind, which had set out to describe reality, finds that its own restlessness prevents such description, and that the abstracted and immobile certainty it sought required, in fact, its own elimination" (99).

12. Regueiro, *The Limits of Imagination*, p. 192.

13. See especially Heringman, "Wallace Stevens," p. 6; Benamou, *Wallace Stevens and the Symbolist Imagination*, p. xxv; and Lentricchia, *The Gaiety of Language*, p. 139.

14. Martz, "Wallace Stevens," p. 145.

15. Bloom, *"Notes toward a Supreme Fiction*: A Commentary," pp. 78, 83.

16. Bloom, *Wallace Stevens: The Poems of Our Climate*, p. 173.

17. Miller, *Poets of Reality*, pp. 217–84. A shorter version of the essay appeared the same year in *The Act of the Mind*, pp. 143–62.

18. Stevens states, "Modern reality is a reality of decreation, in which our revelations are not the revelations of belief, but the precious portents of our own powers. The greatest truth we could hope to discover, in whatever field we discovered it, is that man's truth is the final resolution of everything" (NA, 175). I will return to the concept later in the essay.

19. Miller, *Poets of Reality*, p. 247.

20. Ibid., pp. 247–48.

21. Ibid., p. 248. In more recent discussions of Stevens there is some indication that Miller has modified the view stated here. I will discuss

these apparent modifications later in the chapter. However, it should be pointed out that Miller's possible retreat from this position does not lessen the significance of the reading of Stevens's poetry given in *Poets of Reality*, which has become one of the dominant approaches among the host of critics influenced by Miller.

22. Kermode, *Wallace Stevens*, p. 112.

23. Pearce, *The Continuity of American Poetry*, p. 396. In a recent essay Pearce echoes this early view: "Reality is 'abstract', since to know it under the condition of decreation we must abstract from it the idea of a creator. . . . Sponsored by no one, existing as nothing but uncreated *Ding an Sich*, reality necessarily yields to perception that at long last conceivable idea of a Supreme Fiction" ("Toward Decreation," p. 294).

24. Riddel, *The Clairvoyant Eye*, p. 166.

25. Perlis, *Wallace Stevens*, p. 28.

26. "Stevens uses the word 'idea' in its original meaning of 'direct sense image'" (Miller, *Poets of Reality*, p. 248).

27. "I think that the critic is under obligation to base his remarks on what he has before him. It is not a question of what an author meant to say but of what he has said. . . . This goes to the extent of saying that it would be legitimate for a critic to make statements respecting the purpose of an author's work that were altogether contrary to the intentions of the author" (L, 346–47).

28. My references to Richards, *Coleridge on Imagination*, hereafter cited in the text, are to the third edition; the pagination is the same as that of the 1934 edition.

29. The two-period ellipsis is Stevens's.

30. One may find statements similar to this throughout *Coleridge on Imagination*. Richards notes, e.g., "The more transcendental parts of Coleridge are an indispensable *introduction* (from which we may disengage ourselves later) to his theory of criticism. Rather than dismiss them, we should try to reinterpret them" (p. 18). His reinterpretation is given in psychological terms: "Taken as psychology—not as metaphysics—there is little in such an account of mental *activity* with which a modern psychologist . . . will treat now as other than commonplace" (p. 60). In a passage that Stevens marked, Richards concedes, "Anyone who is well acquainted with Coleridge's ways of discussing Fancy and Imagination will notice that I have, at several places above, translated them in terms which might sometimes have been repugnant, as suggesting mechanical treatment, to Coleridge himself" (p. 84).

31. "When a man has once seen that every single science, except metaphysics, makes use of fictions, he is apt to conclude that the next step for him is to remove these fictions and substitute the Truth. But if he looked closer he would see that human beings cannot get on without mythology. In science, in politics, in art and religion it will be found and can never be driven out" (Bradley, *Principles of Logic*, I, 342; quoted in Richards, *Coleridge on Imagination*, p. 181).

32. By placing *Notes*, first published in 1942, at the conclusion of *Transport to Summer* (1947), Stevens has given a misleading impression of the chronology of this section of the *Collected Poems*.

33. Richards's discussion here may also have furnished Stevens with an early version of what he later termed "decreation." Richards quotes (p. 226) a passage from Richard Eberhart: "It was man did it, man / Who imagined imagination; / And he did what man can / He uncreated creation."

34. These possible links with Richards seem mainly confined to the first section of *Notes*.

35. Valéry has been most frequently cited, perhaps because Stevens quoted his statement that "man fabricates by abstraction" in his preface to Valéry's *Eupalinos*, published fourteen years after *Notes*. In *The Clairvoyant Eye* (p. 294n) Riddel mentions Whitehead and Bradley as possible sources, and John Serio (in "The Ultimate Music Is Abstract") has noted a number of parallels between Stevens's and Ives's uses of the term. Bloom sees a likely connection between Stevens's "first idea" and Peirce's Idea of Firstness, although he concedes that, two years after *Notes* was published, Stevens said he had never read Peirce (*Wallace Stevens: The Poems of Our Climate*, p. 49).

36. Miller, "Theoretical and Atheoretical in Stevens," p. 275. This view, of course, represents a shift from the position Miller had taken in *Poets of Reality*, where he argued for one of these theories at the expense of the other two. His present argument is based on a conception of interpretation suggested by Michel Foucault.

37. Ibid., p. 283.

CHAPTER THREE

1. Bloom, *Wallace Stevens: The Poems of Our Climate*, p. 189; hereafter cited in this chapter as PC. The following works by Bloom have also been cited in the chapter and will be referred to by these abbreviations: *The Anxiety of Influence* (AI), *A Map of Misreading* (MM), *Poetry and Repression: Revisionism from Blake to Stevens* (PR), *The Breaking of the Vessels* (BV).

2. Adams, *The Life and Writings of Giambattista Vico*, hereafter cited as LWV.

3. This volume is now in the Special Collections of the University Library, University of Massachusetts at Amherst.

4. Stevens read *The Life and Writings of Giambattista Vico* sometime between 1935 and early 1941. His reference to it in "The Noble Rider" suggests that it was one of the books to which he refers in a letter to Church in March 1941 (L, 388).

5. Croce's *La Filosofia di Giambattista Vico* was, however, available in English translation, and Croce's championing of Vico is the one exception

to the general neglect of his work until the late forties and fifties. I can find no evidence that Stevens read Croce's study of Vico.

6. Verene, *Vico's Science of Imagination*, p. 22.

7. See ibid., pp. 62, 71.

8. Bloom believes that, although poets' misreadings are more "drastic" than critics', "this is only a difference in degree and not at all in kind" (AI, 95).

9. If Bloom is implying here that the image Stevens attributes to the bootblack is actually his own, he is almost certainly mistaken. Stevens was much taken with this example of primitive image-making, which he says he heard from a man who spent his boyhood as a shepherd, and he used it again in "Imagination as Value" to make much the same point: "I know an Italian who was a shepherd in Italy as a boy. He described his day's work. He said that at evening he was so tired he would lie down under a tree like a dog. This image was, of course, an image of his own dog. It was easy for him to say how tired he was by using the image of his tired dog. But given another mind, given the mind of a man of strong powers, accustomed to thought, accustomed to the essays of the imagination, and the whole imaginative substance changes" (NA, 151).

CHAPTER FOUR

1. The frequent references to Mauron, *Aesthetics and Psychology*, in this and the following chapter will be cited in the text as AP.

2. Milton J. Bates, in his bibliography of the Stevens library, states that Stevens "paraphrased Mauron's argument in the margins rather than mark-ing salient passages" ("Stevens' Books at the Huntington," p. 54). In fact, Stevens did both, as well as preparing a private index on the back flyleaf and laying in a memo page of penciled notes.

3. "I am neither a lecturer nor a troubadour," Stevens wrote to Allen Tate while he was at work on "The Noble Rider" (unpublished letter of 1 March 1941, Huntington Library).

4. This comment, broken into three phrases, appears on pp. 11, 12, and 13 of *Aesthetics and Psychology* beside a section where Mauron draws a distinction between the amateur like himself, whose duty is to inquire into his own reactions to art, and the scientist, whose business is to find an explanation for the reaction.

5. The essence of Mauron's argument for the contemplative state of mind as the key to the aesthetic emotion may be found in Ch. 5, pp. 31–38. Stevens's note is penciled in the margins of pp. 31, 36, and 38.

6. Although the arrangement of the *Collected Poems* would indicate that the composition of the three poems was separated by a number of years, this is misleading. "A Postcard from the Volcano," collected in *Ideas of Order*, did not appear in the first edition published by Alcestis Press in

1935, but was one of three poems added to the trade edition published by Knopf late in 1936. It was probably written within a few months of the lecture Stevens delivered at Harvard in December 1936, "The Irrational Element in Poetry," where he first refers to Mauron. The poems of *Parts of a World*, where "On the Road Home" appears, were written between 1936 and 1942 and published in 1942, the year of first publication of *Notes toward a Supreme Fiction*.

7. The term is Stevens's in his marginal commentary on Mauron's argument, p. 8.

8. The foxes and grapes of both poems suggest an ironic allusion to Aesop's fable. In the fable the fox, unable to attain the grapes, hides his disappointment by concluding that they are sour. The grapes of these poems are, however, accessible and therefore "seemed fatter" and "Made sharp air sharper by their smell."

9. Bloom, *Wallace Stevens: The Poems of Our Climate*, p. 217.

10. NA, 93. The essay that forms the basis of Stevens's analysis is "On Poetic Truth," mistakenly attributed to Stevens by Samuel French Morse in *Opus Posthumous*, pp. 235–38.

11. Stevens's comment is penciled in the margins of pp. 49, 50, and 51 of his copy of *Aesthetics and Psychology*.

12. It is clear, from a letter that Stevens wrote to his publisher on 14 May 1942, that the word *notes* in the title refers to what are now taken to be section titles—"It Must Be Abstract," "It Must Change," and "It Must Give Pleasure." "Each of the three groups will develop or at least have some relation to, a particular note: thus the first note is . . . I IT MUST BE ABSTRACT. . . . There are three notes by way of defining the characteristics of supreme fiction. By supreme fiction, of course, I mean poetry" (L, 406–7).

13. The appeal of nonsense or irrationality for Stevens is treated in more detail in the following chapter.

14. Stevens's 1936 lecture "The Irrational Element in Poetry," which contains the earliest evidence of Mauron's influence on his aesthetics, is not as helpful as it might be on this concept—partly because he uses the term in so many different senses, and partly because the lecture as a whole is vague and diffuse. Since Stevens locates the irrational element in poetry in the interaction between the sensibility of the poet and reality, the lecture is more relevant to Mauron's concepts of sensibility and expression, examined later in this chapter.

15. See the following chapter for a more detailed discussion of "Phosphor Reading by His Own Light."

16. Quite obviously the same focus is required of the artist's audience: "the spectator also should be double-minded. . . . having, thanks to the expressive language of the work, discovered and experienced for himself the artist's state of mind, he should be able to consider this inner landscape with the same passive concentration" (AP, 65).

17. Miller, *Poets of Reality*, p. 248.

18. For examples of such readings, see the discussions of abstraction, the first idea, and decreation in Chapter Two.

19. Bloom, *Wallace Stevens: The Poems of Our Climate*, p. 216.

CHAPTER FIVE

1. See *Letters*, pp. 346–75.

2. "This is a perfect instance of destroying a poem by explaining it" (L, 347). "Here again the explanation destroys the poem" (348). "As I go on with the thing, I am a little horrified by it. Take, for instance, what I said yesterday about the monster. Certainly I never converted the monster into the sort of extension that you are looking for; I never said to myself that it was the world. These things are intact in themselves" (361). "The poem is the poem, not its paraphrase" (362).

3. Although it is impossible to determine exactly when Stevens read *Aesthetics and Psychology*, which was published in 1935, he had almost certainly read it by the time he was responding to Simons's questions.

4. Compare the conclusion of Stevens's late poem "The Planet on the Table" (CP, 532), where the speaker says of his poems:

> It was not important that they survive.
> What mattered was that they should bear
> Some lineament or character,
>
> Some affluence, if only half-perceived,
> In the poverty of their words,
> Of the planet of which they were part.

5. Stevens expressed this same horror in a passage to Simons quoted above.

6. Bloom, *Wallace Stevens: The Poems of Our Climate*, p. 168.

7. Sontag, *Against Interpretation and Other Essays*, p. 7.

8. Pritchard, "Poet of the Academy," p. 851.

9. Stevens's depiction of the first idea—innocent or naive apprehension—in sexual terms is not foreign to his romantic heritage. In Wordsworth's "The World Is Too Much with Us," our lack of intimacy with the world is traced to overfamiliarity, which results in a loss of potency: "we lay waste our powers." Seeing nature only as a too familiar mate, we are unable to respond to an appeal to our virility which an observer freed from custom could describe only as wanton or seductive: "This Sea that bares her bosom to the moon: / The winds that will be howling at all hours, . . . / For this, for everything, we are out of tune; / It moves us not."

10. Harold Bloom observes, correctly I think, that the young man's name is a reference to the Fugitives; i.e., he is Tate or some other member of a group that values tradition: "Stevens charmingly praises himself for not finding his individual talent within tradition" (*Wallace Stevens: The Poems of Our Climate*, p. 235).

11. Bloom postulates that X is Eliot (ibid., p. 151), but it seems likely from the context that Stevens is referring to a more traditional and perhaps less challenging poet—Frost perhaps, who thinks of poetry as a clarifying or ordering of experience, who "lacks . . . complication" and does "not make the visible a little hard / To see" (CP, 311).

12. Miller, "Theoretical and Atheoretical in Stevens," p. 283.

13. Ibid., p. 284.

14. Blackmur, "Examples of Wallace Stevens," pp. 53–54. The essay first appeared in *Hound and Horn* 5 (Winter 1932): 223–55.

15. Ibid., p. 66. Since Stevens read this essay defending his obscurity and offering a theory for it, Blackmur's essay itself may have contributed to Stevens's defense of obscurity in the poems written a few years later.

16. Ibid., p. 52.

CHAPTER SIX

1. See *Letters*, p. 447.

2. "About One of Marianne Moore's Poems" (1948); the quotation is from H. D. Lewis's "On Poetic Truth" (1946), erroneously attributed to Stevens in *Opus Posthumous*, pp. 235–38.

3. My references to *The Life of Forms in Art* will be incorporated into the text as LF. The best-known of Focillon's works, *Vie des Formes* was published in 1934. It presents in a somewhat rigid and doctrinaire manner Focillon's theoretical position as a historian of Western art, which may be characterized generally as anti-idealist. In the preface to the English translation of Focillon's *The Art of the West*, Jean Bony writes that the "definition of an art by its most material qualities is the very foundation of Focillon's method and he applies it in every field to which his researches extended" (p. xvii). Focillon, Bony notes, "denounces the sterility of the idealist aesthetic which even now too often underlies the historian's judgments. We must 'make a decisive break with the outworn forms of idealism, with the idea of the solidity of matter as opposed to the subtle essence and the creative gifts of the spirit'" (p. xvi). "'So long as art is limited to states of consciousness and to generalized ideas, it is no more than a blind turbulence beneath the surface of the mind,'" Focillon argues. "'It must enter into matter, it must accept it and be accepted by it'" (p. xvi).

4. Stevens's copy of *The Life of Forms in Art* is now in the Special Collections of the University Library, University of Massachusetts at Amherst.

5. Kermode, "'Notes toward a Supreme Fiction': A Commentary," p. 183.

6. Bloom, *Wallace Stevens: The Poems of Our Climate*, p. 189.

7. See Stevens, *Letters*, p. 494.

8. Compare Stevens's "The Glass of Water" (CP, 197), published in *Parts of a World* in 1942, in which light reflected in a glass of water "Is the lion that comes down to drink" and the "refractions" are seen as the "metaphysica, the plastic parts of poems" that "Crash in the mind."

9. Stevens's figure of the giant as a "virtuoso" who "never leaves his shape" is probably taken from Focillon's discussion of the same issue treated in canto x, the relationship between the larger world of forms and the technique of the individual artist. Focillon notes that a work of art represents two "intimately related aspects of activity." The first is "the aggregate of the trade-secrets of a craft," and the second is "the manner in which these trade-secrets bring forms in matter to life" (LF, 43). It is, he notes, an oversimplification to think of art as the result only of the first aspect. Technique is not simply "the 'means to an end' " on the part of the artist. "Nor is it, finally, virtuosity," since the artist must be in touch with both aspects of his activity: "The virtuoso is above all else a kind of tight-rope walker. So absorbed is he in his mastery over equilibrium that his dancing is but the endless repetition of the same step—a step whose rhythm he is in constant danger of losing" (LF, 44). Focillon's virtuoso, like Stevens's, never leaves his shape, although Stevens transfers the figure from the artist to his personification of the central poem with which the artist must remain in touch.

10. One apparent consequence of Stevens's reading of Focillon was his more extensive use of the term *form* as a part of his theoretical vocabulary in poems published after 1942. In the poems contained in the final three volumes of the *Collected Poems* the word occurs fifty-eight times, more than double its usage in the first four volumes.

11. Bloom, *Wallace Stevens: The Poems of Our Climate*, p. 293.

12. Ibid., p. 292.

13. Ibid., p. 283; Bloom's italics.

14. In attempting to explain his conception of a supreme fiction, Stevens said: "There are things with respect to which we willingly suspend disbelief; if there is instinctive in us a will to believe, or if there is a will to believe, whether or not it is instinctive, it seems to me that we can suspend disbelief with reference to a fiction as easily as we can suspend it with reference to anything else. There are fictions that are extensions of reality. There are plenty of people who believe in Heaven as definitely as your New England ancestors and my Dutch ancestors believed in it. But Heaven is an extension of reality" (L, 430).

CHAPTER SEVEN

1. See, e.g., Vendler, *On Extended Wings*, p. 246, and Bloom, *Wallace Stevens: The Poems of Our Climate*, p. 254. Bloom finds the "true point of origin" in Shelley's "Ode to the West Wind" and "Mont Blanc."

2. The illustrations in the 1942 edition were changed for the better-known revised edition published in 1948.

3. Vendler, *On Extended Wings*, p. 231.

4. Ibid., p. 235.

5. Blessing, *Wallace Stevens' "Whole Harmonium,"* p. 135.

6. Vendler, *On Extended Wings*, p. 259.

7. Bloom, *Wallace Stevens: The Poems of Our Climate*, pp. 266–67.

8. Davie, "The Auroras of Autumn," p. 170.

9. Vendler, *On Extended Wings*, p. 259.

10. Bloom, *Wallace Stevens: The Poems of Our Climate*, p. 268.

11. Davie, "The Auroras of Autumn," p. 167.

12. Ibid., p. 174.

13. Bloom, *Wallace Stevens: The Poems of Our Climate*, p. 276.

14. Vendler, *On Extended Wings*, p. 265.

15. Ibid., p. 266.

16. Bloom, *Wallace Stevens: The Poems of Our Climate*, p. 275.

17. Ibid.

18. Another Pan-like figure, Capricorn, who had a human figure above the waist and goat legs below, is evoked in the passage in the term *caprice*. Pan and Capricorn have on occasion been confused. When Capricorn routed the Giants by blowing a horn, the noise and the reaction to it were called "panic."

19. Davie, "The Auroras of Autumn," p. 177.

20. Vendler, *On Extended Wings*, p. 268.

21. Ibid., p. 249.

22. Bloom, *Wallace Stevens: The Poems of Our Climate*, p. 279.

23. Ibid., p. 280.

24. See the chapter on Stevens in Regueiro, *The Limits of Imagination*. Although I am not in agreement with Regueiro's conclusion that Stevens achieved what she calls the "unmediated experience," I find her work of great help in charting Stevens's late shift of allegiance from the domination of the imagination outward into reality.

25. Ibid., p. 210.

BIBLIOGRAPHY

Adams, H. P. *The Life and Writings of Giambattista Vico.* London: George Allen & Unwin Ltd., 1935.

Baird, James. *The Dome and the Rock: Structure in the Poetry of Wallace Stevens.* Baltimore: Johns Hopkins University Press, 1968.

Bates, Milton J. "Stevens' Books at the Huntington: An Annotated Checklist." *Wallace Stevens Journal* 2 (1978): 45–61.

Benamou, Michel. *Wallace Stevens and the Symbolist Imagination.* Princeton: Princeton University Press, 1972.

Blackmur, R. P. "Examples of Wallace Stevens." In *The Achievement of Wallace Stevens,* ed. Ashley Brown and Robert S. Haller, pp. 52–80. New York: J. B. Lippincott, 1962.

Blessing, Richard. *Wallace Stevens' "Whole Harmonium."* Syracuse: Syracuse University Press, 1970.

Bloom, Harold. *The Anxiety of Influence: A Theory of Poetry.* New York: Oxford University Press, 1973.

———. *The Breaking of the Vessels.* Chicago: University of Chicago Press, 1982.

———. *A Map of Misreading.* New York: Oxford University Press, 1975.

———. "*Notes toward a Supreme Fiction*: A Commentary." In *Wallace Stevens: A Collection of Critical Essays,* ed. Marie Borroff, pp. 76–95. Englewood Cliffs, N.J.: Prentice-Hall, 1963.

———. *Poetry and Repression: Revisionism from Blake to Stevens.* New Haven: Yale University Press, 1976.

———. *Wallace Stevens: The Poems of Our Climate.* Ithaca: Cornell University Press, 1977.

Borroff, Marie, ed. *Wallace Stevens: A Collection of Critical Essays.* Englewood Cliffs, N.J.: Prentice-Hall, 1963.

Brown, Ashley, and Robert S. Haller, eds. *The Achievement of Wallace Stevens.* New York: J. B. Lippincott, 1962.

Davie, Donald. "The Auroras of Autumn." In *The Achievement of Wallace Stevens,* ed. Ashley Brown and Robert S. Haller, pp. 166–78. New York: J. B. Lippincott, 1962.

Doggett, Frank. "Abstraction and Wallace Stevens." *Criticism* 2 (1961): 23–37.

———. *Stevens' Poetry of Thought.* Baltimore: Johns Hopkins University Press, 1966.

———. *Wallace Stevens: The Making of the Poem*. Baltimore: Johns Hopkins University Press, 1980.

———, and Robert Buttel, eds. *Wallace Stevens: A Celebration*. Princeton: Princeton University Press, 1980.

Donoghue, Denis. "Nuances of a Theme by Stevens." In *The Act of the Mind: Essays on the Poetry of Wallace Stevens*, ed. Roy Harvey Pearce and J. Hillis Miller, pp. 224–42. Baltimore: Johns Hopkins University Press, 1965.

———. "Wallace Stevens and the Abstract." *Studies* 49 (1960): 389–406.

Focillon, Henri. *The Art of the West*, ed. Jean Bony. Translated by Donald King. London: Phaidon, 1969.

———. *The Life of Forms in Art*. Translated by Charles Beecher Hogan and George Kubler. New Haven: Yale University Press, 1942.

Frye, Northrop. "The Realistic Oriole: A Study of Wallace Stevens." In *Wallace Stevens: A Collection of Critical Essays*, ed. Marie Borroff, pp. 161–76. Englewood Cliffs, N.J.: Prentice-Hall, 1963.

Heringman, Bernard. "Wallace Stevens: The Use of Poetry." In *The Act of the Mind: Essays on the Poetry of Wallace Stevens*, ed. Roy Harvey Pearce and J. Hillis Miller, pp. 1–12. Baltimore: Johns Hopkins University Press, 1965.

Hines, Thomas J. *The Later Poetry of Wallace Stevens*. Lewisburg: Bucknell University Press, 1976.

Jarrell, Randall. "Reflections on Wallace Stevens." In *Poetry and the Age*, pp. 133–48. New York: Farrar, Straus and Giroux, 1972.

Kermode, Frank. " 'Notes toward a Supreme Fiction': A Commentary." *Annali dell'Istituto Universitario Orientale: Sezione Germanica* (1961), 173–201.

———. *Wallace Stevens*. London: Oliver and Boyd, 1960.

Lentricchia, Frank. *The Gaiety of Language: An Essay on the Radical Poetics of W. B. Yeats and Wallace Stevens*. Berkeley: University of California Press, 1968.

Macksey, Richard. "The Climates of Wallace Stevens." In *The Act of the Mind: Essays on the Poetry of Wallace Stevens*, ed. Roy Harvey Pearce and J. Hillis Miller, pp. 185–223. Baltimore: Johns Hopkins University Press, 1965.

Martz, Louis. "Wallace Stevens: The World as Meditation." In *Wallace Stevens: A Collection of Critical Essays*, ed. Marie Borroff, pp. 133–50. Englewood Cliffs, N.J.: Prentice-Hall, 1963.

Mauron, Charles. *Aesthetics and Psychology*. Translated by Roger Fry and Katherine John. London: Hogarth Press, 1935.

Miller, J. Hillis. *Poets of Reality*. Cambridge: Belknap Press, 1965.

———. "Theoretical and Atheoretical in Stevens." In *Wallace Stevens: A Celebration*, ed. Frank Doggett and Robert Buttel, pp. 274–85. Princeton: Princeton University Press, 1980.

———. "Wallace Stevens' Poetry of Being." In *The Act of the Mind: Essays* on the Poetry of Wallace Stevens, ed. Roy Harvey Pearce and J. Hillis Miller, pp. 143–62. Baltimore: Johns Hopkins University Press, 1965.

Pack, Robert. Wallace Stevens: An Approach to His Poetry and Thought. New York: Gordian Press, 1968.

Pearce, Roy Harvey. The Continuity of American Poetry. Princeton: Princeton University Press, 1961.

———. "Toward Decreation: Stevens and the 'Theory of Poetry.'" In Wallace Stevens: A Celebration, ed. Frank Doggett and Robert Buttel, pp. 286–307. Princeton: Princeton University Press, 1980.

———, and J. Hillis Miller, eds. The Act of the Mind: Essays on the Poetry of Wallace Stevens. Baltimore: Johns Hopkins University Press, 1965.

Perlis, Alan. Wallace Stevens: A World of Transforming Shapes. Lewisburg: Bucknell University Press, 1976.

Pound, Ezra. "A Few Don'ts by an Imagiste." Poetry 1 (1913): 198–206.

Pritchard, William H. "Poet of the Academy." The Southern Review 15 (1979): 851–76.

Quinn, Sister Bernetta. The Metamorphic Tradition in Modern Poetry. New York: Gordian Press, 1966.

Regueiro, Helen. The Limits of Imagination: Wordsworth, Yeats, and Stevens. Ithaca: Cornell University Press, 1976.

Richards, I. A. Coleridge on Imagination. Bloomington: Indiana University Press, 1960.

Riddel, Joseph. The Clairvoyant Eye: The Poetry and Poetics of Wallace Stevens. Baton Rouge: Louisiana State University Press, 1965.

———. "The Contours of Stevens Criticism." In The Act of the Mind: Essays on the Poetry of Wallace Stevens, ed. Roy Harvey Pearce and J. Hillis Miller, pp. 243–76. Baltimore: Johns Hopkins University Press, 1965.

Schneider, Daniel. Symbolism: The Manichean Vision. Lincoln: University of Nebraska Press, 1975.

Serio, John. "The Ultimate Music Is Abstract: Charles Ives and Wallace Stevens." Bucknell Review 24 (1978): 120–31.

Simons, Hi. " 'The Comedian as the Letter C': Its Sense and Significance." The Southern Review 5 (1940): 453–68.

Sontag, Susan. Against Interpretation and Other Essays. New York: Farrar, Straus and Giroux, 1961.

Stevens, Wallace. The Collected Poems of Wallace Stevens. New York: Knopf, 1954.

———. Letters of Wallace Stevens, ed. Holly Stevens. New York: Knopf, 1966.

———. The Necessary Angel: Essays on Reality and the Imagination. New York: Vintage, 1951.

———. Opus Posthumous, ed. Samuel French Morse. New York: Knopf, 1957.

Tindall, William York. Wallace Stevens. Minneapolis: University of Minnesota Press, 1961.

Tompkins, Daniel. " 'To Abstract Reality': Abstract Language and the Intrusion of Consciousness in Wallace Stevens." *American Literature* 45 (1973): 84–99.

Vendler, Helen. *On Extended Wings: Wallace Stevens' Longer Poems.* Cambridge: Harvard University Press, 1969.

———. "The Qualified Assertions of Wallace Stevens." In *The Act of the Mind: Essays on the Poetry of Wallace Stevens,* ed. Roy Harvey Pearce and J. Hillis Miller, pp. 163–78. Baltimore: Johns Hopkins University Press, 1965.

———. *Wallace Stevens: Words Chosen Out of Desire.* Knoxville: University of Tennessee Press, 1984.

Verene, Donald. *Vico's Science of Imagination.* Ithaca: Cornell University Press, 1981.

INDEX

Adams, H. P., 13, 15, 50, 59; *The Life and Writings of Giambattista Vico*, 12, 15, 43–48, 50–53, 149; on Vico, 44–48, 50–51, 53

Bateson, F. W.: *English Poetry and the English Language: An Experiment in Literary History*, 13
Blackmur, R. P., 140, 141, 211 (n. 15)
Blake, William, 93–94
Bloom, Harold, 6, 77, 108, 114, 119, 150, 169, 170, 171, 207 (n. 35), 208 (nn. 8, 9), 210 (n. 10), 211 (n. 11), 212 (n. 1); on Stevens's use of "abstraction," 20–22; *The Poems of Our Climate*, 21, 59, 60, 62, 90; attack on Stevens's theory of literary history, 42, 59–71; *Poetry and Repression: Revisionism from Blake to Stevens*, 42, 60, 61, 68, 69; on Stevens's anxiety of influence, 54, 59–71; *The Anxiety of Influence*, 59, 61, 62, 63, 64, 66, 67, 70; theory of literary history, 60–71; on *tessera* and *apophrades*, 61–62; misrepresentation of Stevens, 61–71; *A Map of Misreading*, 64, 71; *The Breaking of the Vessels*, 64–65; reductiveness of his theory, 64–68; reading of "The Auroras of Autumn," 182, 186, 187, 188, 192–93
Bony, Jean, 211 (n. 3)
Bradley, F. H., 31, 39, 206 (n. 31)

Burckhardt, Jakob: *Reflections on History*, 13
Burnshaw, Stanley, 82–83

Church, Henry, 12, 13, 23, 24, 25, 27, 171, 204 (n. 38)
Coburn, Kathleen, 28
Coleridge, Samuel Taylor, 28, 29, 30, 31, 32, 35, 37, 38, 39, 41, 45, 63; *The Statesman's Manual*, 33; on the term *idea*, 33–34, 37
Croce, Benedetto, 84, 207–8 (n. 5); *The Defence of Poetry: Variations on the Theme of Shelley*, 13

Davie, Donald, 184–85, 186, 187, 192
Dickinson, Emily, 173
Doggett, Frank, 18–19, 23, 24, 40, 205 (nn. 5, 6); *Stevens' Poetry of Thought*, 19
Donoghue, Denis, 8, 10, 18–20, 22, 23, 40

Eberhart, Richard, 63, 65, 66, 79, 207 (n. 33)
Eliot, T. S., 63, 68, 110, 139, 140, 211 (n. 11); "Tradition and the Individual Talent," 193
Emerson, Ralph Waldo, 69–70, 173, 195

Focillon, Henri, 13, 15–16, 212 (nn. 9, 10); *The Life of Forms in Art*, 12, 15, 148–62, 165, 167–69, 171, 172, 173–76, 180–82, 184,

Vico, Giambattista, 13; on the invention of poetry, 15, 43, 44, 45–46, 47, 57, 58, 92; conception of the hero, 15, 44; human culture as product of creative mind, 15, 44, 50; history as progression of mental states, 43, 44, 47, 48, 50–53, 58; reaction against Cartesianism, 44, 50; *Autobiografia*, 45; *Scienza Nuova*, 45, 47; use of *autonomasia*, 50

Weil, Simone, 21
Whitehead, Alfred North, 39
Whitman, Walt, 65, 68
Williams, William Carlos, 68, 139
Woolf, Virginia, 13
Wordsworth, William, 30, 63, 121, 173, 210 (n. 9)

Yeats, William Butler: *A Vision*, 21